Media, Myths, and Narratives

SAGE ANNUAL REVIEWS OF COMMUNICATION RESEARCH

Volume 15

SAGE ANNUAL REVIEWS OF COMMUNICATION RESEARCH

Media, Myths, and Narratives
Television and the Press

JAMES W. CAREY

Editor

SAGE PUBLICATIONS
The Publishers of Professional Social Science
Newbury Park   Beverly Hills   London   New Delhi

For information address:

SAGE Publications, Inc.
2111 West Hillcrest Drive
Newbury Park, California 91320

SAGE Publications Inc.
275 South Beverly Drive
Beverly Hills
California 90212

SAGE Publications Ltd.
28 Banner Street
London EC1Y 8QE
England

SAGE PUBLICATIONS India Pvt. Ltd.
M-32 Market
Greater Kailash I
New Delhi 110 048 India

Printed in the United States of America

Library of Congress Cataloging-in-Publication Data

Main entry under title:

Media, myth, and narratives.

(Sage annual reviews of communication research: v. 15)
    Bibliography: p.
    1. Television. 2. Journalism. 3. Culture.
I. Carey, James W. II. Series.
PN1992.15.M43   1987   302.2'34   87-36962
ISBN 0-8039-3048-8
ISBN 0-8039-3049-6 (pbk.)

PN
1992.15
.M43
1988
14 7946
Jan. 1990

CONTENTS

ACKNOWLEDGMENTS

A MAJORITY OF THESE PAPERS originated in a Round Table Seminar on Current Research on Television as Myth, Ritual and Storytelling. The seminar was organized and chaired by Robert A. White, Centre for the Study of Communication and Culture, London, along with Stewart Hoover, Temple University, Philadelphia. The session took place at a meeting of the International Communication Association, Chicago, May 22, 1986. I am particularly indebted to Robert A. White for his assistance with this volume.

—James W. Carey

EDITOR'S INTRODUCTION
Taking Culture Seriously

James W. Carey

THE ESSAYS IN THIS VOLUME attempt two things: to elucidate concepts such as myth, ritual, narrative, and story and, then, to apply them to specific phenomena and episodes in televisions and the press. The linkages between concepts and cases are loose and discursive rather than programmed and the distinctiveness of individual voices is greater than the thematic unities among the essays. The essays in all their diversity nonetheless raise a series of disquieting and as yet unresolved questions concerning the status and study of popular culture. In this brief introduction, I want to highlight those unresolved questions against the general background of the continuing crisis in modern culture.

I

In a melancholy essay written for a melancholy time, the literary critic John Thompson announced to the readers of *Commentary* in 1969 "the end of culture" (Thompson, 1969).[1] The apocalyptic excess of the phrase can be forgiven for those were years in which, to quote the title of a Frank Kermode book of the period, everything was overlaid with "the sense of an ending." Each day brought the news that something else we thought enduring—God, Man, the Family—had been put into permanent receivership.

"The end of culture" is surely an oxymoron but the essay, while its mood was elegiac, was meant to be taken literally. Thompson began by announcing that the arts, high culture, had lost "its hold on us." Alas, we still read serious literature, attended concerts and museums; we still occupied our life with the arts but somehow something had changed. Art had lost its capacity to make sense of the chaos of life. Art no longer fused expression and belief for artist and audience. Like religion, with which all the arts had been historically intertwined, art still had its temples and ceremonies, still occupied a region of our lives, but we were often just going through the motions—like churchgoers taking part in a ritual in which they no longer believe: having abandoned the creed and the faith, they soon would abandon the practice. Art had been infected by the worm of self-consciousness, an intense awareness of its own technique and method: the world in truth was not a world but a text. These were signs of a profound alienation between art and the world and between art and its most sophisticated audience. And, the group among whom the alienation was deepest, though here I add to the argument, were the professors professing and criticizing literary art. They believed less in the art they were distantly experiencing than the theories and scholarship with which they were experiencing it. Rather than art, it was criticism that made sense of the chaos of life, but that criticism, like the poetry it displaced, has proven to be but a "momentary stay against confusion."

The self-distancing and alienation Thompson found in our relation to art he generalized to all of culture by a curious and compelling path. He began from the signal intellectual event in the humanities of the 1960s, the Chomskyian revolution in linguistics. Language was, and to some degree still is, the first, deepest, and most unyielding mystery of human activity. Chomsky proposed to dispel this mystery: to bring to the surface the hidden rules, the competencies, the deep structures of language. While we all speak without instruction, without knowledge of language or how we speak, Chomsky proposed to reveal the hidden capacities that lie behind language use. And what, Thompson mused, would happen if some day Chomsky really succeeded in doing what he said he would do, "that is, to explain fully how it is that we learn language and what the incredibly complex and hidden rules are that allow us, normally without even thinking of it, to produce only and all English sentences." Chomsky's success was dreaded by Thompson because to be fully self-conscious of language would constitute the end of culture. Here's why.

The acquisition of language does more than develop a latent biological capacity. Through language one acquires every other part of the teachings of the linguistic community: a veridical map of the world, the rules of conduct within it, the forms of moral regulation appropriate to it. Language embodies the forms of life characteristic of a community: its art, ritual, religion, mythology; its belief and its temper.

In search of that moment when language, culture, and society were fused together, Thompson reverts to Freud's account of *Totem and Taboo:* the beginning of civilization and the origins of democracy in the slaying and cannibalizing of the primal hereditary chieftain and the institution of the incest taboo. Freud described the moment as follows:

> One day the expelled brothers joined forces, slew and ate the father, and thus put an end to the father horde. Together they dared and accomplished what would have remained impossible for them singly. *Perhaps some advance in culture, like the use of a new weapon, had given them the feeling of superiority.* Of course these cannibalistic savages ate their victim. This violent primal father had surely been the envied and feared model for each of the brothers. Now they accomplished their identification with him by devouring him and each acquired a part of his strength. The totem feast, which is perhaps mankind's first celebration, would be the repetition and commemoration of this memorable, criminal act with which so many things began, social organization, moral restrictions and religion.

The advance that Freud links to the use of a new weapon Thompson reconstructs as the discovery of language:

> Before he drove them out, away from his women, he taught them language, and his profit on it was that they killed him. With speech, they could plan this, they could draw up their pact, the pact of culture. They would observe in fear and piety, and in self-protection, his old incest taboos. But most of all, what interests us most of all—because of their love for him that accompanies their hate, and the feelings of guilt this so heavily laid upon them, they relieved their remorse by re-enacting the crime at the totem feast. They brought the father back to life, they worshiped him again and killed him again, suffered their loss and celebrated their success.

> In the totem feast, slaying an animal which had been given the spiritual qualities of the father, they disguised themselves as the totem, mimicked it in sound and movement. . . . They mourned, and then they burst out in loud festal gaiety, unchaining every impulse. . . . Surely it does not require a long exposition to recognize here "the beginnings of religion, ethics, society, and art."

Thompson herein discovers the origins of culture—the moment when language, music, painting, dance, story-telling, ritual, moral regulation, religion, and social organization were undifferentiated and indissoluble. The compact of culture was society, the fusion of all practices into an unself-conscious whole. Society existed not only *by* art, religion, ritual, language; society existed *in* these forms of life.

Thompson's quest is another episode in the nostalgia for origins: the search for a myth that accounts for our beginnings. We need not be swept up in this quest in order to recognize the strategy and the point. Origins determine endings and Thompson has set up his melancholy story as a trajectory from innocence to self-consciousness. The compact of culture has been blown apart by the worm of self-awareness. In William James's lovely phrase, the "trail of the serpent is overall" and the serpent turns out to be us. One by one each of the elements of the old compact has been turned on by the mind itself, by the mind's inwardness, so that each of the mysteries have been dispelled. Each of the ancient cultural practices has been shown to be not in the nature of things, not a representation of the ways of the world, not a mirror of transcendent reality but one more human practice, one more thing we made up along the way to modernity. As a result, these forms can no longer be believed; they can no longer contain an immediate experience, an unmediated apprehension of how the world is put together and how we should conduct ourselves in it. On this reading, primitives have a culture but we do not. The corrosiveness of doubt and distance sets in whenever culture is recognized as culture.

A simple example. There is a line in one of Flannery O'Connor's essays in which she, a serious Catholic, comments that if the Eucharist is a symbol of the body and blood of Christ, she wants no part of it. She believed, or so she wishes us to believe, in the literalness of transubstantiation. What she knows, in her stories more than in her essays, is that once bread and wine are understood as *symbols* of body and blood, they can no longer be taken seriously, they can no longer be believed or experienced. Her language is an attempt to annul, to cancel out, the metalanguage of culture so that the world in its mystery and manners, its full believability, can be experienced.

We recognize with disbelief the heroism of her struggle, but it is not a struggle she or anyone else is likely to win. One element after another of the original compact as fallen into self-consciousness and, therefore, into disbelief. Religion, ritual, art, moral regulation have been sundered out of their original fusion, appreciated for a moment, and then dispensed. "One part after another of our old original pact . . . has been brought into consciousness, where it flares out in brief glory and dries up and blows away." Self-consciousness has infected all our apprehensions. And, as Philip Rahv argued, at the heart of self-consciousness there is always equivocation:

> One can do no more than hope that this heightened and elaborated awareness of the poetic medium, which is after all a kind of wisdom or self-knowledge, will not soon provide us with another melancholy illustration of Hegel's famous dictum that the owl of Minerva begins its flight only when the shades of night are gathering.

We have discovered, in short, our powers to make art, and the discovery has alienated rather than comforted us. We have discovered culture, to use Ernst Cassirer's apt phrase, as "the place of the mind in nature" and the discovery has its tragic side, our separation from what the Germans more elegantly called the *Umwelt*. Intellectuals are the vanguard, the avant-garde, of this punishing self-consciousness, though not quite the vanguard Lenin conceived.

And, what now is left of the original pact? The only thing left unexplained is language and Chomsky proposes to call that too into consciousness: "Language, the act and nature of verbal communications, has moved outwards from immediacy. It has become objectified: awareness examines and seeks to circumscribe it as it does other phenomena." And what consciousness encompasses it does in a way destroy. In our case, it divorces language and belief, as most of our unbelievable theories of art and other things attest; and it divorces language and action, as most of our politics confirms. Now even talk is threatened by self-consciousness:

> Who will take our guilt and allow us to grieve and then to rejoice and be free? But we now know how all those elements of the ancient ritual worked. And so they can't work any more for us. We can only talk and talk and talk. And talk.

II

In a sense, talk is all we have ever had and, in truth, that ought to be good enough. While there are other ways of writing the history of culture, less elegiac and melancholy than Thompson's, they all end in the same question: how are we to take culture seriously? Once we have invented the language of culture—myth, ritual, art, sign, symbol, paradigm; words about words in Kenneth Burke's phrase—how do we avoid destroying or fatally diminishing and distancing the objects of our interest and affection, objects of belief, commitment, and pleasure. We invented the word *culture*, in the first instance, to encompass the foreign and strange—the alien—but we cannot prevent the word from turning back on us and estranging us from our own practices. We counterposed reason to culture in order to distinguish "us" from "them," but ended up discovering that reason had its own culture and rituals. We went out on the ship Enlightenment looking for Man—capital M—and found men everywhere encased not in natural reason but in a diversity of cultural practices. Later still, we realized that the Enlightenment was our culture, our form of life, just one way among many of being in the world. And, as a result, we could never again take it quite so seriously.

The strategies for escaping from this dilemma are as many and as inventive as the desperate mind can conceive. Among the current options are a vicious relativism that blankly accepts the world in its diversity, accepts a completely decentered world and pretends such a world is habitable by humans. The strategy in turn slides into the fashion of postmodernism: a willingness to stick to surfaces and appearances, to glide along on the ice of a culture without depth or elevation, to abjure any meta-narrative that could make sense of human experience, to treat the entire past as a submerged Atlantis waiting to be ransacked for any prize that might be turned up; above all, to annul contemporary life and anneal its divisions by a strategy of playing on its discordant surfaces. In Marshall McLuhan's sense, we can learn to love the whirlpool.

More potent yet are the strategies of dealing with culture by renaming it: in one case, by renaming it *individual desire* or *utility*, in another case, by renaming it *power* or *ideology*. The first alternative, the simple subjectivization of all experience, turning reality into a form of private property, is the deepest American impulse. The second is currently the most formidable intellectual strategy. Both are species of functionalism: one privileging the individual mind, the other privileging group life. While there is little to be said for conceiving culture as merely utility and gratification, one must take much more seriously the strategy of treating culture as power or domination or ideology. Both strategies are magic acts, however, that dispose of the phenomenon by renaming it.

Let me restate our originating question. Once we come to appreciate the full significance of the discovery of culture, How can we avoid falling into melancholy and hopelessness? How can we both appreciate the objects of culture and maintain some critical distance from them? How can we avoid a vicious relativism, a trendy postmodernism, a radical subjectivism, or, most problematically, an extreme functionalism that reduces the rich phenomenological diversity of culture to the single dominating chord of power and ideology? I do know that the essays that follow and their subject matter—the popular arts of television and journalism—pose the problems in a particularly apposite way.

If high culture has lost its hold on us, the same fate now awaits popular culture. Historically, the popular arts have been the most unreflective and spontaneous part of our culture. However clever in their structure, and occasionally mannered in their presentation, they have been, by definition, close to the hard surfaces of life: a source of simple joy and pleasure and a relatively direct apprehension of the world of their makers and users. They are among the last suburbs of the old city of culture to be incorporated into the academy: to be incorporated into a self-conscious and critical tradition. How can we take the popular arts seriously and still allow them to retain a hold on us, to allow them to continue to express our lives rather than merely infecting them?

Thompson's essay contains one admonition: If one begins with a concept of culture that is literary and ahistorical, if one begins within the high arts, within the self-consciousness and alienation that ruptures the relation of audience and text, one ends only in myth and despair. There is a trajectory, a straight line, logically though not chronologically, from Thompson's beginnings to the Frankfurt School's endings: either the power of despair or the despair of power. One must step outside that not so charmed circle that has placed its signature on much cultural analysis and start at a different point.

My suggestion, briefly, is this. We must begin with the attempt to identify the most durable features of our temporal condition, features that are, for good or ill, the least vulnerable to the vicissitudes of the modern age. I have here twisted some words of Paul Ricoeur, words that must be twisted even further to reveal that these durable features are of two different sorts or have two different disciplinary roots. On one side, these features are anthropological and must be recuperated into the present from societies that live outside history. On the other side, they must be recuperated from history, that is, from our own cultural tradition into which they are deeply but specifically embedded.

On the anthropological side, it means facing fully the fact that the human mind has arisen within culture and, therefore, cannot function outside of it. Language, as the primary cultural datum, is not merely an addition to an already formed and functioning species; it is one of the directive aspects of the very constitution of that species. Without humans, no language; but, without language, no humans. A cultureless human is then a contradiction in terms, a mere monstrosity, a cultureless society is unthinkable. "The end of culture" is merely an ironic gloss on the condition we are in: a desire to escape the dilemmas in which we are placed by our biological constitution and cultural realization. In some unknown sense, we made a trade in a past as distant and deep as the setting of *Totem and Taboo:* we surrendered our reliance on genetics as our way of making it in the world in order to become dependent on culture. We are discomforted by this trade because it forces a harsh truth upon us: while we have been released, liberated, from genetics to a significant degree, we have acquired equally tyrannical limitations, the limitations that culture itself imposes on us. We cannot achieve everything we can imagine; only those things permitted by the general and specific capacities of culture. We can neither sink back into a precultural state (though that is both a hope and a fear) nor can we transcend it into a world of pure epiphany, a world without language, conflict, power, or social groups. Linguistic communion and cooperation are made possible by culture. But once such instincts are no longer inscribed into the strand of bases in our DNA, they can only be achieved, however necessary, in culture.

The decay or instability of our cultural resources, the loss of confidence in extrasomatic sources of information, orientation, and moral regulation, is the thing we fear at the deepest level of our beings. A blank confrontation with nameless things and thingless names is experienced not merely as a deficit but as a threat to our ability to function. We are driven forward by the absolute need to construct a cultural frame within which the picture of our lives can be drawn. To create, maintain, and repair reality is the imperative of our biological nature and, therefore, the quest for meaning or lucidity our deepest motive. This quest is not some mere idealism but the profoundest practical task and material activity. The staring point—I think of it as a Weberian one—of our analysis is this quest for lucidity and the task is to elucidate those forms and practices, those durable features, that withstand the vicissitudes of modern life. This recuperation is not merely a means of going primitive, of seeing quasi-universal practices reinscribed in modern life, but a means of constituting the grounds of intersubjectivity: of seeing the experience of others in the light of our own and our own experience in the light of others. To grasp hold of the popular arts with terms like *myth, ritual, pilgrimage, liminality, story, narrative, chronicle*—to state but a select portion of the list—is to see in a miraculously discontinuous world persistent practices by which that world is sedimented and held together. It is to enlarge the human conversation while deepening self-understanding.

If we take the argument to this point only, we can rest content with a functional analysis: the demonstration of the functional equivalence between ancient and modern practices, between the devices employed to produce and reproduce cultures in small, technologically primitive, and undifferentiated societies and those used in modern, industrial, and capitalist ones. But to remain at that point has a number of severe consequences for both our politics and our mental lives. Above all, it does not raise us beyond the despair that John Thompson was brought to by his inspection of cultural practice. More to the point, it leaves us unable to affirm a commitment to absolute values, to support the already fragile status of the human personality, to prevent the already substantial erosion of historical consciousness, and, finally, to counter the pseudoutopian belief that everything can be fixed up by technology and human reason. All this can be summarized in a telling phrase of Lesek Kolakowski: it leaves us committed to the idolatry of politics.

To move beyond this point requires attention to a second set of durable features that are relatively invulnerable to the vicissitudes of the modern age: those embedded in history, in tradition, in our tradition. Because in the first instance, culture refers to some set of construable signs and symbols, some system of meanings—culture is always situated and specific. It is embedded in things: some relatively durable such as artifacts and practices, some relatively transitory like fashions and follies. Just as there is no going behind culture in search of some cultureless biology, there is no going behind tradition for some uncultured, nonhistorical self. Just as there is a way of speaking a language that is not *some* language, there is no way of having a culture that is not *some* culture. However much culture as a system of construed meanings changes in relation to other cultural objects such as technologies and economic practices or other social processes such as conflict and accommodation, such changes are transformations on a given cultural tradition, a tradition that insists on reasserting itself. That tradition is not only the ground of intersubjectivity but it is, at the same time, the single most valuable resource available for sense making and as an underpinning for other practical activities.

The second frame, then, for comprehending the popular arts is against the cultural tradition in which they are embedded and that they continuously express and transform. It is not only that societies are drawn together around some form of consensus narrative that is variable as to style and technique but that consensus narrative is about something: in fact, it is about itself—the continuous reweaving of given patterns of action and signification.

I have scarcely indicated how it is that the alternative though hardly discrepant frames of anthropology and history preserve cultural analysis from the corrosiveness of self-consciousness and relativism. Nor have I indicated how such a position can preserve culture from a reduction to utility or power. And this is hardly the occasion to do so.

But, I should, at the least, say a word about why the subject of power and ideology should be approached through culture rather than, as is now the practice, the other way around.

To suggest rather than complete an argument, let me treat a representative anecdote. A book, one of the most famous pieces of social science of our times, one that is again receiving treatment, is Gunnar Myrdal's work on race relations, *An American Dilemma*. It is, in many ways, a model of careful scholarship and was so treated by the black novelist, Ralph Ellison, when he reviewed it. Ellison praised its care and its brilliance, its moral seriousness and factual accuracy. After such praise, Ellison's hammering at the deficiencies of the book comes as something of a surprise but hammer he does. He puts his opposition to the book this way:

> But can a people . . . live and develop for over three hundred years simply by *reacting*? Are American Negroes simply the creation of white men or have they at least helped to create themselves out of what they have found around them? Men have made a way of life in caves and upon cliffs, why cannot Negroes make a life upon the horns of the white man's dilemma?

Ellison is objecting to treating blacks as simply a reaction formation to the dominant culture, as an expression of the power relations organized around racial lines and to the various ideologies of white supremacy. This is not to say that one can understand blacks without reference to slavery and its aftermath but that blacks cannot be reduced to those relations alone. It is not enough to be agnostic about black culture while describing white domination. Black culture is more than an assertion into the teeth of slavery and discrimination; it is also an expression of a positive way of life despite slavery and discrimination. Ellison is saying this—to approach black culture, including the popular culture of blacks, through the prism of politics and power, is to miss what is also central to their experience: "much of great value, of richness, which, because it has been secreted by living and has made their lives more meaningful, Negroes will not willingly disregard."

The inversion of politics and culture that currently grips our assessment of the popular arts finally contributes to the reciprocal images of victim and victimizer that has so paralyzed our politics. The mobilization of resentment will hardly move us anywhere, even though the moral elevation of the victim makes all of us—even the latest victims, the silent and moral majorities—feel good. As usual in these things, John Dewey said it best. Dewey argued that regard for the happiness of others means "regard for those conditions and objects which permit others freely to exercise their own powers from their own initiative, reflection, and choice." It was precisely in this regard that much social science was deficient:

> The vice of the social leader, of the reformer, of the philanthropist and the specialist in every worthy cause of science, or art, of politics, is to seek ends which promote the social welfare in ways which fail to engage the active interest and cooperation of others. The conception of conferring the good upon others, or at least of attaining it for them, which is our inheritance from the aristocratic civilization of the past, is so deeply embodied in religious, political, and charitable institutions and in moral teaching, that it dies hard. Many a man, feeling himself justified by the social character of his ultimate aim (it may be economic, or educational, or political), is genuinely confused or exasperated by the increasing antagonism and resentment which he evokes, because he has not enlisted in his pursuit of the "common" end the freely cooperative activities of others. This cooperation must be the root principle of the morals of democracy. (Dewey, 1908, pp. 276-277)[2]

The essays that follow contain many beginnings that draw upon anthropology and history and correctly order democratic relations between politics and culture, though they finally remind us of how much remains to be done.

NOTES

1. All quotations, unless otherwise noted, are from Thompson (1969).
2. The precise phrasing is taken from Westbrook (1987, pp. 25-26).

REFERENCES

Dewey, J. (1908). *Ethics: Vol. 5. The middle works of John Dewey.* Carbondale: Southern Illinois University Press.
Thompson, J. (1969). "The end of culture." *Commentary, 48*(6), 46-52.
Westbrook, R. (1987). "Lewis Hine and progressive photography." *Tikkun, 2*(2), 24-29.

PART I

OVERVIEWS

Chapter 1

TELEVISION MYTH AND CULTURE[1]

Roger Silverstone

I HAVE, OVER A NUMBER OF YEARS NOW, been working with ideas that bear on the relationship between television and myth; first in an analysis of the television message as represented by series drama (Silverstone, 1981) and, more recently, in a study of television documentary science (Silverstone, 1985a). The work has been both theoretical and empirical. It has involved narrative-semiotic analysis, the study of the production process, and some work with audiences (Silverstone, 1985b). It is far from complete.

The work as a whole has centered on the particular character of television as text, as process, as mediator of reality. It assumes television's power in contemporary culture, but challenges many of the more familiar ideas about, and more conventional ways of examining, the nature of that power. It also assumes that questions about the medium's potency are not dealt with simply. I have been concerned, above all, with the exploration of television as a story-telling medium, and both implicitly and explicitly, with seeing it as a contemporary expression of a persistent dimension of human culture: as that which preoccupied with the core concerns of daily life—entertaining, reassuring, defining, translating, controlling, pleasing—in the reemerging oral culture of the mid- and late twentieth century.

It is my intention in this chapter to try and extract some of the main themes of the work, to say something of their origins, more about their structure, and then finally indicate where I think they might be heading. The categories that stud it—myth, common sense, ideology, culture, science, and even television—are friable, like new cheese. Touch them and they start crumbling. But they are central. To a great extent they are to be defined in their interrelationship: to talk of science involves demarcating it from common sense; to talk of myth involves distinguishing it from, among other things, science. To talk of television begs the questions both of its specificity as a medium and of its unity.

Inevitably none of these questions arises, or is to be addressed, in a vacuum. The last 10 years have marked, in Europe at least, the rapid development of media and cultural studies; inchoate still, but increasingly secure in its grasp of the central issues of the relationship of the mass media to culture and society. That field has been dominated by the ideas of a few key figures, and by a critical perspective derived ultimately from the work of the Frankfurt School, and more recently of Roland Barthes. There is an enormous amount of value in both; but also much to be challenged. The study of bourgeois culture as ideology, of ideology as mystification, and of mystification as falsehood may be a good part of the story but it is not all of it.

The project as a whole grew out of three very different kinds of perceptions. The first was substantially theoretical, the second almost trivially empirical, and the third a mixture of both.

The first concerned the relationship between the concepts of ideology and culture. The release of ideology from the iron hand of economic determination undertaken by European marxists between the wars, and reinforced substantially since, opened the way for an intrinsic analysis of cultural forms and a more or less systematic enquiry (both theoretical and empirical) into the processes by which particular versions of reality inscribed by those forms came to become dominant and were sustained. The result, particularly in the work of Gramsci, was a theorizing of culture as ideology, as political, and as a key element in the armory of bourgeois domination of contemporary society. But the predominant stress on the mechanisms of cultural domination and its consequent perception of ideology as necessarily distorting failed to address both the question of the mechanisms of hegemonic success (and crucially also its failures) and correlatively the question of the pleasures to be gained (and who is to say that they may not be genuine?) both in cultural production and in consumption. Roland Barthes's (1972) eroticization of ideology in *Mythologies,* which became the most influential text in the field, involves not an explaining, but an explaining away, of the products of the mass media. They are instruments of the subtle work of bourgeois domination from which there is no escape. Culture is the seducer and myth its agent. It is all very well to insist on the historical specificity of particular cultural formations, but cultures change at different rates and in different ways; they are rarely coherent and they can be both embraced and rejected.

I have come to understand culture in terms of the more or less coherent set of values, beliefs, and practices that have an identifiable social location, be it the family, the neighborhood, an age or gender group, a class, or a nation; and ideology as the political inflection of culture, rather like, to mix metaphors, the adding of color to a neutral paint. There is no culture without the exercise of power, but some cultural formations are deeply stained and others clash horribly.

Television's centrality in and for contemporary culture invited attention, above all because of its pervasiveness. On the one hand, television was too easily incorporated into models of domination. On the other (and within a different theoretical tradition), the mechanisms of that domination, particularly in the empirical study of its effects, proved to be beyond effective reach. Something seemed to be wrong, both with the models and with the research. Somehow no one seemed to be asking the right kinds of questions, or asking them sensitively enough.

The way seemed open for an attempt, through the analysis of television's place and significance in contemporary culture, for rethinking the relationship between mass culture and ideology, and above all for inquiring into the social and culture mechanisms that are implicated in the medium's successful penetration of the soul of the everyday.

The second perception, initially entirely trivial and obvious, was based in the recognition that so much of television culture consisted in the display of simple stories, easily recognizable, continually reiterated, and remarkably similar in form and content not only to each other but to other stories in other cultures at other times. There was nothing particularly novel in this perception. Indeed, it has grounded in one way or another much of the recent work in the study of folklore (see Jakobson, 1970). But that, of course, was the point. What was the relationship, if any, between television's stories and the stories told in the myths and folklore of other cultures? And what would the consequences be for an understanding of contemporary culture if any such relationship could be established?

The medium as the message. This was the third perception. McLuhan's (1964) extravagance gets in his way, and his own analysis of television is, paradoxically, his least successful, but there is no gainsaying television's capacity to create its own media environment.[2] The skills it requires, the particular character of its communication, its immediacy, its ephemerality, and its displacement through image and story of customary perceptions of time and space identify it as an oral medium, *par excellence*. No doubt that its orality is compromised by centuries of literacy and print (Ong, 1982); no doubt that it is oral in a different way from the orality of preliterate societies, but equally no doubt that it has contributed to a fundamental change in the patterns of our collective communication and in that change revived and empha-sized many of the cultural forms and preoccupations of the non-, the pre-, or the semiliterate.

These three perceptions, inarticulate and often contradictory as they were and perhaps still are, opened the way to an enquiry into the nature, status, and significance of television in contemporary culture, and, in particular, as it turned out, into an exploration of the relationship between television and myth.

TELEVISION AND MYTH

In what ways can television be said to be like myth? The answer will depend on what theory of myth is to be used, and this in turn will depend on a whole series of assumptions about culture and society in general.

I have used the term *myth* in a broad and multivalent sense. Myth occupies a particular space in culture, mediating between the sacred and the profane, the world of everyday common sense and the arcane, the individual and the social. Myth is a form of speech, distinct in its character, marked by definable narratives, familiar, acceptable, reas-suring to their host culture. Myths are stories. Some are heroic. Most are formulaic. They are the public dreams, the product of an oral culture musing about itself. Myths shade into folktales, more secular, more literal, more narratively predictable or coherent, not asking to be believed in quite the same way, nor marking so insistently the cultural heartland of a society. Myths are associated with ritual, as beliefs to action, both together defining a transcendent and liminal space and time for a people in their otherwise mundane reality. Myths are logical; they are emotional. Myths are traditional. Myths persist, though often in a diluted form, and, like some good wines, do not always travel well without at least changing some part of their character. Different cultures in very different parts of the world, at very different times, seem to tell similar mythic and folk stories. Myths are elementary but often extremely complex; elemental but often quite superficial. Television is like myth. It occupies the same space. It is the space of intimate distance.

What is being identified here and from where does this synthetic characterization come? Its sources are various.[3] They are to be found in philosophy, anthropology, literary criticism, folklore. What they share is the attempt to identify a basic level of cultural experience, manifested in words and deeds throughout history, and concerned principally with the articulation of the core concerns and preoccupations of their host cultures. The precise, or necessary, relationship between the spoken words of myth and the cosmic, or with acts of ritual, or with other expressions of belief are unresolved in the literature. What is, however, consistent is the attempt to identify something in culture that is at the same time elementary, primary, fundamental, and stable, and to locate this in the texts of preliterate societies, texts that in turn seem to ground those societies' sense of themselves, and above all provide the mechanism by which they marshal their forces for social coherence and reassurance. Myth then is both cultural and social, and it is not just the uttered texts but also the contexts of their utterance that are of importance.

The shift of attention to contemporary society is of course precarious. No unambiguous divide separates myth (or the mythic) from other kinds of communication. But then no unambiguous divide separates our society and culture from those that have preceded, or lie adjacent to it. The search for the mythic in contemporary society is grounded only in the plausible expectation that we too perforce must find ways of expressing basic concerns, core values, deep anxieties; and equally we must find ways of expressing publicly and collectively our attempts at resolving them.[4]

The public, broadcast texts of television: images, narratives, icons, rituals are the site of contemporary mythic culture. My exploration of this medium has taken its principal, though not its exclusive, inspiration from the writings of the French tradition of anthropology and sociology: from Durkheim, Mauss, van Gennep, and Lévi-Strauss. In such a brief chapter as this, I can do no more than identify the main elements of their work that seemed both relevant and exciting for an approach to the study of television in society. What follows is inevitably somewhat schematic.

Émile Durkheim, particularly in *The Elementary Forms of the Religious Life* (1915/1971; Durkheim & Mauss, 1963) but elsewhere also, presented an analysis of the intimate relationship between society and religion, between order and awe. The basic social experiences, of the group, of the community, were also religious experiences; the basic experiences of religion, of majesty, of the cosmic, were also social. At the heart of his perception was a recognition, paradoxical and disturbing, of the essentially nonrational core of social experience, and also a recognition of the key significance of the dichotomy of the sacred and the profane for an analysis of culture. Our world, or at least the world of the so-called primitive, he argued, is marked by an essential dichotomy: on the one hand, the world of the everyday: ordinary, mundane, unremarkable; on the other, the world of the holy: exceptional, awesome, intensely ritualized, vital. If our everyday activities keep the ever-present threat of chaos at bay by their unthreatening normality, then our religious activities deal with the same threat by framing it transcendentally, by transforming and controlling it in the crucible of ritual and belief. Durkheim, of course, saw how the gravity and importance of this dichotomy would be eroded with secularization, but, he believed, that this erosion, fueled by the rapidly developing division of labor, would somehow have to be compensated. The space occupied by the relationship between the sacred and the profane would survive; it was functionally necessary; human beings would continue to need it in some form or another.

I have suggested that television, however inadequately, occupies that space and fulfills that function in contemporary society. In Durkheimian terms, television provides a forum and a focus for the mobilization of collective energy and enthusiasm, for example, in the presentation of national events, from coronations to great sporting fixtures, and it also marks a consistently defined but significant boundary in our culture between the domestic and taken-for-granted world and that of the unreachable and otherwise inaccessible world of, for example, show business, Dallas and the moon landings. The first, consistently noted by media analysts in terms of televised ritual (Bocock, 1974; Chaney, 1983; Katz & Dayan, 1985; Shils & Young, 1953), is principally a characteristic of television's content; the second, equally often the subject of discussion, is a product of television's forms and its particular kind of mediation. This latter perception is also reinforced in the work of Arnold van Gennep.

Arnold van Gennep, the Belgian anthropologist, is chiefly remembered for one book and one idea. In his *The Rites of Passage* (1960), he described in some considerable detail the various but essentially similar ways different societies mark crucial events in their culture, or crucial boundaries in their territory, by rituals that acknowledge and give expression to the transition from the profane to the sacred. Births, marriages, deaths, initiations, the crossing of thresholds, the treatment of strangers, are all marked by a set of standardized but highly significant actions that identify the seriousness of the distinction and the awe with which the passage across it is held. Those involved leave a familiar world, enter an unfamiliar one and return on their own, transformed by their experience. I have suggested that the movement into and out of the "liminal," which is what van Gennep called that period or position at the heart of the ritual process and therefore outside the constraints of the normal and the everyday, is a feature of film- and television making, particularly in the documentary representation of the world (Silverstone, 1985a; see Turner, 1969). I also suggest that the medium of television itself marks a threshold in our cultural experience, and that our watching it involves us in a rite of passage, away from and back to the mundane, via an often equally taken-for-granted, but nonetheless significant, immersion into the other worldliness of the screen. Drama has its source, historically, in ritual, and its end in television (Harrison, 1973). Our nightly news-watching is a ritual both in its mechanical repetitiveness, but much more importantly in its presentation, through its fragmentary logic, of the familiar and the strange, the reassuring and the threatening. In Britain, at least, no major news bulletin will either begin without a transcendent title sequence: London at the center of the planet earth (BBC), or Big Ben at the end of swooping flight across the metropolis (ITN), nor end without a sweetener, a "human interest" story to bring the viewers decently back to the everyday. Indeed, the final shot is almost always of the two newscasters tidying their papers and soundlessly chatting to each other, thereby announcing the return to normality.

There is one comment to be made here. Victor Turner, who took the notion of liminality from van Gennep and applied it most constructively in his analysis of social drama, extended it in order to take into account the profoundly different social contexts of the dramatic and the ritualistic in modern society. His category, "liminoid," is an attempt to identify (as is my notion of the mythic) persistence in social and cultural form but in its attenuation and displacement (Turner, 1982). The liminoid identifies not the collective so much as the individual, not the boundary so much as the margin, not the reinforcive so much as the disruptive. The transition to modernity has transformed, in his view, the liminal, but to the point at which it is hardly the same concept. All that seems to remain of the original is the centrality of drama and the integrity of the link between social drama (à la Goffman) and the dramatic display of society on the stage and screen. My feeling is that this is, however suggestive, neither sufficient nor sufficiently accurate as a way of defining the role of television in contemporary society. The paradox is that it is the original concept of the liminal in all its extravagance: of separation, mediation, betwixt and betweenness, the jumbling of categories and the release of *communitas*, that seems worthy of preservation in this context. There is something peculiarly premodern about that status of television in our society that the "liminoid" fails to capture.

Magic! I will quote Marcel Mauss, Durkheim's nephew and collaborator.

[Magic] is still a very simple craft. All efforts are avoided by successfully replacing reality by images. A magician does nothing, or almost nothing, but makes everyone believe he is doing everything, and all the more so since he puts to work collective forces and ideas to help the individual imagination in its belief. (Mauss, 1972, pp. 141-142)

Our high-technology world is essentially a magical one. By whatever mechanism, the boundary between reality and fantasy is constantly being transgressed. In both television drama and documentary, plausibility, verisimilitude, the suspension of disbelief are the key ambitions, the key achievements. In this, television identifies itself as the supreme magician, the mistress of the "as-ifs" of contemporary culture. I shall return to this notion of culture in the postscript to this chapter.

The problem is to establish the mechanism by which such cultural work is undertaken, as well as to explore in some detail the theoretical and empirical grounds upon which such assertions can be made. There are a number of possible ways of doing this. All require delving beneath the surface of the given and the visible, for what is given and visible itself must be explained. The epistemological difficulties are immense and threatening. We live in an empiricist culture; visibility and value are synonymous; our knowledge must be testable; its ambition is to control. The exercise that this theoretical perspective requires, however, is a hermeneutic one; however rigorous and however disciplined, the work is work of interpretation: structure rather than content, the unconscious rather than the conscious, the speculative rather than the immediately testable, the radical rather than the superficial, the ambiguous rather than the certain.

The immense labors of Claude Lévi-Strauss provide an initiating model:[5] Lévi-Strauss is after both the elementary and the elemental in culture: the logic expressive of humanity's persisting rationality, the links between mind and society, the fugue of culture. Lévi-Strauss defines (and defends) his work in the following terms: "As a method that successfully reveals how apparently arbitrary mythical representations link up into systems that link up with reality, natural as well as social, in order to reflect, obscure, or contradict it" (Lévi-Strauss, 1985, p. 122); and then later in the same paper (perhaps disingenuously) limits it: "Its ambitions remain modest: to pinpoint and determine problems, to arrange them in a methodological order, perhaps to solve a few of them, but especially to suggest a useful path to researchers who hope to tackle the mass of problems that are, and will probably long remain, unsettled" (Lévi-Strauss, 1985, p. 137). The substance, the style, and the achievements of Lévi-Strauss's work all appear in these two brief quotations. And notwithstanding the significant criticisms, particularly of the ahistorical and the quirkily ethnocentric nature of his work, as well as the fact (as even he recognizes) that structuralism is no longer fashionable, his analyses of pre-Columbian myth remain of importance.

Lévi-Strauss's claims are for a method that seeks the logic of culture, especially the culture of the other, in an effort to make sense of the practical activities in which human beings engage, above all in the construction of their myths; activities that have as their ambition the creation of order, an intellectual, cognitive order principally, an order that has as its focus the always problematic relations between man and nature.

The other, the "primitive," is rational. The collective products of that rationality in their purest form are the myths that display in the juxtaposition of their elements a logic, a basic, even a biologically defined, logic. This logic is a concrete logic; its terms are taken from the material world, the lived experience of the teller. This logic is a systemic logic, discernible in the body of myths in their own juxtaposition and in their transformational relationship to each other. It is this systemic logic that gives the unique text its meaning.

Part of the attraction of Lévi-Strauss's often enormously detailed and complex textual analyses is the attraction of the strange, of the unfamiliar, being deciphered. Fascinating in themselves, the myths take on a whole lease of new life in his efforts of disciplined translation. The shifting of his theory and method into the analysis of contemporary culture is not, however, without its problems: aesthetic, technical, and philosophical. His own disinclination to do so was based fundamentally on his perception of primitive society as a society without history, and on his belief that the freeze-dry mechanism of structuralist analysis would do no damage to an essentially static culture. Our own society, historical to the core, would not be an appropriate object for analysis. We are in any case too close to it, too much a part of it. It is too familiar. But primitive society is no more without history than ours is entirely dominated by it, and we can place ourselves in a position of analytical strangeness to what is otherwise familiar without too many problems (Latour & Woolgar, 1979). Indeed, much of postpositivist writing in the human and social sciences consistently does exactly that (Geertz, 1980). There are no a priori grounds for not looking at contemporary culture with Lévi-Straussian spectacles, though one must be careful not to look at the sun.

Lévi-Strauss's work is important, therefore, for three things: first, the identification of myth as a basic element of culture; second, the inquiry into the conditions for myths' possibility, and their significance, in and for the societies in which they are generated; third, for suggesting that myths, despite their manifest implausibilities, are coherent and logical and represent, above all, a culture thinking about itself. They are the product of society as ruminator, masticating the essential categories and contradictions in its way of life through a system of stories that preserve and legitimate its identity. Lévi-Strauss's work forces cultural analysis deep into the texts themselves, in a search for an organizing mechanism, and at the same time away from the texts, in search of a model of the relationship between the myths and the society that produces and receives them. The task, of course, is immense. If television is to be perceived as being like myth, in the sense expressed so far in this chapter, then a number of questions need answering and a number of qualifications need to be made. The questions center first on the particular character of television's texts; on the plausibility of producing an analysis adequate to express their diversity as well as their unity. Second, they center on the process of textualization, on the dynamics of a text's emergence and on the relationship between myth and adjacent discourses with which it becomes enmeshed and transforms. Third, they center on the dynamics of their reception; and fourth on their character as ideology, as texts produced in and for societies full of contradictions and inequalities.

The next two sections of this chapter take on the first and then the second of these questions. The third and fourth will be the subject of a brief discussion in the final section, a discussion to which I intend to return again shortly.

But first, a brief résumé. The argument that television is like myth has three dimensions: television presents the content of myth, most significantly in its reporting of major collectively focused and focusing events, like coronations, weddings, or ball games; it presents a communication, which in its various narrative and rhetorical aspects preserves forms of familiar and formulaic story-telling that are the product and property of a significantly oral culture; and it creates by its technology a distinct spatial and temporal environment marked by the screen and marking for all to see the tissue boundary between the profane and the sacred. There is no sense in which I can pretend that television is just myth, or only myth, or all myth. It is just that all its communications are touched with myth, which, like madness, marks it as in, but not of, the everyday.

TELEVISION AND NARRATIVE

The Lévi-Straussian model of narrative with which I began provides both a sociological and a methodological starting point for the analysis of the television text.[6] Both are crucial. The sociology lies in the insistence that text and context (however defined) are crucially interrelated, and that this interrelationship is both structural, constraining and enabling in turn, and dynamic, the product of individual and cultural work both in the creation and in the completion of textual meaning. The methodology consists in the provision of tools for the analysis of the mechanisms, both textual and psychological, that underwrite the text as potentially meaningful.

This double valency, of the text as at once both sociological and semiological, becomes increasingly salient as the analysis of its structure and dynamics develops. But if with Lévi-Strauss the first throw of the analytic dice has been thrown, it is quite clear that the game as a whole is far from over. In the remainder of this section, I will present, tentatively, a model for the analysis of the television text that still owes a great deal to those early beginnings, but that I believe takes into account more recent and also differently inflected work on and in the semiology of television. The object is an ambitious one: It is to provide a framework for the analysis of mass mediated texts that accounts not only for their variety, but also for their generality, to identify their novelty as well as their persistence, and that above all perceives them as the source, site, and consequence of complex and often contradictory cultural work. The aim is to open up the relationship between producer, product, and consumer in such a way as to steer the narrow path between determinacy and indeterminacy. There is no way that it will prove conclusive.

The orienting assumptions are as follows. At the heart of any consideration of the place of television in society and culture lies the text—the inscription (Geertz, 1980, p. 175): the images, words, sounds, and music of film and video, which are recoverable and tangible. Second, that although meaning is theoretically unlimited, it is empirically limited. It is perfectly possible to imagine as many readings as there are readers (and indeed in one sense this must be the case), but in practice only some will be socially significant, and those will be identifiable as expressions of distinct discourse—of class, of gender, of ethnicity, profession, neighborhood, and so on (Morley, 1980). An understanding of the individual act of reading must be grounded in the dynamics of the idiolect, in the private negotiations both with the presented text and with the intersecting and competing discourses in which both text and reader are placed. Third, the television text is complex and multilayered. Television is, in Theodor Adorno's words, "psychoanalysis in reverse."[7] This is an analogy that I wish to take seriously. It is a further topic for the postscript of this chapter.

The model I have in mind is of a hoop, an upturned U with its feet more or less firmly embedded in the sludge of everyday life. At its crown, the text, in all its complexity. At its base, the two contexts of creation and reception. At its sides, the parallel dimensions of mediation: from society and the individual to text; from text to society and the individual. Nothing terribly mysterious so far, except to say that the model of the communication process is no longer that of the syringe, no longer simply one of effects. The two most significant implications of such a model are, first, the recognition of the formal equivalence between the work that creates the text as a material object and that re-creates the work as a "material" one (the quotation marks indicating the changed status of the text once it has been read and incorporated in the act of reception, as a metaphor of the original); second, the recognition that this work of creation and re-creation is undertaken within, and is an expression of, a complex, subterranean, social, and cultural environment, the analysis of which—in its coincidences, contradictions, its patterns of facilitation and constraint—is an essential aspect of the analysis of the mass-mediated experience and the place of the mass-mediated text in daily life. Such an analysis turns the hoop into a circle and the model of mass mediation from a closed to an open one. Let it be said that the ground base of social experience that provides the bedding for the hoop is infinitely complex, multilayered, densely structured, and above all historical. It requires a veritable social geology if it is to be understood fully. Let me call that social geology the anthropology of everyday life. It is not a particularly novel notion, but no analysis of narrative nor of the emergence and reception of texts can be undertaken without it (Bourdieu, 1977; de Certeau, 1984).

In the equation of text and context that the above figuration suggests, the key, as far as the present argument is concerned, is the text itself, its structure, dynamics, and its claims. I have been very concerned over the years with the nature of, especially, the television text, and each time I come to formulate a model, as I am doing now, the model grows— certainly more complex, it is hoped also more sophisticated, more adequate, and more useful (Silverstone, 1983, 1984a, 1984b, 1986).

Whatever else we want to find within a text, we must begin with its content; that which is not just simply and easily seen and heard but that becomes meaningful (or not) in its relationship to the experience of those who create and receive it. If I ask, in a matter-of-fact way, what a television program was about, or what was on the news, I am asking a question about content. For a long time in media studies, the analysis of texts was limited to the analysis of content. But the structuralist-semiological revolution in the analysis of texts, the result in part of an unhappiness with the monochrome of much content analysis, insisted on asking more penetrating questions, particularly in terms of the conditions of possibility of meaning: the how rather than the what of meaning (Burgelin, 1972).

If we ask about the how, we are asking about mechanics and dynamics. More specifically, we are asking about text as technology. I want to refine and qualify this notion immediately. The qualification is that the metaphor should not be taken too literally. The text is not a machine, nor is it hard and inflexible. But the equation technology-text is already, in another context, a familiar one. The instruction to read technology as a text is an instruction to recognize the sociocultural logic and dynamics of machine creation and use, and to release the machine from a position of determinance. In this chapter, the instruction to recognize the text as a technology is an instruction to recognize it first as something material, as something independent of, for example, the act of reading it (and, therefore, to some extent determining that act); and, second, it is to invite the study, and the deconstruction, of its organizing logic and its mechanisms. Of course there is one flaw in the metaphor—I should think at least one. The television text is a technology that is created, more often than not, by people who are not aware of how it works.

There are two principal dimensions to the technology of the text. The first is its narrative structure: what I want to identify as the technology of order. And the second is its rhetorical structure: what I want to call the technology of appeal. Both have semiological and sociological dimensions. The semiology of narrative and rhetoric insists on the exploration and identification of the structural dimensions of the text; the sociological on the relationship between those dimensions and the text's sociocultural context. So to see narrative in terms of a technology of order is to see it, as I have already said in my discussion of myth, as an ordered mechanism for the ordering of experience. And to see rhetoric in terms of a technology of appeal is to see the text as claiming attention through a series of devices that both make it appealing (that is, pleasurable) and make it commanding (that is, legitimate). Of course the achievement of a measure of narrative coherence (insofar as that is the text's ambition) is itself a significant part of its appeal, and hence is rhetorical in the sense in which I have defined it.

I have discussed what I mean by *narrative* many times (Silverstone, 1981, 1983, 1984a, 1984b, 1986). I want here just to sketch what I have taken to be its principal elements. They are simply identified: logic, chronologic; myth, mimesis; story, argument.

The logic of the narrative is the logic of the system from within which a particular story is articulated. It is the logic of the paradigm; a concrete logic, expressing both an essential binariness in the activity of creation and a relationship to the material culture of the creating society. The logic is a Lévi-Straussian logic, and I have shown elsewhere how it manifests itself in the texts of today's television programs, as they attempt a resolution, always provisional and ineffective, of the basic dilemmas of social life: the dilemmas of gender, work, morality, of our relationship to the environment or to the cosmic. Insofar as these texts do indeed display and preserve something of this processual and systemic logic, I have been inclined to regard them as mythic—in the Lévi-Straussian sense.

The chronologic is the logic of the logic of the individual story. The beginning, middle, and end of it; the functional logic of hero, of test, of search, of success and failure. It is a logic much more easily grasped, much more accessible to the analyst and to the layperson. Although both logic and chronologic contribute to the particular balance of familiarity and expectation that must ground our experience of a unique text, it is the chronologic, and its relative predictability, that is more simply identified. Indeed, the fairly consistent simplicity of the structure of television's texts links them in quite obvious ways to the folktales of other oral cultures, and it is on these grounds too that I have argued for a view of television that acknowledges its status as a folk medium.

The concepts of myth and mimesis will appear again in the next section. Suffice it to say here that the television text manifests a concern both within its structure and within its content with the need to present reality (and this is as equally true of dramatic and fictional as it is of factual programming) and that this concern is a product both of the particular character of the medium and of the various narrative strategies, in argument, and above all in the naturalization of the text as a whole, that define a primary dimension of its ordering. The demands of verisimilitude, much more in evidence as a conscious strategy in the production of a fictional text, become both more problematic and more insidious in the presentation of a documentary text, which by its very existence and label masks the artifices involved. This strain toward verisimilitude, toward naturalization, present differentially in all television, is the mimetic.

I have already spent much time discussing the mythic, though in the present context, it has a slightly different connotation: as a formal dimension of the text, rather than as the dominating characteristic of it. I have suggested, particularly in my work on documentary that the mythic, that is, the strain toward a narrative of systemic logic and heroic chronologic, is ever present, but that there is an equally persistent struggle within the narrative framing between myth and mimesis. Whether this is true (and whether it is usefully true) in relation to other genres of programming remains an open, and an empirical, question.

Story and argument are, though by no simple and linear route, the expression of myth and mimesis in the particular individual program. In following a story or an argument (often both at once), the viewer is being guided along paths that draw on, and draw in, the mythic and the mimetic. There is a constant tension between the two that each television program must at least make some effort to resolve.

So much for the semiology of the narrative, though this discussion barely scratches the surface and of course there is much more to be said.[8] What of the sociology? Implicit in all that has been discussed here is that the narrative work, the results of which are displayed in the text, are evidence of a primary aspect of culture, the creation of a mythic order, and that the particular path any single text constructs is a display of the context and contradictions involved in its creation as well as an attempt to resolve them. But the final text is also the product of practical work undertaken in concrete social settings, and as such the product of a pattern of judgments, technical, aesthetic, moral, political as well intellectual, that are the requirements of any negotiation through the competing realities of everyday life. Once again I will have a little more to say on this in the next section.

The second major dimension of the text is its rhetoric (Barthes, 1977; Burke, 1950; Group μ, 1981; Perelman, 1979; Todorov, 1982), the technology of appeal. *Rhetoric* is language in action, "the use of language as a symbolic means of inducing cooperation in beings that by nature respond to symbols" (Burke, 1950, p. 43). Rhetoric has both an aesthetic and a political dimension: to please (appeal) and to command (appeal). It is not the case, of course, that all television programs require action in any direct sense (though advertisements and party political broadcasts certainly do), but they require attention. The classical study of rhetoric, and the more recent "new rhetoric," has been engaged in the description and analysis of the mechanisms (tropes, figures) of persuasive language, and its study has in the United States (though less I believe in Europe) been influential throughout the human sciences. Television is a supremely rhetorical medium.

Effective language presumes that both speaker and audience share a set of orienting assumptions; oratory is both public and ephemeral. The text will have one hearing. It must be heard. The more or less formal language of rhetoric that results must be more or less familiar. In its formality, its familiarity, its ephemerality, its status as a public text, television is a supremely rhetorical medium.

But rhetoric is also part of the exercise of power. Insofar as rhetorical address offers a closed text requiring only a response, then simply in its articulation it becomes a display of power (Bloch, 1974). Rhetoric, in the ritualization of its language and of its setting, and in its assumption and creation of community (which must be both real and imagined) remains a central dimension of contemporary social life. In this too television is a supremely rhetorical medium (though some academic papers run it a close second).

However, the rhetorical texts of television are not simply examples of the *exercise* of power, and therefore are not simply to be perceived as examples of the operationalization of a dominant ideology. They are claims, and, although inevitably skewed by the political structure of modern society, are nevertheless in their individuality the expression of different voices, differently inflected by structure, circumstances, and discourse; factors that affect, of course, both their production and their reception.

The rhetoric of television consists principally in the three dimensions of image, look, and voice (though music will have its own rhetoric) and in the narrative structuring of these separate dimensions into the coherence of the text as a whole. Semiotically speaking, the requirement is for the analysis of the tropes and figures by which the television text constructs itself as real, coherent, pleasing, and persuasive, and this in turn requires close attention to the mechanisms of framing in the organization of the image, in the technologies of recording, and in the arrangement of the spoken words.

Sociologically speaking, the requirement, and the payoff, is the analysis of the mechanisms by which text and context lay claim to each other, and in those claims mediate, through the achievement of a textual order, a momentary resolution of the cultural contradictions of everyday life.

In the next section, I will undertake a brief examination of some of these issues particularly insofar as they have emerged in my recent work on television documentary science.

TELEVISION, SCIENCE, COMMON SENSE

The knowledge that informs everyday life is the knowledge of common sense, and television, if it is to have any purchase at all on our daily lives, must come to terms both in its content and in its forms with that knowledge. The world of common sense is both shared and fragmentary. "Commonsense knowledge is the knowledge I share with others in the normal self-evident matrices of everyday life" (Berger & Luckmann, 1967, p. 37). Commonsense knowledge is practical knowledge, grounded in the taken-for-granted experiences of daily existence: fragmentary, incoherent, and inconsequential. It is also multivalent: an uneven but predictable mixture of evaluative, technical, and aesthetic as well as cognitive judgments.

"Commonsense is not something rigid and immobile, but is continually transforming itself, enriching itself with scientific ideas and with philosophical opinions which have entered ordinary life. 'Commonsense' is the folklore of philosophy, and is always half-way between folklore properly speaking and the philosophy, science and economics of the specialists." (Gramsci, 1971, p. 326)

Writers trying to characterize common sense often do so by reference to its distinctiveness in relation to specialist forms of knowledge (Lyotard, 1984). It has a residual quality, practical, unchallenging, sufficient to maintain the fragile equilibrium of ordinary life. It is closely associated with ritual forms and processes and with the whole panoply of mythic narratives (Geertz, 1975): fable, folktales, proverbs, myths themselves. Everyday knowledge provides a basis for our competence, and the knowledge that it constitutes is wide-ranging, not restricted to the simple determination and criteria of efficiency, but including moral, aesthetic, and practical judgments. It can be identified with core knowledge (Giner & Silverstone, 1985): traditional, slow to change but continually adjusting to, incorporating, defending itself against novelty, variation, challenge, and above all the ever-present but rarely visible threat of chaos.[9]

The effective demarcation of common sense from science is a persisting and thorny philosophical problem. The two discourses, even assuming sufficient coherence to be able to describe them as such, insist on interweaving, compromising their status as discrete. The irony is that even if scientific/philosophical discourse cannot finally separate science from common sense, common sense can and consistently does. We all know when we are crossing the boundary from the customary to the technical, the accessible to the inaccessible, the comprehensible to the incomprehensible, the practical to the theoretical. The boundary between science and common sense may be for common sense a constantly shifting one, but it is a boundary nevertheless. And from the position of common sense, science is neither neutral nor necessarily benevolent. Science can and often does occupy an equivalent space to that occupied by the wild and natural: both intrinsically beyond reach, both together (the one supercultural, the other anticultural) providing common sense with its essential raw material. On the one hand, there is the domain of what might be called nonknowledge: the natural or the primitive; the unknowable, the unpredictable, the uncontrollable. On the other hand, there are the various and often competing specialist accounts of the world, which increasingly seem to have the same qualities.

Myth and mythic narratives are profoundly implicated in the definition and maintenance of commonsense reality, constantly at work translating and reassuring at the boundary between the familiar secure world of the everyday and the unfamiliar, insecure world beyond it (Silverstone, 1981, p. 81). And I am arguing that television is the contemporary expression of myth. Its forms—news, documentary, serial drama—each and together, are daily at work on politics, science, the private, the strange, the challenging, offering accounts of the world with one aim in view: to give pleasure, to provide reassurance (Ang, 1985). And what links television to the world of the everyday are the narratives present in both: the elementary forms of the temporal and spatial and moral ordering of experience (Ricoeur, 1984).

Both television and myth are necessarily participatory: inclusive, synaesthetic in McLuhan's sense. Both television and myth unify: both in their texts which bring together, without shame, the most diverse and otherwise incompatible elements; and in their social claims, discriminating hardly at all in relation to their audience. Both television and myth define and reinforce for the society that generates and receives them, its essential categories: the moral, aesthetic, and cognitive structures that, by their very appearance in text after text, program after program, claim legitimation. Both television and myth are essential ingredients in the exercise of power.

How is the work of translation, incorporation, and reassurance undertaken in the texts of television science? How is the tension between science and common sense expressed or resolved in them? Television documentary science is, in many ways, paradigmatic; what is at issue is the process by which it comes to emerge and be displayed. Empirically, that process is a process of creative, collective work undertaken within an organization and according to conventions that the organization itself requires. That process of work is complex and contradictory. It has as its end product a television text that meets, if it is to be transmitted, the standards and expectations of a genre, a time, a station. It involves above all the transformation of multiple realities into a singular (though still complex) narrative expression (Silverstone, 1985; Singer, 1966). The work of transformation/translation—Karin Knorr-Cetina (1981, p. 132) calls it conversion/perversion in another but related context— consists in television's capacity to create its own culture, its own forms, and impose them on all its subject matter, one way or another. Something we might call science, specialized, inaccessible, literary, often dull and inconclusive, becomes, in the hands of *Horizon* or *Nova* or unequivocally in the hands of Carl Sagan, a drama, an adventure: heroic, powerful, accessible, visual, probably unchallenged.

The resulting texts share, of course, a good deal with those texts that scientists themselves produce to communicate their work: both involve a rhetoric and a poetic structure, both are artful, both seek to persuade and convince (Silverstone, 1986). Television is not, after all, unique in contemporary culture. But each differ, significantly, by virtue of their intended audience, their medium of expression, and their attention. What marks television in this context is its aim to please, and in its presentation of science its attempt to resolve the competing demands of myth and mimesis.

The texts of television science, at least as far as I have analyzed them both in production and in finished form, betray a tension between these competing demands, and that tension in turn is expressed in the formal structure of their narratives. If the mythic in television documentary draws the viewer into a world of fantasy, of the heroic, then the mimetic pulls her or him toward the real. It does so by the label "documentary"; it does so in images that in their presence guarantee fidelity to a separate and unmediated reality; and it does so through its narrative forms, essentially word driven, that define an argument or a logic that by its very invisibility is recognized as natural (Culler, 1975). There are a number of conventional forms through which the mimetic might be expressed: a demonstration, lecture, or argument governed, however loosely, by a structure derived from classical rhetoric; or in a form following a model set by extrafilmic discourse, for example, the chronology of a day's events, the passage of the seasons, a journey. The key to the achievement of the mimetic is in the text's strategies of naturalization; its capacity to make its own technical and aesthetic work invisible; to make the unique or the novel instantly recognizable and familiar. I have suggested that the mythic and the mimetic can be considered as the symbolic representations of the two competing discourses of common sense and science in the television documentary text, and that they are in turn expressed through the particular narrative strategies, still in tension, of story and argument, which, with some qualification, make an appeal, respectively, to emotion and reason (Silverstone, 1986).

The key, then, to the analysis of the place of television in contemporary culture is to be found in television's textuality and in the work of narrative transformation that that implies. The study of the presentation of science looms large in our cultural life (even in its relative infrequency), and television is, once school is over, our main informer (BBC, 1984); but it is also important as a paradigm for the work of television as a whole.

I think this is probably not too grand a claim. The received wisdom, of course, is that the different genres of television: news, soap opera, series and serial drama, documentary and the ads, must be treated as discrete forms and that arguments about narrative and narrative structure particularly as the basis for defining the nature of its textual coherence are misplaced. McLuhan (1967, p. 126), himself, once wrote of television that "there is simply no time for the narrative form borrowed from print technology." I would disagree and point out that such fragmented and apparently nonlinear forms as the news or ads still betray, both in their contextualization and in their fragmentation, a close link with narrative forms, increasingly mythic insofar as it is the logical and the heroic dimensions that define the nature of their appeal. News items are micro-narratives, textually closed, contextually open (they insist on a particular reading but demand to be incorporated into the open structures of everyday life). Their stories are those of heroic exploit and disaster; their concerns are with the cosmic and threatening; their function is the management of anxiety, anxiety that they themselves in part create;[10] they are ritually told at regular and predictable times of day; they make stars of their presenters, both liminal and luminary; they provide the stuff of everyday interaction; we are entirely dependent on them. News is a central dimension of television's output and, like soap opera, almost indigenous to the medium. Both are involved in the crucial work of mediation that marks television as the site of a distinct and persistent dimension of culture. Neither news nor soaps necessarily depends on the simple beginning, middle, and ends of classic and simple narrative, but they are hardly divorced from myth, nor from the essentially close interdependence that all forms of television storytelling have with the everyday.

THE QUESTION OF RECEPTION

My work, until now, has been, essentially, a study in cultural engineering, involving stripping down rather than design. It has focused on the mechanisms, the gearing, of cultural transformation. It has dwelt on forms, or elements, or functions. An engine can be used for many purposes—a tractor or a tank—and an effort at the identification of the basic elements of a given technology will inevitably leave open the question of how such a technology can be and is (and might be) used.

To write about reception is to write, actually, about the creation of ideology and the negotiation of hegemony, but it is done so by reference to the "empiricities" of everyday life. The model of narrative that I sketched out above depends for its support on the two legs of production and reception, both grounded in the discourses and events of everyday life. In a certain sense, there is a formal parallel between the two, each being perceived as routes of narrative emergence, the one into the materiality of textual expression, the other into the "materiality" of quotidian language and social interaction. Both are creative. Both are mediated by experience and by the capacity of both sets of creators—producers and receivers—to find in the text a resolution (partial, provisional) of some aspect of one or many of life's contradictions. Both involve movement between the private and the public, between the individual and the collective. The process as a whole is both significant and signifying, or it is nothing at all, and the successful completion of the cycle is, given the inevitably skewed political structure that provides its basic context, evidence of the fragmentary but continuous pattern of hegemonic work in contemporary society.

The word *successful*, of course, begs the question, but it is a question that we cannot begin to answer until the complex relationship between the text, its claims, its plausibilities, its voices, its myth, and the commonsense understandings and irrationalities of everyday life, contrary, incomplete, unstable, is itself understood. I take this to be the current task of mass media and cultural studies. It concerns not the study of audiences, conceived as more or less passive, more or less removed from the dynamics of family, neighborhood, and the discourses of class and gender relations, but precisely their study as entirely active and embedded. David Morley's (1980; see Lewis, 1985) work announces this project, but there is still much to do. And indeed there are many dangers, not least an incipient romanticism that seems in some current work to grant all power to the reader, and to grant the text a status as infinitely open, dialogically speaking. What is at issue, and what is required, is a thoroughgoing sociological and anthropological immersion into the relatively uncharted territory of everyday life in the pursuit of both the subtleties and the unsubtleties of textual emergence and acceptance. This in turn requires both textual and cultural analysis, both a semiology and a sociology.

I hope my work, and this chapter, goes some way toward identifying some of the elements of the structural links between these various semiological and sociological processes, both cultural and individual, both conscious and unconscious, and their manifestation in the products of, and relationships surrounding, television. There is still an immense amount of theoretical and empirical work to be done, both in the analysis of audiences—individuals, families, classes, nations—and in the development of a coherent historical and structural perspective. There is much work to be done analyzing the variety of the texts of television, how they come to be produced as well as received. The work must be both theoretical and empirical, though not necessarily empiricist. This may be a cliché but if we are to understand the fascinating and important power of television in our society, in terms of myth and ritual or indeed in terms of something else entirely, then nothing else will do.

POSTSCRIPT

Postscripts are for kite flying, or at least this one is. Its purpose is to explore, entirely tentatively, some ideas suggested in the course of my work that bear on the psychodynamics of television as an individual and a cultural experience. I still feel that we are long from grasping what that experience is and that the conventional ways of thinking about, and investigating what we have come to call "effects," and "uses and gratifications" or even "readings" have so far not been able to produce a convincing account of the relationship between the medium and social life. What follows is speculative (hence its appearance in a postscript), but it arises from all the work that I have undertaken hitherto, and I believe it may have some substantial methodological implications.

The starting point is a belief that any analysis of culture must take into account unconscious processes, both individual and collective. Human beings relate and respond to their environment in ways that are neither always rational nor necessarily conscious. We do not always know, nor can we always tell, why we do things, why we believe what we do. Our experiences of ourselves and of others are always mediated. They exist for us in a symbolic realm: of language, communication— always "as-if" (Horton & Wohl, 1956; Vaihinger, 1924). Our culture is the product of work that we undertake to shield ourselves from naked reality, from the chaos of self and other. In this context, I have been struck by the parallel theorizing of three major figures, one a psycho-analyst, one a philosopher, the other an anthropologist. Each is concerned with the exploration of the relationship between the indi-vidual and the social; each is concerned with some aspect of the relationship between identity and experience.

D. W. Winnicott (1974), the British psychoanalyst and key figure in the development of object relations theory (that branch of psycho-analytic theory that seeks to understand personality through the analysis of early experience rather than through the analysis of otherwise unmediated unconscious processes), explored in his work the elementary germs of cultural experience in the initial separation of the infant from the mother. He identified the creation, at this point of separation, of an object, a transitional object, that both separates and links the two individuals who until that point had been indissolubly bound. The transitional object, often materializing in a blanket or some such comforter, becomes the first symbol. It becomes the focus of the feelings that previously belonged to the mother, with whom the child originally entirely identified. It is the first metaphor, standing both for and against the other, and both for and against the child. The transitional object mediates between the child and reality, and initiates the child's involvement in culture.

It is this quality of the symbolic, as a mediator, that lies at the heart of Ernst Cassirer's (1953, 1955) writings, particularly in *The Philosophy of Symbolic Forms*. Cassirer is after the basic mechanisms, in language, myth, and knowledge, by which human beings come to know and represent their world; that knowledge and representation being the result of what he calls the "symbolic function," the dynamic work of mediation that consciousness brings to bear on an otherwise meaningless world. Cassirer traces the various forms that this mediation has taken throughout history, in order for both to establish a philosophical unity to cultural experience and to identify its diversity. In this context, his work on myth is particularly instructive, above all because he finds in it an expressive nonrational symbolism, which he sees as both preceding and opposing science. Myth seeks to unify; it occupies a sacred territory, of awe and power and feeling. In myth, the primitive finds his or her identity. It becomes the focus, the transitional object, between the man, as child, and reality; it too has an elemental character.

The third figure is one we have already met: Claude Lévi-Strauss, who is also concerned with the fundamentals of cultural experience, and who identifies myth as its purest form. Lévi-Strauss finds within myth and ritual what he calls the "totemic operator," the basic mechanism of mythopoesis, the essentially rational structure of the mythic system. Cassirer and Lévi-Strauss differ in their views of myth (Silverstone, 1976), but they are alike in identifying a primary mechanism at the heart of the symbolic, the function of which is the drawing of order out of chaos, and the creation of a form of life that is reassuring in its capacity both to measure and to control unmediated nature. Lévi-Strauss's hope, of course, was that myth would also provide the clue to the basic link between mind and culture, a link that he divined, albeit unconvincingly, in the binary mechanism at the heart of thought and that he presumed to lie deeply embedded in the human brain.

The juxtaposition of his ideas with those of Cassirer and Winnicott should serve the following purpose. It is to suggest that an explanation for the power of the symbolic in general, and of myth in particular, is not to be sought in biology, nor even in behavior, but in the elementary experiences of life, and at the level at which those experiences shape unconscious and conscious thought and feeling.

The implications for the study of television are clear. It is that television, in its mythic character, must be seen as a basically regressive medium; not regressive necessarily in a pejorative sense, but in the sense of putting those who work with it, both as producers and receivers, in touch with elementary thoughts, elementary feelings, elementary both in terms of individual and cultural experience. Douglas Kellner (1982) has talked of the "palaeosymbolic" meanings of television. I have invited consideration of the medium in terms of narrative structures. What both perceptions suggest is that no understanding of the impact, effect, or whatever, of television can be assured without considering the psychodynamics of the medium as a primary cultural force that puts us, the viewers, literally in touch with the basic concerns of life in basically simple and effective ways. In this sense, it is possible to see television as a transitional object.

All this means that research into the place of television in everyday life must be conducted through the analysis of the fine detail of social and psychological interaction in and around the television, into the minutiae of gossip and memory, and into the narratives of personal and familial and national identity into which television's own narratives are, and must be, crucially embedded.

NOTES

1. The writing of this chapter has benefited enormously from the comments of the following, to whom grateful thanks are given: Robert White, James Carey, Horace

Newcomb, James Reeves, Jackie Byars, Gregor Goethels, Stewart Hoover, and Elizabeth Lockwood. Needless to say, none of them bears any responsibility for what follows.

2. For the most recent excursion into the wilds of the technologically determinant, see Joshua Meyrowitz (1985).

3. The literature on myth is enormous, contradictory, and exhilarating. I have tried to summarize some of it, insofar as it bears particularly on the issue of television, in Chapter 3 of Silverstone (1981, pp. 49-84).

4. But it is possible, and often persuasive; see, for example, Marshall Sahlins (1976), Goethels (1981), Wright (1975), and Leymore (1975).

5. Claude Lévi-Strauss (1973, pp. 392-393): "It is as if we were asserting that men have always and everywhere undertaking the same task in striving towards the same objective and that, throughout history, only the means have differed. I confess that this view does not worry me; it seems to be the one most in keeping with the facts, as revealed by history and anthropology, and above all it appears to be more fruitful. . . . If men have always been concerned with only one task—how to create a society fit to live in—the forces which inspired our distant ancestors are also present in us" (cf. Claude Lévi-Strauss [1969, 1973, 1978, 1981]).

6. The literature developing narrative theory is now substantial. My work took on the work of Vladimir Propp, A. J. Greimas, Claude Bremond, Tzvetan Todorov, Christian Metz, and many others. Poststructuralism, following above all Barthes's break with formal models in *S/Z* (1975), has developed rapidly; see, for example, Culler (1975), Sturrock (1979). Recent readers include Harari (1979), Young (1981).

7. Theodor Adorno (1964, p. 480 and p. 479): "Probably all the various levels in mass media involve all the mechanisms of consciousness and unconsciousness stressed by psychoanalysis."

8. This is more than cavalier. Of course, there is a wealth of semiology relevant to, though not always directly focused on, television. For two relatively recent accessible introductions, see Fiske and Hartley (1978), Berger (1981).

9. "Man can adapt somehow to anything his imagination can cope with, but he cannot deal with chaos. . . . Therefore our most important assets are always the symbols of our general orientation in nature, on the earth, in society and in whatever we are doing" Langer (1951, p. 287).

10. For a fascinating recent study of the mass media's role in creating and managing anxiety, see Turner, Nigg, and Paz (1986).

REFERENCES

Adorno, T. (1964). Television and the patterns of mass culture. In B. Rosenberg & D. Manning White (Eds.), *Mass culture: The popular arts in America*. New York: Free Press.

Ang, I. (1985). *Watching Dallas: Soap opera and the melodramatic imagination*. London: Methuen.

BBC Broadcasting Research. (1984). Special report: Research for horizon, "a new green revolution." London: Author.

Barthes, R. (1972). *Mythologies*. London: Jonathan Cape.

Barthes, R. (1975). *S/Z*. London: Jonathan Cape.

Barthes, R. (1977). The rhetoric of the image. In S. Heath (Ed.), *Image-music-text* (pp. 32-51). London: Fontana.

Berger, A. A. (1981). Semiotics and television. In R. P. Adler (Ed.), *Understanding television* (pp. 91-114). New York: Praeger.

Berger, P., & Luckmann, T. (1967). *The social construction of reality.* Harmondsworth: Penguin.

Block, M. (1974). Symbols, song, dance and features of articulation. *European Journal of Sociology, 15*(1), 55-81.

Bocock, R. (1974). *Ritual in industrial society.* London: Allen & Unwin.

Bourdieu, P. (1977). *Outline of a theory of practice.* Cambridge: Cambridge University Press.

Burgelin, O. (1972). Structural analysis of mass communication. In D. McQuail (Ed.), *Sociology of mass communications* (pp. 313-328). Harmondsworth: Penguin.

Burke, K. (1950). *A rhetoric of motives.* New York: Prentice-Hall.

Cassirer, E. (1953). *Language: Vol. 1. The philosophy of symbolic forms.* New Haven, CT: Yale University Press.

Cassirer, E. (1955). *Mythical thought: Vol. 2. The philosophy of symbolic forms.* New Haven, CT: Yale University Press.

Chaney, D. (1983). A symbolic mirror of ourselves: Civic ritual in a mass society. *Media, Culture and Society, 5,* 119-135.

Culler, J. (1975). *Structuralist poetics: Structuralism, linguistics and the study of literature.* London: Routledge & Kegan Paul.

de Certeau, M. (1984). *The practice of everyday life.* Berkeley: University of California Press.

Durkheim, É. (1971). *The elementary forms of the religious life.* London: George Allen & Unwin. (Original work published 1915)

Durkheim, É., & Mauss, M. (1963). *Primitive classification.* London: Cohen and West.

Fiske, J., & Hartley, J. (1978). *Reading television.* London: Methuen.

Geertz, C. (1975). *The interpretation of cultures.* London: Hutchinson.

Geertz, C. (1980, Spring). Blurred genres: The refiguration of social thought. *The American Scholar,* pp. 165-179.

Giner, S., & Silverstone, R. (1885). Comunio, domini, innovacio: Per una teoria de la cultura. In S. Giner Comunio, *domini, innovacio: Per una teoria de la cultura* (pp. 15-55). Barcelona: Laia.

Goethels, G. (1981). *The TV ritual: Worship at the video altar.* Boston: Beacon.

Gramsci, A. (1949). Gli intellettuali e l'organizzazione della cultura [quoted in Antonio Gramsci (1971). *Selections from the prison notebooks.* London: Lawrence and Wishart].

Group μ. (1981). *A general rhetoric.* Baltimore: Johns Hopkins University Press.

Harari, J. V. (Ed.). (1979). *Textual strategies: Perspectives in post-structuralist criticism.* London: Methuen.

Harrison, J. (1973). From ritual to art. In T. & E. Burns (Eds.), *Sociology of literature and drama.* Harmondsworth: Penguin.

Horton, D., & Wohl, R. R. (1956). Mass communication and para-social interaction. *Psychiatry, 29*(3), 215-229.

Jakobson, R. (1970). On Russian fairy tales. In M. Lane (Ed.), *Structuralism: A reader.* London: Jonathan Cape.

Katz, E., & Dayan, D. (1985). Media events: On the experience of not being there. *Religion, 15,* 305-314.

Kellner, D. (1982). TV, ideology and emancipatory popular culture. In H. Newcomb (Ed.), *Television: The critical view.* New York: Oxford University Press.

Knorr-Cetina, K. D. (1981). *The manufacture of knowledge: An essay on the constructivist and contextual nature of science.* Oxford: Pergamon Press.

Langer, S. (1951). *Philosophy in a new key.* Oxford: Oxford University Press.

Latour, B., & Woolgar, S. (1979). *Laboratory life: The social construction of scientific facts.* Newbury Park, CA: Sage.

Lévi-Strauss, C. (1969). *The raw and the cooked: Vol. 1. Introduction to a science of mythology.* London: Jonathan Cape.

Lévi-Strauss, C. (1973a). *Tristes tropiques.* London: Jonathan Cape.

Lévi-Strauss, C. (1973b). *From honey to ashes: Vol. 2. Introduction to a science of mythology.* London: Jonathan Cape.

Lévi-Strauss, C. (1978). *The origin of table manners: Vol. 3. Introduction to a science of mythology.* London: Jonathan Cape.

Lévi-Strauss, C. (1981). *The naked man: Vol. 3. Introduction to a science of mythology.* London: Jonathan Cape.

Lévi-Strauss, C. (1985). *The view from afar.* Oxford: Basil Blackwell.

Lewis, J. (1985). Decoding television news. In P. Drummond & R. Paterson (Eds.), *Television in transition* (pp. 205-234). London: British Film Institute.

Leymore, V. L. (1975). *Hidden myth: Structure and symbolism in advertising.* London: Heinemann Educational Books.

Lyotard, J.-F. (1984). *The post-modern condition: A report on knowledge.* Manchester: Manchester University Press.

Mauss, M. (1972). *A general theory of magic.* London. Routledge & Kegan Paul.

McLuhan, M. (1964). *Understanding media.* London: Routledge & Kegan Paul.

McLuhan, M. (1967). *The medium is the message.* New York: Bantam Books.

Meyrowitz, J. (1985). *No sense of place: The impact of electronic media on social behaviour.* New York: Oxford University Press.

Morley, D. (1980). *The nationwide audience.* London: British Film Institute.

Ong, W. J. (1982). *Orality and literacy: The technologizing of the word.* London: Methuen.

Perelman, C. (1979). *The new rhetoric and the humanities: Essays on rhetoric and its applications.* Dordrecht: D. Reidel.

Ricoeur, P. (1984). *Time and narrative* (Vol. 1). Chicago: Chicago University Press.

Sahlins, M. (1976). *Culture and practical reason.* Chicago: Chicago University Press.

Shils, E., & Young, M. (1953). The meaning of the coronation. *Sociological Review, I*(2), 63-82.

Silverstone, R. (1976). Ernst Cassirer and Claude Lévi-Strauss: Two approaches to the study of myth. *Archives de Sciences Sociales des Religions, 41*, 25-36.

Silverstone, R. (1981). *The message of television: Myth and narrative in contemporary culture.* London: Heinemann Educational Books.

Silverstone, R. (1983). The right to speak: On a poetic for television documentary. *Media, Culture and Society, 5*(2), 137-154.

Silverstone, R. (1984a). A structure for a modern myth: Television and the transsexual. *Semiotica, 49*(1/2), 95-138.

Silverstone, R. (1984b). Narrative strategies in television science: A case study. *Media, Culture and Society, 6*(4), 377-410.

Silverstone, R. (1985a). *Framing science: The making of a BBC documentary.* London: British Film Institute.

Silverstone, R. (1985b). Television and the family. Report presented to the Independent Broadcasting Authority. London: Author.

Silverstone, R. (1986). The agonistic narratives of television science. In J. Corner (Ed.), *Documentary and the mass media.* London: Edward Arnold.

Singer, A. (1966). Science broadcasting. *BBC Lunchtime Lectures*. London: BBC.

Sturrock, J. (Ed.). (1979). *Structuralism and since: From Lévi-Strauss to Derrida*. Oxford: Oxford University Press.

Todorov, T. (1982). *Theories of the symbol*. Oxford: Basil Blackwell.

Turner, R. H., Nigg, J. M., & Paz, D. H. (1986). *Waiting for disaster: Earthquake watch in California*. Berkeley: University of California Press.

Turner, V. (1969). *The ritual process*. London: Routledge & Kegan Paul.

Turner, V. (1982). *From ritual to theatre*. New York: Performing Arts Journal Productions.

Vaihinger, H. (1924). *The philosophy of "as-if."* London: Kegan, Paul, Trench, Trubner.

van Gennep, A. (1960). *The rites of passage*. London: Routledge & Kegan Paul.

Winnicott, D. W. (1974). *Playing and reality*. Harmondsworth: Penguin.

Wright, W. (1975). *Sixguns and society: A structural study of the western*. Berkeley: University of California Press.

Young, R. (Ed.). (1981). *Untying the text: A post-structuralist reader*. London: Kegan Paul.

Chapter 2

TELEVISION AS AN
AESTHETIC MEDIUM

David Thorburn

A WARRIOR'S SWORD

"The life of things is in reality many lives," writes the cultural historian Philip Fisher. To illustrate, he traces the history of a warrior's sword: a sign of manhood and communal defense during the warrior's life, it passes after his death into the hands of the priests of his society, no longer a weapon for use in warfare but a sacred object. Now more often heard of in legends than seen, kept hidden except for ceremonial occasions, the sword takes up its second, its ritualized, and sacred identity. In time, Fisher continues, the society suffers a defeat; the sword along with all valued objects is seized as loot, "converted to treasure by the victors for whom it is a souvenir that reminds them of a victory. It is an object of wealth." Finally, a "higher" civilization destroys all the groups of this warrior society: "Anthropologists take the sword to a museum, classifying it along with cooking implements, canoes, clothing, statues, and toys as an example of a cultural 'style.'" Now it has become an artifact, a source of historical, anthropological and aesthetic contemplation (Fisher, 1975, pp. 587-88).

We can say, I think, that the story forms of a society undergo similar (though not identical) transformations. Homer's oral epics, the plays of Sophocles, Aristophanes, Plautus, even Shakespeare, continue to be experienced as narratives and as performances in our own day, but we fool ourselves when we imagine or pretend that contemporary versions of such texts very closely resemble their original, communal enactments. Even with the story forms of our own century and native culture—the

AUTHOR'S NOTE: This chapter is excerpted from *Story Machine* by David Thorburn, to be published by Oxford University Press. Copyright by the author.

silent film, radio, movies of the studio era—there exists a gap between our contemporary mediated experience of such texts and the actuality of their originating embodiments before audiences who regarded them as objects of use and leisure, no more "valuable" or "artistic" or historically instructive than the jokes and conversations and social encounters that comprised the ordinary blurred continuity of their daily lives. Students of popular culture, and particularly of American television, are crucially entangled in the paradoxes of cultural transformation Fisher's parable describes. In examining television, we inevitably become part of a system or process of "museumization": Appropriating television texts for historical or anthropological or aesthetic use, we transform the medium, conferring upon it something of the dignity accorded to the texts and artifacts already elevated into the "high culture" that is preserved in museums and art galleries and scholarly books and university curricula. The costs and dangers inherent in this enterprise, wherein the most ordinary and habitual usages of a culture are appropriated for intellectual analysis, have come increasingly to preoccupy me, and surely demand closer scrutiny than they have yet received from all who think and write about American media.

BEYOND IDEOLOGY

One partial resolution or solution to the paradoxes mentioned above, however, turns on the recognition that the warrior's sword only imperfectly resembles objects whose original character was essentially aesthetic.

This adjective is problematic, I realize. But I know no other word I can use for the qualities I wish to identify in our popular culture and specifically in our television system. Let us first understand the term *aesthetic* in its descriptive, its cultural or anthropological dimension: not a valuing of "aesthetic objects" but a designation of their chief defining feature—their membership in a class of cultural experiences understood to be "fictional" or "imaginary," understood to occur in a symbolic, culturally agreed-upon imaginative space. This site may be a theater; the intimate, privatized spaces of our experience of television; the vast ritual amphitheaters of the ancient world; the dark communal space of the movie house—any ritualized environment wherein "real" experience is re-presented, re-created, symbolically displayed.

The vase paintings or dramatic rituals or communal legends of the warrior's culture must be said to differ from the sword in this way: their fictive or imaginative, their representational or artistic qualities are inherent from the beginning, and this means that however much is lost in their later survivals—as translated printed texts, say, of original oral performances; or as photographic reproductions or scholarly reconstructions of drawings and paintings on the shards of clay vessels—our later experience of these objects, our understanding of them as symbolic and artistic expression, may be a lesser violence than our appropriation of the sword.

For me, this recognition is the ground for an argument that insists on the centrality of aesthetic perspectives in the study of most forms of popular culture, and especially such forms as films, television programs, and rock concerts, all of which contain narrative or dramatic or spectacular/musical features.

The argument for aesthetic (or, in the case of narrative and dramatic forms, literary) methods seems to me particularly important to articulate in our present intellectual climate because the widespread influence of structuralist and so-called deconstructionist perspectives has clearly sanctioned approaches to popular and elite texts alike that minimize or deny the difference between fictional discourse and other forms of expression. The increasing fashion in film scholarship to seek out what are said to be the ideological structures controlling cinematic discourse has already measurably affected the emerging and far more primitive academic writing devoted to television. The genuine value of such ideological emphases need not be doubted, but their limits need to be more fully recognized and acknowledged.

In the case of literary scholarship, and, to a lesser degree, film scholarship, the prior existence of a complex and widely known field of argument devoted to explication and evaluation creates a steadying background, a counterpoint, against which the newer forms of ideological criticism can be placed and judged. We are not likely, for example, to be misled, our sense of his cultural and artistic significance is unlikely to be simplified, when we are told by a neo-Marxist or structuralist reader that Shakespeare's plays articulate the standard (and historically biased) Tudor view of English history. Or again, an account of Dickens's perhaps unconscious acceptance of liberal-reformist and patriarchal ideologies will scarcely dislodge the large and persuasive body of criticism that establishes his distinction as one of the wisest and most artful of English novelists.

But the absence of such traditional forms of scholarship in the case of many aspects of popular culture, and particularly in the case of television, creates, I believe, special dangers. In these emerging fields of study, a scholarly discourse intent on "deconstructing" texts (and audiences) risks severing itself from the way in which such texts were conceived and experienced by those who created them and by the audiences who consumed them. Lacking a systematic history of television programming, much less a body of analysis attempting even the most elementary aesthetic discriminations—as between, say, *Gilligan's Island* and *M*A*S*H*, or between the *Mod Squad* and *Police Story* or that fine series' culminating refinement, *Hill Street Blues*—we are unlikely to be instructed by accounts of television purporting to lay bare its ideological substructures, its hidden assumptions about sexual or familial or racial conflict.

I don't mean that searching out such meanings is wrong, of course. But I do mean that such topics can't be meaningfully addressed by a scholar oblivious to what I'm calling the literary or aesthetic dimensions of television programs. The argument for the centrality of aesthetic perspectives in the study of television, as I conceive it, then, is not only, not even primarily, an argument for an evaluative criticism aiming to disclose the thematic density and formal excellence of particular programs, though that remains for me a crucial enterprise. The most compelling justification for essentially literary perspectives in television study—or, at the very least, in the study of television's fiction programming—is that such perspectives are necessary for the basic work of historical and cultural interpretation. Because television fiction is a body of drama or narrative that relies on conventions of characterization, plotting, and, especially, of genre, and that employs strategies of editing and camera movement drawn from our culture's 80-year saturation in forms of visual story-telling, a scholarship oblivious or insensitive to these aesthetic ground-features of the medium will be radically enfeebled. Even the simplest account of the evolution or historical development of the medium must be capable of recognizing, for example, how the genre-formulas that have dominated television have altered over time, must be sensitive to the ways in which particular performers bring particular thematic associations with them as they move from role to role, and must be alert to the nuances of tone that particular writers and creators and even directors introduce into television programs.

A concrete example will perhaps help to clarify the dangers of ignoring such literary perspectives. In a widely cited section of his history of American broadcasting, Erik Barnouw perceives a virtually conspiratorial fit between the corporate imperialism of John Kennedy's foreign policy and the content of prime-time television. In a subsection of *Tube of Plenty* (1975), provocatively titled "Paranoid Pictures Presents," Barnouw cites the increase of spy series in the mid-1960s as proof that an aggressively self-righteous imperialism, pitting American good guys against evil communist bad guys, was being promulgated by television. TV entertainment, we are informed, was "an integral part of the [Vietnam] escalation machine" (p. 377).

But the evidence chiefly cited to support this judgment consists of six spy series, at least four of which have a subversively antic or parodic energy that undermines or radically qualifies Barnouw's view of them as forms of propaganda aiming "to harness the nation . . . for war" (p. 376). Such political themes are hard to take seriously, for example, in *Get Smart* (cited by Barnouw) in whose characteristic pilot episode an evil dwarf named Mr. Big holds the world's cities for ransom using a doomsday device, called (after its inventor) "Dante's Inthermo" (Eisner & Krinsky, 1984, p. 281).

The reductiveness of Barnouw's analysis of spy series of the 1960s is, as this example shows, partly a consequence of his indifference to their aesthetic character. Of the six series that constitute his chief evidence, three are explicit parodies, *Get Smart, The Man from U.N.C.L.E.*, and *The Girl From U.N.C.L.E.,* and a fourth, *I Spy* (Bill Cosby's first star vehicle on television), is at least as interested in joking and comic badinage and in the rich improvisational intimacy of the friendship between Robert Culp and Cosby as in the conventional muscle-flexing of the typical spy story. These texts can scarcely sustain the argument that they are significant cold war propaganda. It is more plausible, in fact, to see their mocking attitude to the whole genre of the spy-narrative as instances of a countertendency in the popular arts, whose effect is to expose the foolishness and emptiness of the conspiratorial worldview embedded in straight or serious spy fiction. Barnouw cites details from a few episodes from these series, and he recognizes and even praises the improvisational energy of *I Spy*. But he can't escape his reductive idea of TV series as instruments of propaganda, and so all but ignores questions of tone and atmosphere. The bizarrely improbable plots, the extravagant, almost campy villains, the audiovisual complexity in these programs register if at all for Barnouw as mere "novel surface features" in ideological fables all demonstrating that "Americans lived . . . among unscrupulous conspiracies that required a response in kind" (p. 372). His error, I'm suggesting, is a literary one; he radically misreads these texts because he does not grant sufficient weight to their aesthetic qualities.

Of course, I don't mean to suggest that Erik Barnouw, more participant-observer than objective scholar (though still an indispensable authority on the economic history of broadcasting), can fairly represent contemporary schools of ideological criticism. There is an emerging, ideologically grounded scholarship devoted to television that is far subtler and more persuasive than Barnouw's unselfconscious civic-mindedness. But I think my example instructive nonetheless, for the reductiveness in Barnouw's reading *is* characteristic of most journalistic interpretations of television, and also of much social-scientific work on the medium, even including that of George Gerbner's Annenberg school of neo-Marxist statistical interpretation, perhaps the most influential body of American "academic" writing on television.

Other more theoretically sophisticated perspectives, such as those of Todd Gitlin (1983) and those of Raymond Williams (1975) and other members of the British cultural studies group—suggestively represented in such collections as Michael Gurevitch et al.'s *Culture, Society and the Media* (1982) and Len Masterman's *Television Mythologies* (1984)— offer more nuanced, indisputably helpful readings of television's ideological substructures. Fiske and Hartley's *Reading Television* (1978), an essential book, can be said to represent the best of both the semiotic and the "neo-Marxist" strains in recent cultural theory. But even these perspectives are often limited by an implicit anticapitalist program, the assumption that a medium so embedded in the economic and political order of advanced technological capitalism must be "demystified" so we can see its corruption.

This is helpful but too partial a view, for the medium is not uniquely corrupt: all new systems of communication and technology are controlled by the nexus of economic, political, and social forces governing the cultures in which they appear. The relevant task is not merely to "deconstruct" or expose the ideological assumptions embedded in television texts, but to explore the range of freedoms permitted the text by the cultural rules and ideological pressures that ultimately *but not in every dimension* confine it.

Comparative perspectives are helpful here, though rarely invoked. The Nazis, Raymond Williams (1975, p. 24) shrewdly reminds us, had systematic plans to use television as an instrument of state control. There would be no private ownership or use of television receivers in Goebbels's scheme for the medium; instead, television screens were to be placed in public spaces, refining and monstrously enlarging the state's project of ritualized mass indoctrination. Such potential alternatives to the American advertiser-based system of television ought to remind us that there will be critical differences in the nature and degree to which particular communications systems obey their cultural masters.

Moreover, to imagine such alternatives as Nazi prime time—or to think comparatively about Russian or South African or British television—is to see more clearly that what I'm calling aesthetic methods of interpretation—an attentiveness to tone, to plot and character, to visual strategies, to the workings of narrative and symbolic texts—are essential to the task of describing and judging such systems. In fact, one way to explain the rare authority of such writers as Fiske and Hartley is to recognize that their accounts of television programs are far more attuned than most ideologically oriented readings to aesthetic registers of meaning. To understand our television system, I want to insist, even in its historical and ideological dimensions—to understand the medium as a cultural force—we must be sensitive in part to literary matters; we must be able to read these texts in something of the way in which the audience experiences them: as stories or dramas, as aesthetic artifacts, whose meaning will be fully available only if we employ, along with other interpretive methods, the strategies of reading traditionally used by critics of literature and film.

TOWARD AN AESTHETIC ANTHROPOLOGY

In estimating the importance of aesthetic or literary perspectives on television, it is instructive to compare prevailing American attitudes toward television with the attitudes held less than a generation ago toward our homegrown movies and moviemakers. Many film scholars have pointed to the irony that America's recognition of her own achievement in the art of film lagged far behind that of Europe. Our genre movies came finally to seem valuable to us, the film critics have shown, only after the French *nouvelle vague* directors had legitimated for educated Americans the myths and conventions of those direct ancestors of today's police and detective series, the films of Bogart and Cagney and Edward G. Robinson.

This change in American attitudes toward the movies—more accurately, this change in the attitudes of our educated classes—is the more instructive, and grows more ironic, when we consider how its emergence is tied to the decline of the movies as a form of popular art. Through the 1950s and the 1960s, as critics of the American film lost their defensiveness and began to speak with the same confidence (and also, alas, often the same specialized jargon) as the literary critics, the American film itself was being supplanted by television as America's principal medium of popular narrative. (In 1951, in the early dawn of the television age, 90 million Americans attended the movies each week; by 1959, weekly attendance had fallen to 43 million; today the vast majority of Americans attend the movies only two or three times *per year*.) As the Hollywood studios and their vast machinery for star-making and film manufacturing receded into history and as there emerged a generation of reviewers, critics, and, finally, university professors whose deepest experience of art had occurred in the movie houses of their childhoods, the American film came to be detached or liberated from its identity as a consumer item, a mere commercial product, and to be located within an aesthetic field.

This recognition of the essential *artistic* dimension of the Hollywood commercial movie was and remains an intellectual achievement of great magnitude, for it permitted fundamental new perspectives on the cultural history of the United States, profoundly complicating our understanding of the workings of our economic system and altering our understanding of the nature and possibilities of art itself. The most significant implication of this recognition, an implication still only partially explored by film critics and historians, is this: *capitalist greed, the crassest of alliances between commerce and modern technology, may constitute the enabling conditions of a complex narrative art.*

But, as I've already suggested, this recognition, which was the work of years and many scholars, was in certain respects a belated one. By the time it had been fully lodged in the educated consciousness, in our museums and our universities—Abbott and Costello transfigured to an artifact, joining Euripides and warriors' swords—the American film itself was no longer a habitual experience for the mass of our population, having yielded to television not only its ability to incite our contempt for manufactured entertainment but also its status as our central institution for story-telling.

It is certain that this distance was a necessary prelude to our recognition of the cultural importance and aesthetic value of the movies. But it is essential to observe that television itself is now four decades old and that the respect the film scholars and reviewers routinely bestow on even the most insignificant monster movies has almost no counterpart in our discourse concerning television.

To describe television as an institution for story-telling is not, of course, to identify all of its functions in our society. But the term does identify what has always been and will no doubt continue forever to be one of television's dominant functions; and it has the further advantage of helping to expose the crude denial of history that is inherent in prevailing behaviorist and McLuhanite theories about our media culture. Television is unique, unprecedented in human history, these perspectives naively but aggressively assume: the medium has no past, no ancestors. But the moment we recognize that television has a story-telling function, we open ourselves to vastly instructive continuities, we link television to a past more central to it than the behavior of the FCC since 1948 or even—useful as such vital history will be, of course—the stories of Paley, and Goldenson, and the legatees of Robert Sarnoff; and we begin also to acknowledge (or should we say, recover) something of the way it has actually been experienced by viewers.

To define television as (partly) an institution for story-telling is, I'm suggesting, not to flatter the medium nor to grant it a false dignity, but simply to name one of the ways, perhaps the most significant way, in which it has actually functioned in American lives: as an instrument for continuity as well as change, a communication system devoted most of the time to entertaining as many of us as possible with stories and fables that earlier media and story systems had told before. To conceive of television in this way, as the best film scholars conceive their topic, as John Cawelti conceives the task of studying popular culture, is to commit oneself to what might be described as an "aesthetic anthropology," wherein one strives for a simultaneous awareness of TV programs as manufactured cultural artifacts *and* as fictional or dramatic texts.

TELEVISION AS
CONSENSUS NARRATIVE

Such a perspective grounds our sense of television simultaneously in real experience, in the economic and cultural forces that shape it, and also in a long history, a continuity of story-systems—institutions of mythmaking and popular narrative—that extend back into Western history to at least the time of Homer. This continuity, which has a centrally aesthetic dimension, is implicit in Fiske and Hartley's notion of television's "bardic" function (1978, pp. 85-100) and also in Newcomb and Alley's account of television as a "choric" medium that speaks with a communal voice like that of the chorus in Greek tragedy (1983, pp. 31-34).

Extrapolating from these sources, I would identify, in a tentative and speculative spirit, a kind of narrative system I believe is common to most societies if not to all, a recurring, distinct cultural formation to be called *consensus narrative*. I avoid the adjective *popular* to achieve a clearer neutrality, and to identify as a chief feature of consensus narrative the ambition or desire to speak for and to the whole of its culture, or as much of "the whole" as the governing forces in society will permit. Many forms of narrative and performance will exist in most societies and will rightly be called popular, but nearly all will address particular subgroups or classes within a society, as country music or Broadway theater or wrestling or rock concerts do in contemporary America; as bear-baiting and Petrarchan sonnets and the popular ballad and public executions did in the London of Shakespeare and Marlowe.

Consensus narrative, in contrast, operates at the very center of the life of its culture, and is in consequence almost always deeply conservative in its formal structures and in its content. Its "assignment"—so to say—is to articulate the culture's central mythologies, in a widely accessible "language," an inheritance of shared stories, plots, character types, cultural symbols, narrative conventions: a "popular" language because legible to the common understanding of a majority of the culture, as the legends and heroes of Troy and the complex conventions of a formulaic oral poetry confined to dactylic hexameters were known to Homer's audience, as the conventions of the revenge play and the dense verbal textures of the Elizabethan pentameter were known to Shakespeare's, or as the segmented abrupt rhythms and formal and thematic conventions of situation comedy are known to contemporary Americans.

Perhaps there are cultures, or historical eras within particular societies, wherein no form of consensus narrative can emerge, or wherein several media or theaters of communication reinforce and partly contend against one another as carriers of the culture's consensus. And, of course, in any society not only its story-systems but many other practices and institutions will be devoted to articulating an ideology that affirms existing cultural arrangements and values. But the central story forms in a culture have a special significance, partly because they appeal across boundaries of class and wealth and age and gender, affecting to speak to everyone, and partly because their status as "entertainment" and as "fiction" licenses forms or degrees of expression that are otherwise prohibited or denied in actual social practice. Systems or institutions of consensus narrative are thus always complex mirrors of their societies, essential artifacts to which we must turn if we wish to understand ourselves, our ancestors, and our filiations with the past. I have in mind primarily, of course, such story-systems as those I've already mentioned or implied: the oral-formulaic narrative of Homer's day, the theater of Sophocles, the Elizabethan theater, the English novel from Defoe to Dickens and a little beyond, the silent film, the sound film, television during the Network Era.

These, and perhaps many other story-mediums, share central features: they are ritualized, habitual experiences for their audiences; they are profoundly traditional in their formal or stylistic strategies and in their recurring plots, characters, and themes; and they can be seen, I believe, to undergo a similar process of development or evolution.

Whether we consider the oral-formulaic medium that culminated in the poems of Homer or whether we examine later systems of story-telling or communication, a similar pattern of development is visible. Most simply, this pattern is one of self-discovery, in which the new medium begins by repeating and imitating the forms and strategies of its ancestor-systems and gradually, through accident and experiment, discovers more and more thoroughly its own uniqueness.

The novel, for example, is born as an amalgam of older forms—the romance, the picaresque tale, certain forms of religious narrative such as puritan autobiography, various forms of journalism and historical writing. At first it combines these elements haphazardly and crudely. Then, nourished by a large and eager audience that makes novel writing a highly profitable enterprise, the novel begins to distinguish itself clearly from these earlier forms, to combine its inherited elements more harmoniously and judiciously, and to exploit the possibilities for narrative that are uniquely available to fictional stories printed in books.

The same principle can be seen in the history of the movies, which begin crudely, borrowing assumptions taken from older media such as theater and still photography and then evolving methods that exploit with greater and greater subtlety the unique properties of the motion picture camera and the particular qualities inherent in the environment of the movie house.

The evolution of these systems of entertainment and communication is always immensely complicated by the rivalry of competing systems, by the economic structures that shape and support such systems and that are in turn altered themselves as the new media root themselves in people's lives. Improvements in technology and in methods of distribution and access further complicate the development of such media. In the case of film, for instance, decisive changes follow upon the advent of sound, the development of lighter, more mobile cameras and of more sensitive film stock; and seismic shifts in the very nature of film, in its relation to its audience and its society, occur with the birth of television. Perhaps most significant of all, media systems and institutions for story-telling alter and extend their possibilities as their audiences grow more comfortable with them, learning the special codes and conventions such institutions generate and rely upon. This distance between *Fred Ott's Sneeze* (1893)—only seconds long, produced in East Orange, New Jersey, in the world's first movie studio—and Chaplin's *Modern Times* (1936) is a rich, decisive emblem for these interacting processes, these enabling conditions of consensus narrative.

I believe such story-systems present even greater challenges to adequately "thick" description than the immense complexities involved in understanding a Balinese cock fight as Clifford Geertz would have us understand it. In his suggestive essays in *The Interpretation of Cultures* (1973), Geertz offers powerful arguments for the centrality of aesthetic perspectives in the reading of all forms of cultural ritual, urging us to bring to the cock fight the same respect for complexity and the same attentiveness to dramatic ritual as we bring to a reading of *Macbeth* (pp. 448-453). There can be no rational dissent from this expectation, but I wonder if forms of narrative, at least the most coherent and significant of them, are not more taxing still in their claims on the interpreter, because they do not merely embody cultural assumptions and values, they consciously articulate, examine, and judge such matters themselves. Narrative and dramatic texts, that is to say, do not merely express or display a culture's notions of masculinity, risk, nobility, the power of fortune or catastrophe as the cock fight (among other things) does for Geertz's Bali; such story-forms will in addition be *about* these topics, will try to examine and to understand them, as *Macbeth* examines and understands these and other aspects of its culture.

Insisting on this distinction between art and artifact, I'm clinging, I recognize, to an outmoded humanism, which wants still to believe that there is a significant difference between art and entertainment, the former having value for us not only as a cultural artifact but also intrinsically, because it is beautiful and wise. In this perspective, to supply some concrete examples, Thomas Heywood—Shakespeare's popular contemporary, whose *A Woman Killed with Kindness* (1603) is one of the originating melodramas of the English-speaking world—is an entertainer, as worthy as the cock fight of our sustained historical or anthropological attention; but Shakespeare is an artist who demands (and rewards) a wider, deeper, and ultimately less specialized atten- tiveness. Or again, Wilkie Collins is a superior entertainer who sustains a rich suspense in his stories of Victorian crime and mystery, a writer whose assumptions about social class, marriage, crime, and punishment are culturally or historically revealing; but Dickens is an artist whose equally suspenseful mysteries articulate in addition a complex under- standing of these defining Victorian and modern themes.

Increasingly, though, I find myself reluctant to press this distinction too austerely because the margins separating art from entertainment are so difficult to locate, and because so many works of art—and especially so many instances of consensus narrative—are partial achievements, arresting and powerful intermittently, but lapsing often to incoherence or easy stereotypes or mechanical formulas of plot and character. Because movies are a collaborative and commercial art, as many film critics have come to acknowledge, the perfect masterpiece is very rare.

But the intelligence and energy of the performers, the craft or art of the director, the cinematographer, the editor may redeem banal scripts, complicate and subvert stereotypes, and offer us complex pleasures.

So acknowledging this partialness is not a retreat from the archaic evaluative humanism I'm defending; it's just a necessary qualification. Our understanding of television will be crippled, I'm suggesting, if we refuse to describe and evaluate the differences between Gilligan and Hawkeye Pierce, for example, or between *I Led Three Lives* and *I Spy*.

In any event, the most crucial feature of consensus narrative is shared by all members of the class, even the least "artistic": consensus narrative is always a deeply collaborative enterprise. Such stories are created, or constituted, by an elaborate web of transactions or interactions or contested collaborations: between the text and its audience, which brings to the story-experience a critical historical and aesthetic literacy; and between the individual text and its ancestors and competitors in the same genres; and between the text and the rules and constraints as to subject matter and form imposed by the dominant economic and social order; and even between or among the community of creators—teams of oral poets or singers, performers, directors, technical specialists, writers, producers—who actually produce the text.

This communal and collaborative dimension of consensus narrative helps to explain why such story-forms are confined by the dominant pieties of the cultures they inhabit, explains their apparent lack of originality, their formulaic character. But it also explains their special power to articulate what my old humanist teachers would have called the wisdom of the community. This crucial aspect of consensus narrative is, in my view, minimized or (often) entirely denied by most of the ideologically grounded scholarship devoted to film and television. The "dominant ideology" that is said to govern these and other forms of consensus narrative is neither so rigid nor so oppressive as current semiotic and neo-Marxist perspectives seem to assume, and the relationship between the audience and the text is more complex, more active and vital than such perspectives acknowledge (Abercrombie & Turner, 1978; Newcomb & Hirsch, 1984).

The conservatism of consensus narrative, that is to say, makes it a chief carrier of the lore and inherited understanding of its culture, as well as society's idealizations and deceptions about itself. That inherited understanding is no simple ideological construct, but a matrix of values and assumptions that undergoes a continuous testing, rehearsal, and revision in the culturally licensed experience of consensus narrative. If consensus narrative is a site or forum in which the culture promulgates its mythologies of self-justification and appropriation, it is also the "liminal space," as the anthropologist Victor Turner names it, in which the deepest values and contradictions of society are articulated and, sometimes, understood (1967, pp. 93-111; 1977, pp. 94-130).

Some lines from Shakespeare wonderfully illustrate this principle and can stand as an emblem for the collaborative and communal wisdom of consensus narrative. Late in *Cymbeline*, two young men sing a haunting dirge over the corpse of one they believe to be a comrade:

> Fear no more the heat o' the sun
> Nor the furious winter's rages;
> Thou thy worldly task hast done,
> Home art gone, and ta'en thy wages;
> Golden lads and girls all must,
> As chimney-sweepers, come to dust. [IV.2.258]

These lovely simple lines link human death with the cycles of nature, a commonplace idea, I suppose, but brought alive, renewed, by the very clarity and directness of the phrasing, by the decisive, end-stopped rhymes, and by the odd mingling of the familiar or the much-spoken with the abrupt muscular economy of the stressed syllables that begin each line and with the tetrameter rhythms. Though the specific decisions are no doubt Shakespeare's, we can hear in the Biblical phrasing a collaborative energy that aligns the poem's sentiments with a long tradition of proverbial and religious understanding. The last two lines quoted above are the most memorable and potent in the poem, I think, for they are the most humanly specific and disturbing, extending the text's argument to the ambiguously consoling recognition that wealth and station, even youth itself, must come home to the grave: "Golden lads and girls all must, / As chimney sweepers, come to dust." The beauty and genius of these lines belong not only—perhaps not even mainly—to Shakespeare, but to the culture that speaks with and through him. For, as Hugh Kenner (1971, pp. 122) reports, even today in Shakespeare's native Warwickshire, dandelions, those common weedy yellow flowers that appear in early spring, are called "golden lads" in their first blooming and then are called "chimney-sweepers" when they go to seed, their sturdy yellow caps transformed to a delicate spume of white filaments, the entire flower metamorphosed into the smalfened image of a chimney sweeper's broom. The metaphoric richness of the lines is not compromised by this colloquial meaning; on the contrary, the poem achieves a stunning enhancement or deepening of its argument when we know that the very terms used to describe human mortality actually name the phases in the life of a common flower. Here as so often elsewhere in his work, Shakespeare recovers and speaks the familiar wisdom of his culture, the wisdom of consensus narrative.

A FABLE FOR OUR
MEDIA CULTURE

I began with a fable about a warrior's sword, and want to end, as a way of complicating my argument one last time and also as a way of crystallizing and completing it, with another fable—this one transcribed from my imperfect memory of a science fiction short story I read as a teenager perhaps 30 years ago.

Millenia from now, the planetary archaeologists of an advanced civilization come across a dead Earth, whose ruins they sift for artifacts of a vanished culture. In one promising site, yielding other fragments of a highly technologized society, the Centuran archaeologists discover a flat metal canister containing a spool of semitransparent celluloid on which images or signs are inscribed. Inferring projectors after laborious study, the aliens construct one and project the film:

> Tiny bipeds in rapid and spasmodic motion. Projectiles, machines, perhaps vehicles, racing and careening through a dizzyingly colored and rapid visual field. Explosions. Frantic collisions—acts of aggression? sexual encounters?—between bipeds and between bipeds and vehicles.

These frantic images, we are told, will baffle generations of Centuran scholars, who will construct elaborate theses concerning the civilization inscribed in the celluloid artifact, and whose deepest powers will be spent in a fruitless effort to decode the hieroglyphs that appear in its final frames: A Walt Disney Production.

The author of this wry fable intended a simpler irony than we can enjoy. He meant, I'm sure, to expose the absurdity and inadequacy of the popular culture as an expression of our civilization. Writing in the 1950s, he expects a response to Hollywood entertainment no longer possible in our age of film archives and Ph.D. programs in film history. Of course, he is right in a way that should still haunt us, but I believe anyone who thinks seriously about our media culture must have a different sense of the task of deciphering the world according to Disney. And we ought also to see—I hope the foregoing has helped us to see—that the key missing element for our Centurans, the clue or solution to the mystery of their film, would be an awareness of aesthetic conventions, a power to read that alien text with something of the literate eye of an American moviegoer of the studio era.

The best understanding of television, I am trying to say, will be reached by those among us who can achieve something of the outsider's objectivity or partial neutrality but who can remain also something of a native informant: alive to the lies and deceptions inscribed in and by the medium, aware of its obedience to advertising and the ideology of consumption, yet responsive also to its audiovisual complexity and to its status as America's central institution for story-telling.

Television Series Cited

Get Smart
9/18/65-9/11/70   138 episodes NBC, CBS
30-min. com.
c: Mel Brooks with Buck Henry
ep: Leonard Stern, Arne Sultan
p: Burt Nodella, Jay Sandrich, Arnie Rosen, Jess Oppenheimer, Chris Hayward
dph: Meredith Nicholson, Robert H. Wyckoff
m: Irving Szathmary
prod. co.: Talent Artists

Gilligan's Island
9/26/64-9/4/67   98 episodes CBS
30-min. com. 36 b&w; 62 color from 65
c: Sherwood Schwartz
p, ep: Schwartz, Jack Arnold, William Froug, Robert L. Rosen
theme: Schwartz and Georgy Wyle
dph: Richard Rawlings
prod. co. : Gladasya-UATV

The Girl from U.N.C.L.E.
9/13/66-8/29/67   29 episodes NBC
60-min. spy-spoof
ep: Norman Felton
prod. co.: MGM

Hill Street Blues
1/15/81-5/12/87   NBC
60-min. police series

c, ep: Michael Kozoll and Steven Bochco
p, ep, w and d include Bochco, Gregory Hoblit, David Anspaugh, Anthony
    Yerkovich, Scott Brazil, Jeffrey Lewis, Sascha Schneider, John Butler,
    David Milch
dph include John Butler, William Cronjager, John C. Flinn
theme: Mike Post
prod. co.: MTM

I Led Three Lives
7/53-6/65   117 episodes Syndicated
30-min. spy series b&w
Based on the memoir by Herbert A. Philbrick
cons: J. Edgar Hoover
prod. co.: ZIV

I Spy
9/15/65-9/2/68   82 episodes NBC
60-min. spy series
ep: Sheldon Leonard
p: Morton Fine, David Friedkin
dph: Fleet Southcott
theme: Earle Hagen
prod. co.: A Three F Production; filmed at Desilu Studios

The Man from U.N.C.L.E.
9/22/64-1/15/68   105 episodes NBC
60-min. spy series
dev.: Sam Rolfe
ep: Norman Felton
p: David Victor
dph: Fred Koenekamp
theme: Jerry Goldsmith
prod. co.: MGM

M*A*S*H
9/17/72-9/19/83   251 episdoes CBS
30-min. com. series
c: dev.: Larry Gelbart
ep: p., w. and d. include Gene Reynolds, Burt Metcalfe, Gelbart, Allan Katz,
    Alan Alda
dph: William Jurgenson, William Cline, Dominick Palmer
theme: Johnny Mandel
prod. co.: 20th Century Fox Television

The Mod Squad
9/24/68-8/23/73 124 episodes ABC
60-min. police series
c: Buddy Ruskin
dev: Tony Barrett, Harve Bennett, Sammy Hess
ep: Aaron Spelling and Leonard Goldberg; Danny Thomas
dph: Fleet Southcott III
m: Earle Hagen
prod. co.: Paramount

Police Story
9/25/73-8/23/77 NBC
60-min. police anthology, cont. irreg. through 79 in 2-hr. episodes.
c: prod. cons.: Joseph Wambaugh
dev: E. Jack Neuman
ep: Stanley Kallis, David Gerber
dph: Emmet Burgholz
theme: Jerry Goldsmith
prod. co.: David Gerber Prods./CPT

REFERENCES

Abercrombie, N., & Turner, B. S. (1978). "The dominant ideology thesis." *British Journal of Sociology, 29*, 149-70.

Barnouw, E. (1975). *Tube of plenty.* New York: Oxford University Press.

Cawelti, J. (1976). *Adventure, mystery, and romance.* Chicago: University of Chicago Press.

Eisner, J., & Krinsky, D. (1984). *Television comedy series.* Jefferson, NC: McFarland.

Fisher, P. (1975). "The future's past." *New Literary History, 6,* 587-606.

Fiske, J., & Hartley, J. (1978). *Reading television.* London: Methuen.

Geertz, C. (1973). *The interpretation of culture.* New York: Basic Books.

Gitlin, T. (1983). *Inside prime time.* New York: Pantheon Books.

Gurevitch, M., Bennett, T., Curran, J., & Woolacott, J. (Eds.). (1982). *Culture, society and the media.* London: Methuen.

Kenner, H. (1971). *The Pound era.* Berkeley: University of California Press.

Masterman, L. (Ed.). (1984). *Television mythologies: Stars, shows and signs.* London: Comedia/MK Media Press.

Newcomb, H., & Alley, R. S. (1983). *The producer's medium.* New York: Oxford University Press.

Newcomb, H., & Hirsch, P., M. (1984). "Television as a cultural forum." In W. D. Rowland, Jr., & B. Watkins (Eds.), *Interpreting television* (pp. 58-73). Newbury Park, CA: Sage.

Turner, V. (1967). *The forest of symbols.* Ithaca, NY: Cornell University Press.

Turner, V. (1977). *The ritual process.* Ithaca, NY: Cornell University Press.
Williams, R. (1975). *Television: Technology and cultural form.* New York: Schocken Books.

Chapter 3

MYTH, CHRONICLE, AND STORY
Exploring the Narrative
Qualities of News

S. Elizabeth Bird and Robert W. Dardenne

ALTHOUGH NEWS ACCOUNTS ARE traditionally known as *stories*, which are by definition culturally constructed narratives, little serious study has been made of the narrative qualities of news, and what constructing "stories" actually means. Many journalists continue "to think in terms of freedom of the press, objectivity, fairness, impartiality, balance, the reflection of reality, true representation, readily accepting a clear distinction between fact and opinion, and so on" (Halloran, 1974, pp. 14-15), treating discussion of the relationship between news and story with suspicion. "Scandals," such as the Janet Cooke affair or the more recent revelations that *New Yorker* writer Alastair Reid used fictional devices in his factual accounts, result in recriminations and "back-to-basics" appeals (see Murphy, 1985).

The pretense is maintained that every news story springs anew from the facts of the event being recorded. If it is true that "you can put six reporters in a court and they can sit through six hours of court verbiage and they'll come out with the same story" (Chibnall, 1981, p. 86), journalists prefer to see this as a vindication of objective reporting rather than the triumph of formulaic narrative construction. Rhetorical and structural devices are seen simply as methods to convey information accurately and effectively, and the perceived gulf between fact and fiction is defended ever more vociferously. "It is very simple. . . . The writer of fiction must invent. The journalist must not invent" (Hersey, 1981, p. 25).

In other disciplines, meanwhile, the study of narrative and story is becoming increasingly important, as emphasis focuses on texts as cultural constructions. Cultural anthropologists have not only rediscovered narrative as an important element in the cultures they examine, but have also begun reflexively to rethink their ethnographic narratives—their news stories—which had long been treated as objective accounts of reality (Marcus, 1982). As Bruner (1984) warns:

> There may be a correspondence between a life as lived, a life as experienced, and a life as told, but the anthropologist should never assume the correspondence nor fail to make the distinction. (p. 7)

Even in such an apparently "objective" discipline as physical anthropology, questions are being raised about the cultural conventions that shape such narratives as the scientific account of human evolution (Landau, 1984).

Historians have always debated the difference between events and stories about events: "Objective" history is now largely seen as naive—"a failure to take into consideration the initial distinction between a physical event which simply occurs, and an event which has already received its historical status from the fact that it has been recounted in chronicles, in legendary stories, in memories etc." (Ricoeur, 1981, p. 276). Like news, history and anthropology narrate real events, and their practitioners are finding that to understand their narratives, they must examine how they are constructed, including the story-telling devices that are an integral part of that construction.

In this interdisciplinary discussion, we consider the news genre as a particular kind of symbolic system. We aim to explore some of the questions arising from the serious consideration of news as narrative and story, and hence the troubled relationship between "reality" and "stories about reality." Media scholars are already studying the narrative paradigm in order to understand the nature of news (for example, Bennett & Edelman, 1985). We aim to advance that discussion by drawing together converging ideas from several fields of inquiry and relating them to this growing communications literature. We believe that from this may come a clearer understanding of the context in which journalists construct news stories, and how these stories relate to the culture of which they are both a reflection and a representation.

APPROACHES TO THE
STUDY OF NEWS

Running through most American writing on news is the assumption that there are two kinds of news, variously called "hard" versus "soft," "important" versus "interesting" (Gans, 1979), "news" versus "human interest" (Hughes, 1968), and "information" versus "story" (Schudson, 1978). Hughes, for example, claims that news articles either edify or entertain, and this either/or split has become a taken-for-granted, if constantly qualified, assumption in American journalism.

This assumption has held back productive discussion of the narrative qualities of news in two ways. First, it has hindered us from seeing news as a unified body that exhibits clear themes and patterns that have little to do with important/interesting splits. It leaves us viewing news within a traditional "transmission model"—essentially from the point of view of the professionals who created this dichotomy. There is little to suggest that audiences experience the world as so neatly divided.

Second, this assumption blinds us to the structural qualities of individual stories. It is accepted that "hard" news is informative and factual, while "soft" news is diverting. In ideal terms, this split is supposed to be dictated by content—certain types of news simply "are" hard, others soft. These qualities are intrinsic in the events being narrated. This perception blinds us to the way narrative devices are used in all news writing, maintaining the illusion that the structural devices used in hard news are merely neutral techniques that act as a conduit for events to become information, rather than ways in which a particular kind of narrative text is created.

We believe that to understand what news as narrative is and does, we must put aside the important/interesting dichotomy and look at news stories as a whole—both as a body of work that is a continuing story of human activity, and as individual stories that contribute to that continuing one. Considering news as narrative does not negate the value of considering news as corresponding with outside reality, as affecting of being affected by society, as being a product of journalists or of bureaucratic organization, but it does introduce another dimension to news, one in which the stories of news transcend their traditional functions of informing and explaining. The news as narrative approach does not deny that news informs; of course readers learn from the news. However, much of what they learn may have little to do with the "facts," "names" and "figures" that journalists try to present so accurately. These details—both significant and insignificant—all contribute to the larger symbolic system of news. The facts, names, and details change almost daily, but the framework into which they fit—the symbolic system—is more enduring. And it could be argued that the totality of news as an enduring symbolic system "teaches" audiences more than any of its component parts, no matter whether these parts are intended to inform, irritate, or entertain.

NEWS AS
MYTHOLOGICAL NARRATIVE

News is part of an age-old cultural practice, narrative and story-telling, that seems to be universal (Rayfield, 1972; Scholes, 1982; Turner, 1982). As narrative, news is orienting (Park, 1944), communal (Dewey, 1927), and ritualistic (Carey, 1975). The orderings and creations in narrative are cultural, not natural; news, like history, endows past events with artificial boundaries, "constructing meaningful totalities out of scattered events" (Ricoeur, 1981, p. 278). So, rather than considering the "accuracy" of facts and their correspondence with an outside reality, we can consider them as contributing to the narrative, as elements in a human ordering of elements.

One of the most productive ways to see news is to consider it as myth, a standpoint that dissolves the distinction between entertainment and information. By this we do not mean to say that individual news stories are like individual myths, but that as a communication process, news can act like myth and folklore (Bird, 1987). Bascom (1954), in a classic statement on the functions of folklore, writes that it serves as education, as a validation of culture, as wish fulfillment, and as a force for conformity, while Malinowski (1974) considered myth to be a "charter" for human culture. Through myth and folklore, members of a culture learn values, definitions of right and wrong, and sometimes can experience vicarious thrills—not all through individual tales, but through a body of lore. As Drummond (1984) writes:

> Myth is primarily a metaphorical device for telling people about themselves, about other people, and about the complex world of natural *and* mechanical objects which they inhabit. (p. 27)

Myth reassures by telling tales that explain baffling or frightening phenomena and provide acceptable answers; myth does not necessarily reflect an objective reality, but builds a world of its own (Frye, 1957).

The mythical qualities of news, particularly television news, have been remarked on (Hartley, 1982; Knight & Dean, 1982; Smith, 1979). For news, too, is a way in which people create order out of disorder, transforming knowing into telling. News offers more than fact—it offers reassurance and familiarity in shared community experiences (Mead, 1925-1926); it provides credible answers to baffling questions, and ready explanations of complex phenomena such as unemployment and inflation (Jensen, 1977). Consuming the news has been compared to religion (Gerbner, 1977), ritual activity (Carey, 1975), celebration (Capo, 1985), and play (Glasser, 1982; Stephenson, 1964). For through the ritualistic narrating of tales (including news), myths are acted out, transformed, and re-created in a "ritual process" (Turner, 1969). As a symbolic system, myth and news act both as a model of and as a model for a culture (Geertz, 1973).

For example, myth outlines the boundaries of acceptable behavior by telling stories, such as the Apache moral narratives that criticize social delinquents, "thereby impressing such individuals with the undesirability of improper behavior and alerting them to the punitive consequences of further misconduct" (Basso, 1984, p. 34). As Drummond (1984) notes, "Of the several boundary conditions, or cultural continuums, that define human identity, the one that holds our interest longest and last is what makes us like and unlike others" (p. 21).

So all news media report crime and deviant behavior, and not primarily as a duty to inform; the average reader does not require the quantities of information offered on crime. While it is possible to argue that readers need to know about crime in order to guard against it, or to bemoan the amount of crime news while saying it is what the "morbidly curious" public demand (Haskins, 1984), a central meaning of crime news is symbolic:

> Such news is a main source of information about the normative contours of a society. It informs us about right and wrong, about the parameters beyond which one should not venture and about the shapes that the devil can assume. A gallery of folk types—heroes and saints, as well as fools, villains and devils—is publicized not just in oral tradition and face-to-face contact, but to much larger audiences and with much greater dramatic resources. (Cohen & Young, 1981, p. 431)

Each individual crime story is written against a backdrop of other crime stories, drawing from them and adding to them. Readers rarely remember details of crime stories, and they do not "use" the information in their daily lives (Graber, 1984). Instead, the stories become part of a larger "story" or myth about crime and values. Graber (1984) and Roshier (1981) both point out that media do not reflect actual crime rates. If information were the only purpose of crime reporting, it would make sense to report all major crimes, such as burglaries and car thefts, so that readers could be on their guard. Instead, 26% of all news-reported crimes in Chicago are murders (Graber). Graber and Roshier show, however, that readers' estimates of actual crime rates are much closer to reality. Readers do not only consume news as a reflection of reality, but as a symbolic text that defines murder as more noteworthy than car thefts. News stories, like myths, do not "tell it like it is," but rather, "tell it like it means." Thus news is a particular kind of mythological narrative with its own symbolic codes that are recognized by its audience. We know, when we read or hear a news story, that we are in a particular "narrative situation" (Barthes, 1982) that requires a particular kind of stance to be understood.

TELLING THE STORY

But how, in terms of individual news accounts, are the myths—the continuing stories—actually narrated? Myth has meaning only in the telling; cultural themes and values exist only if they are communicated. Obviously there is no single myth or narrative that is merely repeated, yet to continue to have power, myths must be constantly retold. Rather, themes are rearticulated and reinterpreted over time, themes that are derived from culture and that feed back into it. Stories are not reinvented every time the need arises; instead, "you constantly draw on the inventory of discourse which have been established over time" (Hall, 1984, p. 6).

Folklorists discuss the oral tradition in terms of an ideal "story," an archetype that does not exist but that is re-created in individual tellings. Thus we have a "story" of Cinderella, of which there is no definitive version, but that we recognize as the same "story" regardless of variation. At a broader level, we know a "Cinderella" story when we hear one—"Cinderella" is a heavily encoded term in our culture. Every so often the story is retold, restructuring diffuse images "all of which will be organized, integrated or apprehended as a specific 'set' of events only in and through the very act by which we narrate them as such" (Herrnstein Smith, 1981, p. 225).

In a news context, Darnton (1975) recalls writing crime stories that, while recording actual events, were rooted in conventional, larger stories, such as "the bereavement story":

> When I needed such quotes, I used to make them up, as did some of the others . . . for we knew what the "bereaved mother" and the "mourning father" should have said and possibly even heard them speak what was in our minds rather than what was in theirs. (p. 190)

Cohen (1981) makes a similar point in assessing how the British media defined the 1960s "mods and rockers" as "folk devils," describing interviews with them as not necessarily faked but as "influenced by the reporter's (or sub-editor's) conception of how anyone labelled as a thug or a hooligan *should* speak, dress and act" (p. 275).

Much of the mythical quality of news derives from such "resonance"—the feeling that we have written or read the same stories over and over again. The principle of consonance (Galtung & Ruge, 1965) ensures that events that may actually be different are encoded into frameworks that are already understood and anticipated. News "conveys an impression of endlessly repeated drama whose themes are familiar and well-understood" (Rock, 1981, p. 68). Frayn (1981) neatly satirizes this process in his "demonstration that in theory a digital computer could be programmed to produce a perfectly satisfactory daily newspaper with all the variety and news sense of the old hand-made article" (p. 71). Frayn's point is that such is the formulization of news that we need draw only on the existing body of news to create new configurations constantly.

So, as Lévi-Strauss (1972) notes, "we define myth as consisting of all its versions" (p. 217), or, to put it the opposite way, each version feeds from and nourishes the totality of the myth itself. As Frye (1957) comments, "Poetry can only be made out of other poems; novels out of other novels. Literature shapes itself" (p. 287).

Journalists, however, resist the view that news also shapes itself:

> Because of our tendency to see immediate events rather than long-term processes, we were blind to the archaic element in journalism. But our very conception of "news" resulted from ancient ways of telling stories. (Darnton, 1975, p. 191)

Indeed, "news values," which journalists often imply are something intrinsic in events, to be deduced using "news sense," are culturally specific story-telling codes. These values, summarized by Chibnall (1981) as "rules stressing the relevancy of: The Present, The Unusual, The Dramatic, Simplicity, Actions, Personalization and Results," are just those values that any storyteller uses in creating a tale. Stories never "reflect reality" and tell of mundane, everyday events. They are about the different and the particular, which yet represent something universal—just as is news.

In practical terms, news values, rules, and formulas are essential for journalists to do their jobs. Reporters may have to write many stories in a week, or they may have to move to a different community and start writing about it immediately. They can comfortably do this with all the story-telling tools at their disposal, giving them a skeleton on which to hang the flesh of the new story. It is the same skill as that of the Yugoslav epic poet described by Lord (1971):

> He can hear a song once and repeat it immediately afterwards—not word for word, of course—but he can tell the same story again in his own words. (p. 26)

The oral poet uses a "common stock of formulas" that give "the traditional songs a homogeneity" and create "the impression that all singers know all the same formulas" (Lord, p. 49), much as "most stories are simply minor updates of previous news or new examples of old themes" (Graber, 1984, p. 61). More than any other kind of story-telling, the time frame of the daily newspaper resembles oral narrative. The six crime reporters who leave the courtroom with the same story may be writing about reality, but their "story" emerges as much from the stories that have gone before as from the facts of the case in court.

CHRONICLE

While the "story-telling" aspect of news is clearly important, however, much of news can hardly be called "story" in any accepted sense—the daily background of routine stories in terse, inverted pyramid style, recording accidents, unremarkable crimes, day-to-day local or national government business. At the extreme local level, the small-town weekly lists the visitors to the town and who left for vacation, while at the national level, Washington correspondents detail the arrival and departure of foreign dignitaries at the White House. Exactly how people read this kind of news is unclear, although it seems that they scan it for general patterns, and forget details (Graber, 1984).

These accounts are not "stories" designed to engage the mind, but "chronicles" provided as a record that something noteworthy has happened (White, 1981). This is not to imply that, unlike stories, chronicles simply record reality, although this seems to be how they have come to be perceived by news professionals. In fact, they are a vital element in the continuing mythological process. They provide us with the backdrop of events that tell us the world is still going on and that things we value still matter. The interminable (to the outsider) bulletin board of neighborhood comings and goings tells us that the local social structure endures, while the White House bulletins tell us that the government is continuing reliably.

Chronicles are not stories, but are still vital, myth-repairing narratives. And the recognition of qualitative differences between chronicle and story are not peculiar to our culture. In predominantly oral cultures, important events may be narrated as chronicle, in listing of wars, genealogies, and so forth. In some sense, they are akin to what historians once called "objective" history. For instance, the African Ndembu distinguish clearly between *nsang'u* (chronicle) and *kaheka* (story). Turner (1982) describes how a sequence of events involving Ndembu royalty may be told in either narrative style:

This sequence may be told by a chief of putative Lunda origin in his court
... as an *nsang'u*, a chronicle, perhaps to justify his title to his office. But
episodes from this chronicle may be transformed into *tuheka*, "stories"
and told by old women to groups of children huddled near the kitchen fire
during the cold season. (p. 67)

When told as "story," the accounts are embellished with rhetorical
flourishes, songs, and personal touches, and it is through stories that the
people "really" understand the events in human terms. Turner emphasizes that the difference between chronicle and story lies not in the
quality of the events, but in how they are narrated. "As in other cultures,
the same events may be framed as chronicle or story. . . . It all depends
where and when and by whom they are told" (p. 68). He stresses the
more ritualized aspect of the chronicle, which involves a kind of roll call
of events deemed newsworthy. Through chronicle, the overall structure
of the myth is emphasized, although individual "stories" are not.

The parallels between this and news narratives are clear. News does a
great deal of chronicling, recording newsworthy events in a routine
fashion—"the routinization of the unexpected" (Tuchman, 1974).
Judgments of what deserves to be chronicled change over time—simply
tracing the changes in news chronicles can tell us a great deal about a
culture and its dominant values.

The narrative form of chronicle essentially derives from the discursive
form *logos*, which the Socratic philosophers distinguished from *mythos*,
or story (Fisher, 1985) and became identified as "objective," in all forms
of narrative, be they history, news, or social science. The perception
developed that the chronicle was the real way to inform, while the story
merely entertained, and within journalism the two became distinguished
in both form and content in the hard/soft dichotomy (Bird & Dardenne,
1986; Schiller, 1981; Schudson, 1978). Chronicle is no more a reflection
of reality in all its aspects than story is. Just as the Ndembu king
chronicles events to make a point, historical chroniclers and news
writers select whom and what is newsworthy. The "great man"
syndrome in traditional history is mirrored in news chronicles.

IMPLICATIONS

Where does an appreciation of the narrative qualities of news take us?
First, anthropologists use the study of narrative to find an entrance
point into a culture, arguing that texts, like rituals, art, games, and other
symbolic configurations, are cultural "models" that encode values and
guides for behavior (Colby, 1966, 1975). If we study these models, of

which news narratives are a type, we can learn about the values and symbols that have meaning in a given culture.

Like Colby, Rice (1980) drew on earlier work by Bartlett (1932), which showed that members of different cultures retell stories in different, culturally determined ways. Rice found that Americans, when asked to retell Eskimo tales, did so in predictable ways, adjusting the tales to the American "story schema":

> The suggestion here is that cultural schemata are . . . responsible for a sort of "selective perception" of the world which is common to members of a given culture and which has the effect of imparting a characteristic interpretation to the phenomena under consideration. (Rice, 1980, pp. 161-162)

So just as Americans "mend holes" in Eskimo tales, journalists are likely to do the same in their stories of real events, and they will do so in culturally prescribed ways. In other words, journalists, as members of a particular culture, are bound by the "culture grammar" (Colby, 1975) that defines rules of narrative construction, a realization that changes the notion of an "objective" transposing of reality. Seeing news as narrative representing culture thus allows us to study it as a symbolic model of cultural values (Corrigan, 1984), in an attempt to uncover the particular configurations characteristic of a given culture's news. We tend to assume that news media in different cultures have different aims and emphases, but we are not very clear on what these might be. It will also be valuable to examine how and why the narrative genre of news has changed over time as culture changes (e.g., Smith, 1975).

At the same time, journalists, while obviously part of a culture and bound by its narrative grammars, are also specialists trained in particular narrative techniques that may sometimes be at odds with the overriding cultural conventions, and a closer examination of the variety of narrative techniques used by journalists may be in order.

The narrative devices used in news writing are widely seen as ways to organize information clearly and effectively, with story-telling as such tending to be reserved for events deemed "soft" or human interest. The inverted pyramid form, using lead, frequent attribution, and so on is at its most stylized in the newspaper staples of accident, crime, and other routine accounts—the type of story that "writes itself" for the experienced journalists—but it is used in more elaborate ways for much "hard news." The most striking feature of this style is that it is very different from traditional story form (Scholes, 1982). The lead comes first, dispensing with suspense, while explanation, rather than developing through the story, may follow the "result" of the events described. While still contributing to the continuing myth, it is chronicle, not story, and as such has significant narrative consequences.

For while the inverted pyramid is an efficient device for the writer, it may be a disaster for the reader. Readers ignore much of a newspaper because the subject does not interest them, but they may also ignore a great deal because the narrative form repels them. The inverted pyramid style encourages partial reading (Graber, 1984), and it may help ensure that readers forget much of what they do read. As Scholes (1982) writes, to become a "story," a narrative must be ordered in a particular way, usually presenting cause-and-effect relationships in a logical progression; Ricoeur notes that in order for readers to follow a story, "Explanations must . . . be woven into the narrative tissue" (1981, p. 278). Stories must have "narrativity"—be recognizable as stories—if readers are to understand them properly:

> It may even be that no long form of discourse can be received by a reader . . . unless it allows and encourages a certain amount of narrativity in its audiences. (Scholes, 1982, p. 64)

Increasingly, work on narrative reveals that readers respond to information presented in "story" form, regardless of content. Donahew (1983, 1984) conducted an experiment to measure the physical response of readers to news accounts of the Jonestown mass suicides, containing the same facts but structured differently. His conclusion:

> Messages written in narrative style generated significantly greater arousal and mood change responses than those presented in the traditional newspaper style. (1984, p. 155)

The common assumption that readers prefer "human interest" stories only because the content is more interesting overlooks that these are the same stories that are usually written in traditional story form. Roshier (1981) stresses the interdependence of form and content when he discusses the readers of the *News of the World*, a British "sensational" Sunday paper. These readers have an unusually high recall of the "titillating" crime stories they enjoy, and while this memorability is obviously inherent in the subject matter, in addition,

> it is achieved by the use of relatively long reports with a literary style that often unfolds the plot like a novelette, with headlines which are suggestive without giving much away. (Roshier, p. 48)

Likewise, Robins and Cohen (1981) offer an explanation for the unlikely popularity of Kung Fu films among British working-class youth:

There is an objective correspondence between *some* oral traditions in working-class culture and some genres produced by the media. It is a correspondence of form rather than content, and where it doesn't exist, the impact of the mass media on working-class consciousness is entirely negligible. (p. 484)

So people respond to and process accurately information presented in story form. Much of the information in newspapers and broadcast news is thus difficult to process, and may actually be perceived as barely comprehensible (Rayfield, 1972). La Baschin (1986) discusses studies that show the average television news viewer recalls only one in nineteen of the stories presented in a news program. As Benjamin wrote much earlier this century, "every morning brings us the news of the globe, and yet we are poor in noteworthy stories" (1969, p. 39).

This is not to say that some news is not efficiently communicated in stylized, chronicle structure. Much routine news performs the chronicling function, and, while details may not be recalled, the overall symbolic pattern is strengthened. Thus "crime is understood as a permanent and recurrent phenomenon and hence much of it is surveyed in the media in an equally routinized manner" (Hall et al., 1981, p. 352).

Journalists know, however, that the stylized account often will not do the job. They feel the need to "humanize" events—which, though rarely expressed as such, is the need to write a story. In order to explain, journalists are constantly reverting to the story form—attributed quotes take on the nature of dialogue, a point of view develops, details are added that turn a statistic into an unemployed miner or a bereaved parent. Whether in history or in news, the demands of narrativity ensure that events are most completely understood when they are transformed into story. Certain types of news (like unroutine crime) and certain types of audiences (particularly working class) are given the full story treatment, while most "serious" news is not. And while undoubtedly many readers have learned the particular narrative code of objective reporting, the majority of readers show a marked inability to process political news in anything but the broadest of terms (Graber, 1984).

Journalists find themselves poised uneasily between what they see as two impossible ideals—the demands of "reality," which they see as reachable through objective strategies, and the demands of narrativity. They face a paradox; the more "objective" they are, the more unreadable they become; while the better storytellers they are, the more readers will respond, and the more they fear they are betraying their ideals. So journalists do some chronicling, some story-telling, and a lot that is something of both. Every so often something comes along (like Janet

Cooke or Alastair Reid) that makes them try to redraw the line, which invariably becomes instantly smudged once again.

WHOSE STORY?

Perhaps most significant, the consideration of the narrative qualities of news enables us to look more critically at whose values are encoded in news—whose stories are being told. If anthropologists Colby and Peacock (1973) are right, the study of narrative should be at the center of any consideration of news in its cultural context:

> The subtle and undercover techniques of narrative as art, which do not obviously aim to control, may seduce people into letting their guard down. . . . The rise of the mass media, which lend themselves more to stories than sermons, strengthens the position of expressive culture. Expressive forms, including narrative forms, might well assume increasingly important roles in social control. Should this occur, the study of narrative will become increasingly relevant to the student of society. (p. 633)

American cultural studies have tended to adopt a consensual framework; Carey (1983) has commented on the "frequent and telling criticism that cultural studies in the United States, undercut as it is by the cheery optimism of pragmatism, inescapably fails to consider power, dominance, subordination, and ideology as central issues" (p. 313). The consensual approach accepts that news is part of and not apart from the rest of culture, but fails to appreciate that, as a mediated symbolic system, news does not stand in an identical position in culture as, say, oral tradition.

Even in the few discussions of news as story or myth, analysis rarely goes beyond saying that news tells stories about cultural values. Thus Barkin (1984) notes that journalists play a role in "affirming and maintaining the social order" (p. 32), tacitly assuming that there is indeed a recognized set of values to which all members of a culture subscribe.

Certainly, the story-telling or news values Barkin notes are culturally shared:

> There must be villains and heroes in every paper, and the storylines must conform to the usage of suspense, conflict, the defeat of evil, and the triumph of good that have guided the good sense and artistry of past storytellers and controlled their audience's ability to respond. (Barkin, 1984, p. 30)

The journalist-storyteller is indeed using culturally embedded story values, taking them from the culture and re-presenting them to the culture, and is thus akin to the folk storyteller who operates in a "communal matrix" vis-à-vis the audience (Cawelti, 1978).

A journalist, however, is also creating stories out of events that audiences are unfamiliar with, where they do not have their own experiences in which to place those events. In this case, newspapers and other media are much closer to the "mythological matrix," where although "the genres are a communal possession rather than individual creations," nevertheless

> the creator-performer is given a special authority, he is somewhat distanced from the audience and tends to become more so as the culture develops, to the degree that many versions of the mythological matrix develop a separate caste of creator-performers who are specialists in the performance of mythology. (Cawelti, 1978, p. 298)

In the mythological matrix, the audience tends to put faith in those "specialists" who have access to the "truth," at least in those areas that are unfamiliar. Myth, like news, rests on its authority as "truth." Television news, with its presenters seen in person by its audiences, has co-opted the storyteller/mythmaker role so effectively that it is now regarded as the most authoritative and hence "truthful" source of news (Sperry, 1976).

In newsmaking, journalists do not merely use culturally determined definitions, they also have to fit new situations into old definitions. It is in their power to place people and events into the existing categories of hero, villain, good and bad, and thus to invest their stories with the authority of mythological truth. Thus Hall (1975) agrees that news writing is a "social transaction" that picks up on existing cultural conventions, just as Eason (1981, p. 27) calls it an "interactive process." Nevertheless,

> at the same time, the producers hold a powerful position vis-à-vis their audiences, and they must play the primary role in shaping expectations and tastes. (Hall, 1975, p. 22)

Sperry (1976) argues that this process is in no way ideological. She maintains that in producing news stories, "if the story form you have chosen is a heroic tale, then there must be a protagonist and an antagonist. It is not political favoritism but simply a formulaic understanding of how the world operates" (p. 137). This view, however, begs the question of how these assignments are made; who is hero and who villain is not a question of random selection to fit existing formulas.

As Schudson (1982) argues, "the power of the media lies not only (and not even primarily) in its power to declare things to be true, but in its power to provide the forms in which the declarations will appear."

Increasingly, it is up to the media to "place" such groups as strikers (Glasgow University Media Group, 1976, 1980), peace demonstrators and other protesters (Gitlin, 1980; Halloran et al., 1970), feminists (Tuchman, 1978), drug users (Young, 1981), and homosexuals (Pearce, 1981). Hartmann and Husband (1971) found that white children who had little contact with black people were more ready to see race relations in terms of conflict (as the issue was usually defined in the media, in accordance with news/story values) than were those with personal experience of black neighbors. For the media, using existing narrative conventions and "maps of meaning" (Hall et al., 1981), construct reality to conform to those maps, and assign meanings to new realities. It is here that the "ideological effect" (Hall, 1977) is perceived:

> Ideology is not a collection of discrete falsehoods, but a matrix of thought firmly grounded in the forms of our social life and organised within a set of interdependent categories, which constitute a network of established "given" meanings embedded in the "assignment" of events to the "relevant" contexts within these pre-established cultural "maps of meaning." (Morley, 1981, p. 371)

Journalists have to make these "assignments" or "news judgments" quickly, and inevitably resort to existing frameworks. "Normality" is good, difference bad or deviant (or amusing). The media ultimately tend to "legitimize the American system by the deference they pay to its structures, its values, and its elected and appointed officials" (Graber, 1984, p. 207). The assignments reflect the interests of the status quo, whether the form chosen for the account is story or chronicle. The result is that the prevailing maps of meaning have come to be perceived as "natural" and "common sense," blinding us to the fact that even "common sense" is culturally derived (Geertz, 1983):

> This confusion of authority and legitimacy with objectivity makes the news an active agent in the construction of a narrow but compelling version of reality—a version that is communicated so broadly and filled with such familiar symbolism that other versions seem biased or distorted. (Bennett et al., 1985, p. 51)

So, in tracing the story-telling patterns in news, we must be aware that journalists are not only drawing on those patterns, they are also actively reshaping them, constantly "repairing the paradigm" (Bennett et al., 1985). It is a process that is more complex than either a consensual model or a manipulative model, which assigns all the control to the media, and sees media as somehow outside of, yet affecting, culture. Rather, media are very much part of culture, but with a particular kind of privileged status within it. The media's narrative reshaping will be most successful when this can present new information in such a way that it accords with readers' existing narrative conventions, and can be accommodated within them. The media cannot create mythology out of nothing, but it is more than the "passive transmitter" of myth that has been suggested (Gans, 1979, p. 294). Such media-shaped perceptions may then become part of the common cultural framework, to be drawn on again by journalists in a continuing dialectical process.

CONCLUSIONS

It is important to begin looking more critically at the narrative qualities of news. While news is not fiction, it is a story about reality, not reality itself. Yet because of its privileged status as reality and truth, the seductive powers of its narratives are particularly significant. As Johnson (1983) writes, narrative forms are more than literary constructions; they give people a schema for viewing the world and for living their lives. "Human beings live, love, suffer bereavement and go off and fight and die by them" (p. 32).

News has the function of chronicling, and it does so in the backdrop of narratives recounting "newsworthy" events, written so that no one need read beyond the lead. Chronicling repairs the myth on a day-to-day basis, assuring us of continued order and normality while plotting the parameters of this normality. Yet it cannot fully explain and make things seem "real," because it lacks comprehensible narrativity.

Thus journalists know that events seem more real to readers when they are reported in story form; when they do this they find themselves slipping into the mire of "fiction" and hauling out the lifebelts of objectivity and fact. For the "best" and most readable and convincing stories are those constructed most tightly, so that sides are clearly delineated—stories make a point. Thus according to White (1981), "Narrativity, certainly in factual storytelling . . . is intimately related to, if not a function of, the impulse to moralize reality" (p. 14).

Journalists' training, steeped in the ideology of objective reality, leads them to speak in one narrative voice. Within the existing news paradigm, they frame the problem of "the impulse to moralize reality" in terms of fact/fiction or true/false dichotomies, and fall back on the technique of chronicling. Rather than constantly trying to redraw lines, however, we might do better to consider Tuchman's observation that "being a reporter who deals in facts and being a storyteller who produces tales are not antithetical activities" (1976, p. 96). We might think how journalists could learn to create stories that can be processed by their readers, but that speak in other narrative voices. Journalists do tend to tell the same stories in similar ways; the telling of one story by nature excludes all the other stories that are never told.

REFERENCES

Barkin, S. M. (1984). The journalist as storyteller: An interdisciplinary perspective. *American Journalism, 1*(2), 27-33.

Barthes, R. (1982). Introduction to the structural analysis of narratives. In S. Sontag (Ed.), *Barthes: Selected Writings* (pp. 251-295). London: Fontana-Collins.

Bartlett, F. C. (1932). *Remembering*. Cambridge: Cambridge University Press.

Bascom, W. R. (1954). Four functions of folklore. *Journal of American Folklore, 67*, 333-349.

Basso, K. H. (1984). Stalking with stories: Names, places, and moral narratives among the Apache. In E. M. Bruner (Ed.), *Text, play and story: The construction and reconstruction of self and society* (pp. 19-55). Washington, DC: American Ethnological Society.

Benjamin, W. (1969) The storyteller: Reflections on the work of Nikolai Leskov. In H. Arendt (Ed.), H. Zohn (Trans.), *Illuminations* (pp. 83-109). New York: Schocken.

Bennett, W. L., & Edelman, M. (1985). Toward a new political narrative. *Journal of Communication, 35*, 156-171.

Bennett, W. L., Gressett, L. A., & Haltom, W. (1985). Repairing the news: A case study of the news paradigm. *Journal of Communication, 35*, 50-68.

Bird, S. E. (1987). Folklore and media as intertextual communication processes: John F. Kennedy and the supermarket tabloids. In M. L. McLaughlin (Ed.), *Communication Yearbook 10*. Newbury Park, CA: Sage.

Bird, S. E., & Dardenne, R. W. (1986). *News and storytelling: Reevaluating the sensational dimension*. Paper presented at the Sensationalism and the Media Conference, Ann Arbor, MI.

Bruner, E. M. (1984). The opening up of anthropology. In E. M. Bruner (Ed.), *Text, play, and story: The construction and reconstruction of self and society* (pp. 1-16). Washington, DC: American Ethnological Society.

Carey, J. W. (1975). A cultural approach to communication. *Communication, 2*, 1-22.

Carey, J. W. (1983). The origins of the radical discourse in cultural studies in the United States. *Journal of Communication, 33*(3), 311-313.

Capo, J. A. (1985). Some normative issues for news as cultural celebration. *Journal of Communication Inquiry, 9*(2), 16-32.

Cawelti, J. G. (1978). The concept of artistic matrices. *Communication Research, 5*(3), 283-305.

Chibnall, S. (1981). The production of knowledge by crime reporters. In S. Cohen & J. Young (Eds.), *The manufacture of news: Social problems, deviance and the mass media* (pp. 75-97). London: Constable.

Cohen, S. (1981). Mods and rockers: The inventory of manufactured news. In S. Cohen & J. Young (Eds.), *The manufacture of news: Social problems, deviance and the mass media* (pp. 263-279). London: Constable.

Cohen, S., & Young, J. (Eds.). (1981). *The manufacture of news: Social problems, deviance and the mass media.* London: Constable.

Colby, B. N. (1966). Cultural patterns in narrative. *Science, 151,* 793-798.

Colby, B. N. (1975). Culture grammars. *Science, 187,* 913-919.

Colby, B. N., & Peacock, J. L. (1973). Narrative. In J. J. Honigman (Ed.), *Handbook of social and cultural anthropology* (pp. 613-636). Chicago: Rand McNally.

Corrigan, D. (1984). Valuation and presentation conventions in news communications: A formula for measurement. *Journal of Communication Inquiry, 8*(2), 29-45.

Darnton, R. (1975). Writing news and telling stories. *Daedalus, 104,* 175-194.

Dewey, J. (1927). *The public and its problems.* Chicago: Swallow Press.

Donahew, L. (1983). Newswriting styles: What arouses the reader? *Newspaper Research Journal, 3*(2), 3-6.

Donahew, L. (1984). Why we expose ourselves to morbid news. *Proceedings of symposium on morbid curiosity and the news* (pp. 154-191). Knoxville, TN.

Drummond, L. (1984). Movies and myth: Theoretical skirmishes. *American Journal of Semiotics, 3*(2), 1-32.

Eason, D. L. (1981). Telling stories and making sense. *Journal of Popular Culture, 15*(2), 125-129.

Fisher, W. R. (1985). The narrative paradigm: In the beginning. *Journal of Communication, 35,* 74-89.

Frayn, M. (1981). The complete stylisation of news. In S. Cohen & J. Young (Eds.), *The manufacture of news: Social problems, deviance and the mass media* (pp. 71-74). London: Constable.

Frye, N. (1957). *Anatomy of criticism.* Princeton: Princeton University Press.

Galtung, J., & Ruge, M. H. (1965). The structure of foreign news. *Journal of International Peace Research, 1,* 64-90.

Gans, H. (1979). *Deciding what's news.* New York: Pantheon.

Geertz, C. (1973). *The interpretation of cultures.* New York: Basic Books.

Geertz, C. (1983). Common sense as a cultural system. In *Local knowledge: Further essays in interpretive anthropology* (pp. 73-93). New York: Basic Books.

Gerbner, G. (1977, June). Television: The new state religion? *Et Cetera,* pp. 145-150.

Gitlin, T. (1980). *The whole world is watching.* Berkeley: University of California Press.

Glasgow University Media Group. (1976). *Bad news.* London: Routledge & Kegan Paul.

Glasgow University Media Group. (1980). *More bad news.* London: Routledge & Kegan Paul.

Glasser, T. L. (1982). Play, pleasure and the value of newsreading. *Communication Quarterly, 30*(2), 101-107.

Graber, D. A. (1984). *Processing the news: How people tame the information tide.* New York: Longman.

Hall, S. (1975). Introduction. In A.C.H. Smith (Ed.), *Paper voices: The popular press and social change 1935-1965* (pp. 1-24). London: Chatto & Windus.

Hall, S. (1977). Culture, the media and the "ideological" effect. In J. Curran, M. Gurevitch, & J. Woolacott (Eds.), *Mass communication and society* (pp. 315-348). London: Edward Arnold.

Hall, S. (1984). The narrative construction of reality: An interview with Stuart Hall. *Southern Review, 17*(1), 3-17.

Hall, S., Chritcher, C., Jefferson, T., Clarke, J., & Roberts, B. (1981). The social production of news: Mugging in the media. In S. Cohen & J. Young (Eds.), *The manufacture of news: Social problems, deviance and the mass media* (pp. 335-367). London: Constable.

Halloran, J. D. (1974). *Mass media and society: The challenge of research.* Leicester: Leicester University Press.

Halloran, J. D., Elliott, P., & Murdock, G. (1970). *Demonstration and communication: A case study.* Harmondsworth: Penguin.

Hartley, J. (1982). *Understanding news.* London: Methuen.

Hartmann, P., & Husband, C. (1971). The mass media and racial conflict. *Race, 12*(3), 268-282.

Haskins, J. (1984). Morbid curiosity and the mass media: A synergistic relationship. *Symposium on morbid curiosity and the news* (pp. 1-50). Knoxville, TN.

Herrnstein Smith, B. (1981). Narrative versions, narrative theories. In W.J.T. Mitchell (Ed.), *On narrative* (pp. 209-232). Chicago: Chicago University Press.

Hersey, J. (1981). The legend on the license. *Yale Review, 70*(1), 1-25.

Hughes, H. M. (1968). *News and the human interest story.* New York: Greenwood Press.

Jensen, M. C. (1977). *The sorry state of news reporting and why it won't be changed.* (Speech to New York State Publishers Association, Rochester, NY)

Johnson, R. (1983). *What is cultural studies anyway?* Birmingham: Birmingham University, Centre for Contemporary Cultural Studies.

Knight, G., & Dean T. (1982). Myth and the structure of news. *Journal of Communication, 32*, 144-161.

La Baschin, S. J. (1986). The ritual of newswatching: Why more news isn't better. *Et Cetera, 43*(1), 27-32.

Landau, M. (1984). Human evolution as narrative. *American Scientist, 72*, 262-267.

Levi-Strauss, C. (1972). *Structural anthropology.* Harmondsworth: Penguin.

Lord, A. B. (1971). *The singer of tales.* Cambridge, MA: Harvard University Press.

Malinowski, B. (1974). *Myth in primitive psychology.* New York: Negro Universities Press.

Marcus, G. E. (1982). Rhetoric and the ethnographic genre in anthropological research. In J. Ruby (Ed.), *A crack in the mirror: Reflexive perspectives in anthropology* (pp. 163-172). Philadelphia: University of Pennsylvania Press.

Mead, G. H. (1925-1926). The nature of aesthetic experience. *International Journal of Ethics, 36*, 382-393.

Morley, D. (1981). Industrial conflict and the mass media. In S. Cohen & J. Young (Eds.), *The manufacture of news: Social problems, deviance and the mass media* (pp. 368-392). London: Constable.

Murphy, J. E. (1985). Rattling the journalistic cage: New journalism in old newsrooms. *Journal of Communication Inquiry, 8*(2), 8-15.

Park, R. (1944.) News as a form of knowledge. *American Journal of Sociology, 45*, 669-686.

Pearce, F. (1981). The British and the "placing" of homosexuality. In S. Cohen & J. Young (Eds.), *The manufacture of news: Social problems, deviance and the mass media* (pp. 303-316). London: Constable.

Rayfield, J. R. (1972). What is a story? *American Anthropologist, 74*, 1085-1106.

Rice, G. E. (1980). On cultural schemata. *American Ethnologist, 2*, 152-171.

Ricoeur, P. (1981). The narrative function. In J. B. Thompson (Ed.), *Paul Ricoeur: Hermeneutics and the human sciences* (pp. 274-296). New York: Cambridge University Press.

Robins, D., & Cohen, P. (1981). Enter the dragon. In S. Cohen & J. Young (Eds.), *The manufacture of news: Social problems, deviance and the mass media* (pp. 480-488). London: Constable.

Rock, P. (1981). News as eternal recurrence. In S. Cohen & J. Young (Eds.), *The manufacture of news: Social problems, deviance and the mass media* (pp. 64-70). London: Constable.

Roshier, B. (1981). The selection of crime news by the press. In S. Cohen & J. Young (Eds.), *The manufacture of news: Social problems, deviance and the mass media* (pp. 40-51). London: Constable.

Schiller, D. (1981). *Objectivity: The public and the rise of commercial journalism.* Philadelphia: University of Pennsylvania Press.

Scholes, R. (1982). *Semiotics and interpretation.* New Haven: Yale University Press.

Schudson, M. (1978). *Discovering the news: A social history of American newspapers.* New York: Basic Books.

Schudson, M. (1982). The politics of narrative form: The emergence of news conventions in print and television. *Daedalus, 111*(4), 97-112.

Smith, A.C.H. (1975). *Paper voices: The popular press and social change 1935-1965.* London: Chatto & Windus.

Smith, R. R. (1979). Mythic elements in television news. *Journal of Communication, 29,* 75-82.

Sperry, S. L. (1976). Television news as narrative. In R. Adler & D. Cater (Eds.), *Television as a cultural force* (pp. 129-146). New York: Praeger.

Stephenson, W. (1964). The ludenic theory of newsreading. *Journalism Quarterly, 41,* 367-374.

Tuchman, G. (1974). Making news by doing work: Routinizing the unexpected. *American Journal of Sociology, 79,* 110-131.

Tuchman, G. (1976). Telling stories. *Journal of Communication, 26*(4), 93-97.

Tuchman, G. (1978). *Making news: A study in the construction of reality.* New York: Free Press.

Turner, V. (1969). *The ritual process: Structure and anti-structure.* Chicago: Aldine.

Turner, V. (1982). Social dramas and stories about them. In *From ritual to theatre: The human seriousness of play* (pp. 61-88). New York: Performing Arts Journal Publications.

White, H. (1981). The value of narrativity in the representation of reality. In W.J.T. Mitchell (Ed.), *On narrative* (pp. 1-23). Chicago: Chicago University Press.

Young, J. (1981). The myth of drugtakers in the mass media. In S. Cohen & J. Young (Eds.), *The manufacture of news: Social problems, deviance and the mass media* (pp. 326-334). London: Constable.

PART II

TELEVISION

Chapter 4

ONE NIGHT OF PRIME TIME
An Analysis of
Television's Multiple Voices

Horace M. Newcomb

THE PROBLEM I ADDRESS IN THIS CHAPTER has to do with the degree to which television is an "open" or "closed" textual system. I approach this topic by analyzing a particular text, but the perspective I present extends far beyond this text. I am arguing that television is an extension and elaboration of other popular culture processes, and suggesting that what we now see in television is common to all popular cultural media when they reach the stage of serving as a *central story-telling system* in a particular social and historical setting. Television, in this view, is the latest, perhaps the most totalizing version of what I have elsewhere referred to as a "cultural forum" (Newcomb & Hirsch, 1983).

I also argue that this pressing question regarding television's sociocultural function is not in any way divorced from problems related to the aesthetic foundations of television. We do not yet fully understand how television works as an expressive form. Certainly we have moved beyond early studies that assumed television to be no more than an amalgam of stage, screen, and radio, and beyond early descriptive studies of television's generic patterns as perhaps its defining characteristics. But we are still working to grasp the full implications of its density, its reflexivity, its seriality, and its mixture of narrative styles. Here I demonstrate some ways in which recent approaches to discussion of television's textuality shed powerful light on its sociocultural roles. Again, by implication, I think this blend of formal and social analysis indicates important potential for reformulating some of our most basic questions about popular culture in many of its previous forms.

Traditional commentary on television, as on other forms of popular culture, has emphasized its closed nature. Focusing on patterns of stereotypy, and repetition, on redundancy of format, narrative structure, apparatus, and theme, these studies have denied to television the power of social criticism and cultural discussion. The latest version of such analyses is perhaps Hal Himmelstein's *Television Myth and the American Mind* (1984).

I argue, however, for a perspective that seeks difference, that looks for varying points of view, even to the point of conflict, in television presentations (Newcomb, 1984; Newcomb & Alley, 1983; Newcomb & Hirsch, 1983). Such an approach is increasingly common in critical television studies. Thorburn's 1976 concept of "the multiplicity principle" in television points the way for much of this work. Fiske and Hartley (1978) with their notion of "bardic television" come at the problem in a somewhat different way, and individually, both have explored the problem even more thoroughly (Fiske, 1986; Hartley, 1984). Silverstone (1981) uses a complex, anthropologically based concept of myth to deal with television's multiple meanings. Ellis (1982) expresses the possibility of a multiplicity of meanings, but ultimately argues more strongly for closure and containment. As early as 1980, Eco argued for the instability of the television text, and in his most recent work (1986), to which I will return later, makes an even clearer case for such assumptions. Allen, in his masterful study of soap opera, indicates an elegantly simple scheme for the circulation of textual information that can be applied to the whole of television (1985). Browne (1984) presents another overview of the medium that, in his view, explains its power to limit and control meaning, but that I hope to demonstrate here is essential to understanding the multiplicity of television meanings that cannot be contained. Certainly Hall, in the now essential essay, "Encoding/Decoding" (1980), outlines in a fundamental way the significance of television's range of meanings.

To clarify this position further, let me state here that not one of these explanations, my own included, suggests that television's *primary* thrust is toward the expression of values, attitudes, political positions, or moral perspectives that challenge central, received, dominant perspectives. All of them recognize the conservative and conserving power of television and, by implication, any central story-telling system. Indeed, this is a commonplace. The fundamental question regards the *degree* of what I will call cultural negotiation, the ongoing struggle over signification that can be seen as the ground of shared, conflicted social meaning and social action. All the scholars cited above see this struggle as a fundamental, defining characteristic of television and popular culture.

For all of them, it is now essential to examine and analyze change as well as stability, to emphasize questions of potential as well as of accomplishment. Television must be seen as dynamic rather than static, as processural rather than merely as a product, as fissured and contradictory rather than monolithic, polysemic rather than univocal.

Only in this way can theories of textuality and the analysis of specific texts serve to match audience responses. While ethnographic studies of the experience of television remain crude, they have already indicated a wide range of audience readings and uses of television texts (see Ang, 1985; Katz & Liebes, 1984; Liebes, 1984; Morley, 1980; Wolf, Meyer, & White, 1982). Certainly one of the key texts in this discussion, again taking us beyond television, is Radway's *Reading the Romance* (1984). And I would add, to bolster all this work from a nonethnographic, nonempirical, but thoroughly theorized perspective, de Lauretis's superb *Alice Doesn't* (1985).

Put still another way, all these considerations can be related to a fundamental sort of textual instability, characteristic of post-modernist, recombinative forms of imaginative expression. In some views, perhaps put forward most strongly by Jameson (1979) and Gitlin (1983, 1987), there is no real "negotiation," no potential critique here. Instead, we have only a pastiche—free-floating signifiers with no ground from which to discern, judge, select, and act. I am inclined to accept this possibility with what we have traditionally taken as "high art" forms—I will include the experimental, the avant garde, the meta-fictional—forms often more "about" the processes of art than about more generalized human experience. But I am unwilling to apply the judgment to popular culture. The latter, in my view, still stays closer to the lives most people lead, and cannot allow itself to fold into meaningless mush. As the most basic ethnographic studies have demonstrated, audiences for these materials read in such personalized, idiosyncratic, locally determined ways that it becomes impossible to "read off" the text any totalizing, determining response. To do so, ironically, is to revert, in textual-cultural theory, to the crude "indoctrination" theories of "direct effects" models now rejected even by mainstream social scientific approaches to communication. In fact, as I hope to show later, the very economic forces that drive commercial television in various capitalist systems cannot allow this to happen.

To begin making a case for some of these assertions, I want to take as a "text" an entire night of prime-time television (7:00 to 10:00 PM, Central Standard Time) aired on the three commercial networks on Thursday, October 3, 1985 (see Appendix Tables 1, 2, and 3). Obviously, such a "text" cannot exist for a single viewer without the use of videotape and time to replay the recordings. Here, however, I describe some of the central elements *made available* by this text for various viewers who might have seen parts of it. My own reading, of course, is also personalized, but the persona is that of the critic attempting to "see more" than other individualized viewers. To do this, I break the master text into various "strips," which could exist as actual texts experienced by viewers, the several enjammed hours potentially watched by a given viewer. I am *not* arguing that viewers experience television as undifferentiated, blurred strips. I suspect that viewers mark all sorts of breaks, that they clearly distinguish among programs, that they even forget what they watched prior to a new moment of viewing. I *am* arguing that the strip is the best unit of analysis to capture what was *offered* the viewer in a given period of viewing, and I suggest that meaning can be altered by juxtaposing different parts of potential strips, different clusters of meaningful elements.

I "idealize" these strips, however, for analytical purposes, "changing the channel" only at program breaks, foregoing any discussion of commercials, and radically reducing the scope of this discussion. There are 81 possible paths through this nine hours of television, counting *only* those paths that change channels at program breaks. An infinite number of paths exist for the pathological channel shifter, a species undoubtedly growing in number with the rapid diffusion of remote television control devices.

My first step will be to follow the path I ordinarily take on Thursday nights, the only night of the week when I was inclined, during the 1985 TV season, to watch three hours of television in a single evening. Throughout my initial comments, I rely on Bakhtin's notion of dialogue, and emphasize the heterological nature of television. I have made a case for this approach elsewhere (Newcomb, 1984), and hope to demonstrate its utility in this analysis. Later, however, I bolster this perspective with other theoretical approaches to television, showing how they add to the power of dialogic analysis even while they are best understood in the context of the dialogic nature of mass communication.

My evening begins at 7:00 PM with *Magnum, P.I.,* on CBS. At 8:00 I move to NBC and stay with that network for *Cheers, Night Court,* and *Hill Street Blues.* If I choose not to watch anything during this period, it is the two comedies from 8:00 to 9:00, for the simple reason that comedies are not my favorite television form, and I will use that time for other matters if needed. I will always make an effort to see the first and last shows in the list.[1]

The *Magnum* episode in this strip is, in several ways, quite conventional. The narrative technique is straightforward, without flashback or radical intercutting within contemporaneous time. It addresses political questions overtly. And it draws on Magnum's personal past for much of its significance.

In the opening sequences, two dolphins swim underwater. What appears to be a scene set in the ocean turns into a tank where animals are being trained for a show. The trainer does not notice two sinister-looking characters, who slip behind him and render him unconscious.

We cut to Magnum's quarters, where regular characters Rick and T. C. amuse themselves by examining Magnum's high school yearbook. They comment on his status as football hero and remark on the girls with whom he is pictured. They also find a picture of a friend who is about to arrive in Hawaii, a friend whom Magnum plans to meet. She is not particularly beautiful, and we learn that she is the "intellectual" who helped Magnum pass his English literature course and remain eligible for football. On his way out the door, Magnum meets Higgins, who asks a favor. Higgins has been designated a nonofficial delegate to a human rights conference, nonofficial because the host, President Kole, the dictator of a fictional African country, is not approved of by the British consulate. When Higgins explains his position, Magnum remarks:

> So you want me to help you through the moral ambiguities and contradictions of this difficult situation?

Higgins replies:

> Don't be ridiculous. I'll be busy. I want you to deliver my security code and letters of introduction to the yacht.

We then cut to the hotel where Magnum is to meet his friend. In a bit of exposition, we see Kole's opponent responding to a reporter who comments on the fact that Kole holds banquets while his people starve.

Magnum meets his friend, Goldie, but does not recognize her because she is now quite beautiful. As they drive to the harbor, where Magnum will deliver Higgins's papers, she explains how she changed. Her nose was broken in the Chicago riots of 1968. She keeps thin by running in antihunger marathons. In short, she is active in many "causes" and establishes her political position clearly. This identification continues as she realizes Magnum is visiting Kole's yacht. Outraged, she asks if he knows how many times she's demonstrated against Kole. The following exchange takes place.

> M: Just because I'm not demonstrating doesn't mean I agree with him. Maybe the meetings will do some good.
> G: They're just a smoke screen, a token gesture.

M: How can you be sure it won't do any good?

G: I don't think Kole should be given any more chances.

M: You're just like you were in high school. Anybody who disagrees with you is a bad guy.

G: Are you defending Kole?

M: No. I don't like him any more than you do, but at least they got him talking. Of course that's not as exciting as running in marathons or ducking rocks in riots, but it's a hell of a lot more constructive.

They decide not to fight, and Goldie asks if she can hire him to find something. Puzzled, he agrees, and we learn in the next sequence that she is associated with the animal park from which a dolphin has been stolen. In the course of the conversation, her activist character is reasserted as we discover that she took a job at the park to free the dolphins as part of an animal rights movement. She thinks her associates simply freed the animal, unaware that its mate will die if it is not returned. She wants Magnum to help her find her associates and recover the dolphin. He agrees, and on the way to his car, he calls to her, stops her, and leans down to tie her shoelace. In a voice-over commentary, he remarks:

There's something a little frightening about a girl who can't keep her own shoelaces tied trying to save the world. You know she's bound to spend the rest of her life tripping over her ideals, just like those shoelaces. But you also know there's no way to talk her out of those causes.

Later Higgins informs the two of them that he has received a ransom note, and we realize that Goldie's associates lack her pure motives. Higgins is appalled at Goldie's intentions, but when she quotes Emily Dickinson on the value of life, he is won over, capping her quotes, line for line. Magnum and Goldie go to meet the "dolphin-nappers" and find they are set up to be murder victims. They escape, and later trace the vehicle used by the villains through the identification of a logo. On their way to meet the technician who has modified the van, Goldie and Magnum discuss his tour of duty in Vietnam.

G: While you were fighting, I was marching in demonstrations.

M: I know.

G: Not that I regret protesting, it's just that I never stopped to think about you. I'm sorry.

M: We both did what we thought was right.

Magnum and Goldie meet Rodney, the van customizer, and request his help in identifying the van driven by the villains. They comment on his distinctive logo. At this point, he protests strongly. He doesn't produce "logos," he says, but "signatures." "Logos" he asserts, "appear on toilet doors in airports. Signatures appear on genuine pieces of art." He proceeds to give them a complex philosophy of art and culture. "I have a surrealist vision of the wheel. We live in an age, a culture, on wheels. So I figure, Michelangelo and Salvador Dali got to sign their work. Now who's gonna say my custom jobs can't be called art." Formerly employed to do sophisticated technical work for the Marine Corps, Rodney is now "totally into aesthetics, custom body jobs, special wheels, van art. A man's vehicle is his castle. I figure what you drive says a lot about a person."

Apparently no more than a digression, this discussion gives Magnum a clue. The van was redesigned to hold a dolphin tank, and Rodney remembers seeing an apparatus that could only be a rig for strapping a bomb to a dolphin. The criminals, it turns out, are not after money. They want the dolphin to carry an explosive charge to Kole's yacht, killing him and destroying the human rights conference. From here we are involved in action, as Magnum races to the docks where he and his associates save the day, in part by luring the dolphin-bomb from his course by playing the plaintive cries of his mate under water.

I have summarized at far greater length than I will with other programs in order to anchor the remainder of my analysis and to demonstrate the density of this episode. While it could be written off as "just entertainment," just "another detective show," with a "predictable" plot and "stereotypical" characters, such a reading would miss much of the show's cultural power. A dialogic analysis would focus on the conflicting personal generic patterns developed in character zones. It would distinguish between continuing characters, which in this series are extremely well developed, and guest characters. Goldie, as the primary guest character, is clearly used as a rhetorical device to represent naive and optimistic idealism. Her attention to causes is undercut by that naïveté, her lack of analysis. But it is also refreshing, and is not depicted cynically. The fact that the most serious character, Higgins, and the central narrative agent, Magnum, agree with many of her judgments reinforces her perspective.

But this "ideological" exchange (which brings in Vietnam, the submerged narrative topic always active in this text) is also inflected in other ways. Discussion ranges from the appropriate role of athletics in American education to extended commentary on a major American poet, to a philosophical commentary on mobile culture. As is often the case in *Magnum, P.I.*, the plot of the episode is *little more than a pretense for examining complex character relations and ideas about contemporary culture.*

The manifest content, focusing on idealistic versus sophisticated attitudes toward social problems is shaded by far more powerful discourse systems. The choice of Goldie, the "intellectual" young woman, as spokesperson for idealism is inflected by a discourse of "the feminine" and all the comments on Dickinson are part of that discourse, as is the dying female dolphin who waits for her mate's return. The discourse of "human rights" is both overt and occulted in discussions of the artist's freedom, Vietnam, and questions of "trained animals." The controlling discourse of "maleness," exemplified in the root genre of the private detective, in the patterns of violence, power, and control, ultimately binds the "feminine" into a highly traditional cultural position. But it does so with a version of "masculine" far more flexible, far "softer" if you will, than most traditional detective shows. Even the patronizing gesture of tying the shoelace is performed in a nurturing and caring manner. Positions are not, in other words, given, read easily from large generic patterns. Rather, they are won, and as we shall see later, won over extended time as well as in contained plots.

Moving now to *Cheers*, I notice immediately that many of the same themes are at work, both at a manifest level, and in the controlling discourses that underlie the plot. I will refer to these matching expressions as *resonance*, trying to indicate the overlapping, but shaded relationships among them. Here, for example, two versions of naive idealism are presented. One is in the character Woody, the assistant bartender. "Naive" is perhaps a generous term for Woody, for he is best described as the "fool" of the show, and understanding his role fully would require an analysis of that role in American and European cultural history and folklore. The second version is presented in Diane, one of the two principal characters in the show. Like Goldie in the *Magnum* episode, Diane is given to causes, is an exhibitionist of her intellectual accomplishments, and often presented as rather silly.

In this particular episode, she learns that Woody pines for a girlfriend left behind in Indiana. She arranges for the girl to come to Boston, where, in another resonance with *Magnum*, Woodie fails to recognize her because of physical changes. It seems that "back home in Indiana," both Woody and his girl were grossly fat. Since coming to Boston he has become quite trim, and she, too, has slimmed to a petite figure. Once united, however, they begin a massive eating binge. Quickly several people at the bar notice they are substituting food for sex, and we have an extended interchange on Freudian versus Skinnerian analyses and remedies. Ultimately, Diane and Sam take Woody and his girl to dinner for a lesson in behavior modification. The younger couple decide they don't want to modify, they want sex, and go off to have it. Sam and Diane, meanwhile, gorge themselves to *avoid* sex, which was the bedrock—so to speak—of their previous romantic involvement. The viewer, of course, would need a three-and-a-half year knowledge to catch the full range of allusion and development in this episode. Diane's "expertise," like Goldie's, is made to look somehow inept, but the comic frame suggests that there is no appropriate "knowledge" in the world to instruct characters in the difficulties of personal relationships.

When placed after the *Magnum* episode, we have in this segment of *Cheers* other inflections on "maleness," "femaleness," "sexuality," "science," and "moral laws" that were presented in the earlier program. In the very different generic frame, despite *Magnum*'s comic aspects, all the commentaries take on slightly different meanings. Those variations are further distinguished by character histories, series development, and generic history.

To illustrate this further, we need only move on to the next program in this strip, *Night Court*. This show is frequently a plotless set of comic encounters among bizarre characters made up of those who staff and those who are brought before a New York night court. The immediate generic progenitor of the show is *Barney Miller*.

This episode of *Night Court* focuses on a defendant who has disturbed the peace. He believes he is a Venusian, and longs to return home. Much of his plight is built on not-so-veiled references to the popular movie, *E.T.* He is dying because of Earth's (America's) abuse of the ecosystem, its corrupt values, its moral decay. Actions taken in the court, actions designed to depict him as "insane," serve only to corroborate his point of view; "our logic" makes us look like the insane party. And in one scene, the defendant absorbs a huge jolt of electricity, indicating that we should at least assume the possibility that he *is* from Venus.

A subplot of the show involves Assistant District Attorney Dan Fielding, a regular character on the program. Dan is competent at his job, but single-minded in his pursuit of sex. In this episode, he arranges a date with a sexual adventuress whose appetites seem to outrun his own. Because the Venusian holds the entire court hostage, however, he almost misses his date. Drugged with the food designed to quiet the Venusian, he literally crawls out the door, drooling and panting after the woman. The next morning she swoons at his sexual prowess, but refuses to repeat the experience because it could "never be as good." Unfortunately, Dan remembers nothing—except some vague memory of sexual behavior involving a baseball catcher's mitt.

The combination of prominent discussion of extreme sexual activity with a critique of America's inability to exist rationally in nature and society provides us with an almost random set of discourses. All of them are inflected in bizarre comic fashion. And to do full justice, we would have to consider whether or not such a presentation continues the classical tradition of comedy as social critique or whether, in this case, the comic defuses any significant difference of opinion.

Taken in combination with the two preceding shows, however, we have an overt extension of the dialogue on male-female relations, on the moral base for social actions, and on the role of social law and higher laws in human interaction. Again, my point is not to suggest that viewers make all these connections, even if they follow the strip. Rather, it is to suggest that these varying, yet related, aspects of the issues are present in the text.

And this presentation is complicated further by the most complex narrative of the strip, *Hill Street Blues* (*HSB*). Because of the continuing nature of this program, much of the internal meaning is dependent on familiarity with character histories, ongoing plot developments, and general sociocultural contexts. For the nonfamiliar viewer, there are no strongly marked beginnings or endings, no particular closure. But there are many subplots, interwoven stories, and character relationships that combine to resonate with the *previous shows* in the strip.

Issues of gender, family, race, and ethnicity are chief among the discourses examined here. But the governing pattern is one of genre. At one level, this means that all the ideas presented here are inflected by the sense of grim *"urbanness"* on which the show is constructed. And, at an even higher level of signification, the cultural codes of *realism* and *melodrama* order and arrange the rhetoric and the significance of the ideas surrounding these themes. While there is, then, a great deal of humor, it is not the sort of humor that has informed my previous hour of viewing, nor even the sort that modified the world of the detective genre. I "know," because of visual coding, dialogue, and event, that I am supposed to take this show more "seriously" than the others I have watched. Without referring to the attitude of the professional critic, I think it is fair to say that the dialogic function of *HSB*, in this or any other strip that it concludes, is to shadow all previous content with this new, more complete, "seriousness." The viewer is invited to reconsider previous viewing in light of this newer style. Indeed, in the extra-textual discourse surrounding and positioning television, the show has functioned in this way, as a form of legitimation for the medium as a whole, a point of ultimate comparison, of aesthetic touchstone, of historical or evolutionary capstone.

If I take a specific example, it will have to deal with the discourses of "the law" and the "moral base of the law" that have been woven into the previous two hours of viewing. *HSB* emerges as closer to *Night Court* in this regard than to *Magnum, P.I.*, despite the silliness of the comedy and the seriousness of the detective program. For the bizarre world of *Night Court* also presents us with an urban world falling apart, a world in which only extreme perspectives and behavior serve as points of comparison. For all its openness, there is a kind of moral surety in *Magnum* that is missing in the frantic attempts to maintain order in *HSB*. *Night Court* offers a comic, almost comforting version of that lack of order.

But in the final scene of this episode of *HSB*, a policeman lies dying in a filthy alley. He is a young man, a former law student, a man who has succumbed to the lure of gambling. He owes excessive amounts of money that he cannot pay. His one escape was to alter the evidence against a criminal, but he could not bring himself to do it. When he confronts his bookie, he tries to put on a brave front and walk away. The bookie's "enforcer" first beats him. And when the policeman fights back, he stabs him. In a horrifying scene, the wounded policeman drags himself, screaming in pain, through grimy puddles, to his car radio and calls for help.

The episode ends. We know the next will tell us more about his plight, but it will introduce even more problems. They will never end. Our "discussion" of "the law," with its related discussion of maleness and femaleness, authority and power, family and community, will continue on a horizontal serial plane. But it will also continue to work its way up and down the viewing schedule.

To illustrate this fully, we must alter the viewing strip. Consider, for example, what happens if I "change the channel" in another direction after viewing *Magnum*. If I switched to ABC instead of NBC, my choice is to view *Lady Blue*. Here, in a classic case of gender role reversal, a conventionally beautiful young woman plays a tough and violent Chicago police detective. The narrative form is straightforward and conventional, clearly an action-adventure show. The episode focuses on the interaction of street gangs with illegal aliens from Latin America. The gangs are exploiting the aliens, but are also at war with one another, their antagonisms drawn along ethnic lines.

Ethnicity comes to the fore in the plot in the form of a *Romeo and Juliet* romance between teenagers from rival ethnic communities. The gangs violate one another's territory and perform various violent acts. The most harrowing of these occurs when one gang invades the funeral of one of their victims, removes the casket, throws it into the street, and fires repeated pistol shots through the casket into the corpse.

But overriding all these events is the *gender* of Kate, Lady Blue. Her character is, in terms of cultural coding, more overtly "male" than any in the entire night of programming. She adopts the fierce attitude of a competent purveyor of violent enforcement of law. But she inflects that through a personal vision that rivals the most conservative call for "law and order."

Read as a "response" to *Magnum*, she becomes the "male" challenge to his "female" qualities as nurturer, mentor, protector. Read against any of the characters in *HSB*, she expresses an almost irrational code of "machismo," despite a specific scene in which she disavows the insanity of "perverse macho codes." The only *HSB* characters who approach her extreme attitudes are Howard Hunter, the SWAT team leader, and Fletcher Daniels, Chief of Police. Both these characters are often portrayed as self-parodies, undercut by their extremist views and actions. In *Lady Blue*, we are invited to take these attitudes seriously. Nothing in the show's presentational style, its dialogue, or its actions invites us to question the premises. The placement of the woman in the central role provides an ambiguous, internal dialogue—offering new roles and new capabilities, but linking them to male-dominant discourse in terms of both political content and personal style.

Stylistically, a comparison of *Lady Blue* with *HSB* makes the former appear dated. The violent, but ultimately easy, resolutions to problems, the relentless single-focus of the narrative, the visual coding, all alert the viewer of *HSB* that this is an "old-fashioned" police show. Ultimately, the comparison makes it a "simplistic" show, an anachronism. The moral and political "vision" of the show cannot be saved merely by substituting "female" for "male." We "know," after *HSB*'s entry into television, that the city is not like this, and finally *Lady Blue* can potentially be read as comedy, not as realism, or even as melodrama. Just as *HSB* has given us a new way to evaluate and "place" television through its aesthetic codes and its thematic complexity, so *Lady Blue* can be seen as a parody on all of television, on television as it "used to be."

But there are others ways to "read" this strip. This model of a more inclusive text also invites me as viewer, by providing me with alternatives, to read for specific thematic development. Because gender is so prominently under discussion here, I can read Kate "with" and "against" other females in the text. I can compare her with Goldie in *Magnum,* with Diane and Carla in *Cheers*, with the meek public defender or the sexual aggressor in *Night Court*, and with the highly professional public defender, Joyce Davenport, and the powerfully competent police sergeant, Lucy Bates, in *HSB*. *Lady Blue*, more than any other show in the strip, activates this discussion of gender. Without this show, I might not have considered working my way forward and backward, remembering, comparing, evaluating, sorting among female characters and representations of gender.

But I need not have seen that show. I can view *Magnum* and decide not to change the channel in either direction. If I use as the middle "term" of my text the show that immediately follows *Magnum*, another comic detective show, *Simon & Simon*, everything shifts again.

The included episode focuses on romantic relationships. We watch four couples, two of them involving the same woman, come together or fall apart. The two brothers who form the show's title team both decide to make long-term commitments to the women with whom they are involved. In the end, the women reject them. These matters are presented quite seriously, despite the comic overtones of many episodes in the series. The considered choices are life-changing, and the issues presented at the level of cultural discourse are "marriage," "family," and "commitment." All these things are "under discussion."

Thinking *back* to *Magnum*, my concerns are redirected toward the question of personal commitment to public causes, and toward questions of "friendship" and "mutual support." All this is done within the confines of a very conventional mystery plot that, as in *Magnum*, is pretense for the consideration of the personal and social issues cited. Thus my response to *HSB* shifts toward the subplot involving the mayor's drug addicted son, and the pain his family is forced to endure. The fact that the mayor is black adds yet another dimension to the "discussion." Attention is also directed toward the subplot involving Detective Belker and his girlfriend as they discover that she is pregnant. He asks her, "What are we going to do?" And she replies, "Nothing."

I believe that the notion of the "strip as text" is now clear, and I have no intention of switching through more of the night's option. Suffice it to say that the dialogic, heterological nature of these texts would be altered even more if I began my night not with *Magnum*, but with most American viewers and the *Cosby Show*. To arrive at the conclusion of *HSB*, having begun with a story in which a small child and her father learn gentle lessons of social and personal responsibility, would be to experience a very different text. The pain of the black mayor's family in *HSB* would necessarily be contextualized by the love and care of the Huxtables in the *Cosby Show*. Similarly, my notion of family would be altered if I ended with *Knots Landing* instead of *HSB*. There, the discourse of "family" is under the constant strain common to the soap opera focus on kinship as the primary system of social meanings. And had I ended with *20/20*, I would have seen features on the AIDS virus, the panic surrounding it, and the research regarding its treatment. With the stories' special focus on the death of Rock Hudson, all the notions of romantic love would have been doubly activated. And I would have seen a feature on tracking dogs and the controversy surrounding the use of their discovered evidence. The legal system, notions of evidence, questions of crime all come to the fore. I could also have attended a feature on children's nightmares, again opening discussion of "family" and "childhood."

The primary argument against this process of what I refer to as television's, and, by extension, popular culture's, cultural forum, is that ultimately all the variation is constrained and contained by its appearance *as* television. In this argument, either the commercial nature of the medium in this society, or the casual way in which the medium is used, reduce all difference to a profound sameness. I suggest, however, that this conflicted mixture of meanings and sociocultural problems and ideas is the essence of television. To say that it is somehow "reduced" to this, misses the point. Its sameness *is* difference.

I want to conclude, then, by supporting this idea with several recent attempts to define overarching aspects of the medium and, in so doing, show how they all move toward a view of television as an "open" textual form.

The first is drawn from Robert Allen's *Speaking of Soap Operas,* and builds on the strip analysis I've demonstrated. One of Allen's central arguments is that in soap opera, what appears to be a form of informational redundancy is far more than that. He calls attention to one of the features of soaps, their tendency to present the same information over and over. This is one of the formal characteristics of soaps that make them so vulnerable to parody.

Allen's point, however, is that this circulation of information is not redundant, it is repeated, meaningful, inflection. He sets up character constellations as a soap opera paradigm, then shows how, as information about one set of characters is passed through all the other sets, the syntagmatic nature of the narrative unfolds. Report of an infidelity, an unwanted pregnancy, an illness moves through the community of characters. Each report *means* something different to each pair or triangle or family. It is this circulation of information that literally drives soap opera narrative. Events occur, but it is concern *about* events that interests the audience.

My point here is that this model serves equally to define the process of television as a meta-narrative. The constant recirculation of crucial cultural information in varied contexts makes it possible not only to speak in terms of textual and formal considerations such as genre, blurred genre, character, and action; it also enables us to come to different understanding of audiences. Audiences who prefer certain program types, or who have certain habitual viewing patterns, or rely on certain networks, receive particularized views of this information. By modeling the varied textual interactions possible in television, we can come to a more complete understanding of the cultural contradictions, the problems and the approaches, offered to the mass audience.

In one sense, this model is static. Just as we can take any given episode of a soap opera and analyze the circulation of meaning, so we can take any given night of television and analyze it in a similar manner. But soap opera is paradigmatic of television in yet another way—in terms of its seriality. This seriality is based on the assumption that change is possible—in human experience, in the narratives built from that experience, and therefore in the meaning we take from the narrative and put back into experience.

It is in this regard that Eco (1986) has recently suggested that television's reliance on serial textuality is a return to a very old aesthetic, one we must learn to understand. Television, and other forms of serial art are, in his view, a return to a pre-Romantic aesthetic, and allow us to witness "the birth of a new aesthetic sensibility much more archaic, and truly post-post-modern" (p. 180). This art is built on repetition and redundancy, patterns devalued since the Romantic turn. They are somehow psychologically appropriate to our time, he suggests.

> In a contemporary industrial society, instead [of eighteenth and nineteenth century societies] the social change, the continuous rise of new behavioral standards, the dissolution of tradition, requires a narrative based upon redundancy. Redundant narrative structures would appear in this panorama as an indulgent invitation to repose, a chance of relaxing. (p. 165)

These regularized patterns are, of course, overflowing with variation, with the novelty of individual episodes and plots. Eco merely reminds us that we take pleasure in both familiarity and novelty, and to privilege one over the other is a mistaken understanding of a complex aesthetic development, a return to the archaic uses of narrative.

> What results from these reflections is clear. The focus of the theoretical inquiry is displaced. Before, mass mediologists tried to save the dignity of repetition by recognizing in it the possibility of a traditional dialectic between scheme and innovation (but it was still the innovation that accounted for the value, the way of rescuing the product from degradation and promoting it to a value). Now, the emphasis must be placed on the inseparable knot of scheme-variation, where the variation is no more appreciable than the scheme. (p. 180)

This "inseparable knot of scheme-variation" is what I have tried to emphasize in the previous analysis. For it is only through the combination of redundancy and innovation that either is able fully to speak, fully to be understood, to be translated into social reality.

Again, however, I want to push Eco beyond the notion of the individual texts of television and toward the master text of the medium at large. It is the entire history of television that now forms the "scheme" on which the "variations" are worked. Generic evolution, all the way to the contemporary blurred genres, is part of the ground of all television texts, related by their similarities as well as their differences. We need only think of the "recovery" of old texts in rerun, and of the variations in their meanings "then" and "now," to grasp this sense of the larger textual nature of the medium. The expansion of cable television services, and the voracious appetite of cable for program content has made this historical comparison an exciting field for criticism. We are learning more about television history now than at any time in the past. And when these shows, or the return of their characters in new versions, are slotted into the contemporary schedule, the dialogue becomes overt.

Both Allen and Eco offer us ways of understanding the status of television texts, and the status of television *as* text, more fully. They focus, however, on formal characteristics of the medium. I have applied those formal qualities to larger patterns of television and, in so doing, approach questions of television as industry. It is to this material base of the medium, and to the ways in which material and formal properties coincide, that we must turn in conclusion.

One of the most powerful explanations of this level of analysis has come in Nick Browne's essay, "The Political Economy of the Television (Super) Text" (1984). Browne focuses on "the direct role of economy in shaping the form of American television texts" (p. 175). In so doing, he quickly comes to the conclusion that "the schedule determines the form of a particular television program, and conditions its relation to the audience" (p. 176). It is necessary, then, for reasons somewhat different from those I have suggested, to examine the "supertext" of television including all commercials, announcements, and so on. Similarly, again for different reasons, Browne posits the existence of a "megatext" of television, which "consists of everything that has appeared on television" (p. 177). This concept suggests that the *history* of the schedule is a topic for fruitful analysis.

Ultimately, Browne finds a totally sinister result from this interaction of material economy and textual economy: "Television's serial forms serve to continue the subject along the itinerary of habituated consumption" (p. 178), or "the actual commodity, then, is the ultimate referent of the television discourse" (p. 181), and finally, "in the television age, consumption and social control have become linked" (p. 181). What is overlooked here is the sense in which the American material economy, admittedly based on consumerism with enormous destructive effects, is also an economy of cultural semiotics, quite capable of contradicting and altering those effects. In other words, Browne's powerful perceptions of the ways in which the supertext and megatext work overlooks other linkages of meaning, linkages without which we must reach, with Browne, the pessimistic conclusion that social change is all but impossible. We can, then, come at this material aspect of television's internal dialogue by examining John Hartley's (1984) notion of television's necessary "semiotic excess," a notion most fully elaborated by John Fiske.

Fiske's strategy, one that I have tried to adopt here, is to maintain a critical attitude, fully cognizant of the power of dominant ideology, but to demonstrate how that ideology is fissured and open, capable of change. Here is Fiske's formulation:

> In order to explore how the relative openness of the television text might allow for ideologically contradictory readings we need to investigate the notion of semiotic excess. This has some affinities with both the "preferred reading" and the deconstructionist schools: it shares with the former the belief that dominant ideological values are structured into the text by the use of dominant codes and thus of dominant encodings of social experience. But it shares with the latter the belief that the dominant reading does not exhaust the semiotic potential of the text. In a popular work of art these codes and their formal relationships must conform to the conventions of encoding and decoding that the dominant ideology has established as its natural signifying practice, because without them the reader expectations would be defeated and popularity would be at risk.

> The theory of semiotic excess proposes that once the ideological, hegemonic work has been performed, there is still excess meaning that escapes the control of the dominant and is thus available for the culturally subordinate to use for their own cultural-political interests. The motivation to use semiotic excess for particular, possibly oppositional sub-cultural purposes, derives from the differences between the socio-cultural experiences of the producers and readers. Hodge and Tripp (forthcoming) are in no doubt about what happens when the meanings that TV seems to prefer are in conflict with those used to organize the reader's perception of the world: "non television meanings are powerful enough to swamp television meanings." This brings us to the fuller definition of "popularity," its sense of being "of the people, serving the grass roots interests of the subordinate." (pp. 17-18)

I have quoted at length because I want to offer a full account of how Fiske deals with the problem that has informed this chapter, the problem of *relative* openness with television. Still, I will go beyond Fiske's notion, by pushing the concept of semiotic excess into Browne's notion of super- and megatexts, into Eco's concept of the knot of seriality linking scheme and variation, and into Allen's notion of meaningful alterations that occur in the syntagmatic circulation of paradigmatic content.

With the larger concepts of "text," including diachronic as well as synchronic texts, serial as well as episodic texts, the excess multiplies. Even more important is the notion of the strip as a viewer-activated text. In discussing this kind of text, I have, as I said in beginning, idealized. I have not discussed the ways in which commercials offer differing organizations of the world, or the ways in which news-spots interrupt generic flow. I have not suggested that one could draw entirely different meanings by watching parts of programs, or by lapsing into conversation *about* part of the program, thus missing other parts.

Instead, I have simply tried to show that within these programs there is significant variation. I argue that this sort of variation accounts for both popularity and banality, for maintenance and change. Much of this argument is dependent on this somewhat macrocosmic view of television. I would like to close with a microcosmic example.

In the night's episode of *Magnum*, there comes a moment of great debate over animal rights and their relation to human needs. Goldie convinces Higgins that her position in freeing the dolphins is justifiable. He quotes Emily Dickinson to corroborate her view. Then, however, Goldie wants to accompany Magnum to try and rescue the dolphins. He refuses, citing the danger. These guys don't talk about change, he says, implying their violent intentions. She calls him up short, citing his own defense of the ongoing discussion of human rights with Kole, the dictator. Higgins comes to her defense, again quoting Dickinson:

> We never know how high we are
> 'til we are called to rise.
> And then, if we are true to plan

Here Higgins falters, forgetting the line. It is Magnum who speaks:

> Our statues touch the skies.

This is a moment of apparent novelty, when the detective, the Vietnam veteran, the violent man, offers up the poem, and halts the narrative for a moment. The music shifts, the other characters look at him. He has altered the discourse. Read through the meta-narrative of television, through all the other detectives that have preceded him in a meta-syntagm built on notions of crime, violence, control, and order, he has altered that discourse as well. And in a "vertical" manner, his moment will alter the discourse of the remainder of the evening.

For the familiar viewer, this comes as a minor surprise. We would not have expected Dickinson, perhaps, but there is much poetry in Magnum. My point is only that everything shifts in this small instance of internal dialogue, where character behavior, meaning, representation, and significance place everything in suspension. It is in such moments, I think, that television is open to our appropriation, and to appropriating us in different, less frightening ways than we have generally recognized.

APPENDIX TABLE 1
Thursday Night Network Television Schedule, 10/3/85

Time	NBC	CBS	ABC
7:00	*The Cosby Show*	*Magnum, P.I.*	*The Fall Guy*
7:30	*Family Ties*		
8:00	*Cheers*	*Simon & Simon*	*Lady Blue*
8:30	*Night Court*		
9:00	*Hill St. Blues*	*Knots Landing*	*20/20*

APPENDIX TABLE 2
Thursday Night Network Schedule, 10/3/85

Time	NBC	CBS	ABC
7:00	Domestic Comedy	Private Detective	Comedy Adventure/Crime
7:30	Domestic Comedy		
8:00	Workplace Comedy	Private Detective	Police Detective/ Procedural
8:30	Workplace Comedy		
9:00	Police Procedural	Domestic Melodrama	News Features/ Investigation

APPENDIX TABLE 3
Thursday Night Network Schedule, 10/3/85

NBC:

7:00 *The Cosby Show*/Domestic Comedy

Comedy star Bill Cosby portrays an affluent Philadelphia obstetrician whose office occupies a portion of his home. His wife, a successful lawyer, works outside the home. They are the parents of five children, one of whom is away at college. The plots revolve around common domestic misunderstandings, generally focused on the foibles of raising children. Small moral lessons are embedded in each episode.

7:30 *Family Ties*/Domestic Comedy

The fictional Keaton family lives out life in the American suburbs. Father and mother, Steven and Alise, are presented vaguely as having been "hippies" in the 1960s. Much of the comedy rises from the fact that their children have a different set of social values. Alex, oldest son, has grown through high school and now attends college. His stated ambition is to be the supreme capitalist. Oldest daughter, Mallory, is devoted to her personal appearance, to boys, and to every aspect of material life. Youngest daughter Jennifer, exhibits the wisdom of young children often found in domestic comedy. In the end, the children accept the wisdom of their parents, and the plot-created materialism disappears in the face of "love" and "warmth." (Michael J. Fox, the actor who portrays Alex, has become a popular film star and border-line teen idol.)

8:00 *Cheers*/Situation Comedy

A cast of regular characters meet weekly at a male-dominant, sports-oriented Boston bar. Sam, owner and bartender, is a former baseball player who almost reached stardom, but fell victim to alcoholism. He is now sober. Woody, his assistant, is a "dumb" character from the Midwest. He replaced another assistant, Coach, also "dumb," when actor Nicholas Colasanto died. Diane, a waitress, is a "well-educated" but hopelessly naive young woman given to exhibiting her "intellectualism" in obnoxious ways. Carla, another waitress, is Diane's opposite. Streetwise, mother of children born out of wedlock, lover of sports, foul of mouth, she plays the acerbic foil to almost all characters. Norm and Cliff are bar regulars who have major roles and provide much comedy. Major plots revolve around the on-again/off-again love relationship between Sam and Diane, which is presented openly as a case of rampant sexual attraction.

8:30 *Night Court*/Situation Comedy

A bizarre nonrepresentational comedy set in a New York night court. Comedian/magician Harry Anderson portrays youthful Judge Harry T. Stone, and presides over a continuing parade of outlandish characters who appear, for some reason or another, in night court.

9:00 *Hill Street Blues*/Police Procedural (open-ended serial narrative)

Any generic designation is inadequate for this show at this time. It is best described as an open-ended serial narrative. Its primary focus is on procedural police work, and cases remain open for several weeks at a time as the narrative moves among various plots and subplots. But there are also large doses of comedy and a heavy element of melodrama. Indeed, it would be more accurate to refer to the show as a police melodrama because emphasis is invariably placed on the private and emotional reactions/lives of the characters involved in the plots. A large cast populates the show. All characters, even temporary characters, are finely drawn.

CBS:

7:00 *Magnum, P.I.*/Private Detective (with comic overtones)

Thomas Magnum, played by popular media star Tom Selleck, is a private detective working in Hawaii. He is something of a comic con-man to his friends, living off the generosity of an absent best-selling author, Robin Masters. He lives on the Masters's estate as a "security specialist," but must continually make his way with Higgins, major domo of the estate and, as a retired Sergeant-Major in the British service, the punctilious antithesis of Magnum. Magnum also uses the services of two other friends; Rick, a hotel club manager, and T. C., owner of a helicopter tourist service. These two, like Magnum, are veterans of the Vietnam war. Many of the episodes of the series deal with Vietnam-related issues, while others have a strong and over comic direction. Although the series does wrap up each episode, it has a strong continuing quality in which events from past episodes play an important role in current events.

8:00 *Simon & Simon*/Private Detective (with comic overtones)

Rick and A. J. Simon, brothers, are owners of a private detective agency. Differences in their character traits provide much of the comic element in this series. As with *Magnum, P.I.*, crime is often inflected through the comic. This series is set in San Diego, and makes use of local settings in many plots. Rick Simon is also a Vietnam veteran, and again as in *Magnum,* some plots focus on this issue. On the whole, however, the series offers conventional crime-adventure-comedy.

9:00 *Knot's Landing*/Family and Social Melodrama (prime-time soap opera)

This show was the progenitor of *Dallas*, though the latter appeared first on television. While developing what was to become *Knot's Landing,* producer-writer David Jacob was told to look for more "exotic" material. *Dallas* was the result. *Knot's Landing* appeared later. It began the study of four families who lived in the same suburban cul-de-sac. In "sopa opera" fashion, the narrative chronicled their romantic and melodramatic life in contemporary Southern California. Increasingly, the plot has expanded, to take in more characters as we have experienced the dissolution of families, remarriages, the appearance of new characters, and so on. Mystery and intrigue, usually involving big business and shady politics, often make up plot material, with con-voluted romantic adventures always linked to these other subjects.

ABC:

7:00 *The Fall Guy*/Comic Action Adventure

Lee Majors (formerly the six-million dollar man) portrays Colt Seavers, a professional Hollywood stuntman. He is also a professional bounty hunter, working on contract to capture bail-jumpers and jail-escapees. But much of the show is presented humorously, often building on the lack of respect granted to stuntmen, who do the "hard work" of moviemaking. The show is filled with stunt work—high-speed chases, car crashes, falls, high-dives, and so forth. Colt is accompanied in most of his misadventures by his inept cousin, Howie, who is his accountant, but wishes to be a stuntman, and Jody, a lovely female companion who is "just a friend."

8:00 *Lady Blue*/Police Procedural

This show is no longer on the air. It appeared first as a made-for-television movie, obviously designed as a pilot for a series. It later surfaced as part of the regular schedule because of high ratings for the pilot. It focused on a beautiful woman police detective on the Chicago police force. Kate, the detective, was the complete exemplar of a "New Right" political perspective, preferring to shoot certain types of criminals rather than bother with court proceedings. She wields a large handgun with great skill and delight, and is often quick with "Clint Eastwood-style" aphorisms, as when she holds the pistol on an overweight criminal and asks, "How would you like to lose forty pounds—the hard way?"

9:00 *20/20*/News Magazine

20/20 is the most successful of another network's responses to CBS's *60 Minutes.* Hugh Downs, former host of NBC's *Today Show* hosts this program and provides transitions among its usual three stories. The stories range from expose to soft features. Various ABC reporters provide the narration and focus for each separately produced piece. Barbara Walters and Geraldo Rivera are the two most familiar presenters (though Rivera has recently left this show and ABC). In most cases, Downs speaks with the presenter of each individual piece during a brief moment "on the set" of *20/20*, and the two comment on follow-up material, the seriousness of the problem, the pleasure of the more entertainment-oriented pieces, and so on.

NOTE

1. At the time this essay was written, this schedule no longer existed. In the face of strong (catastrophic) competition from the *Cosby Show, Magnum, P.I.* was moved to Wednesday nights at 9:00 P.M. (EST) in the fall of 1986. In that spot, it regained some of its popularity, sometimes besting the popular *Dynasty* in the ratings, and was renewed for the 1987-1988 television season. The *Magnum, P.I.* slot was filled by a family-child-oriented series, *The Wizard.* Similarly, *Hill Street Blues,* never a strong contender, was

moved to Tuesdays at 8:00, opposite the new hit *Moonlighting*. After a few weeks of drubbing there, NBC moved the show to 9:00. At the time of this writing, all evidence indicated that the show would not return in the fall of 1987—but predictions about television, even in scholarly print, should be taken with large grains of salt. The series was replaced by another Stephen Bochco creation, *L.A. Law,* a show that exhibits many of *HSB*'s characteristics in a different setting. *Lady Blue* lasted half a season and is now forgotten by most of the population that rejected it. The *Fall Guy* moved on to lucrative syndication, replaced by a sometimes brilliant history-documentary program, *Our World.* That show was followed by *The Colbys,* a *Dynasty* spinoff starring Charlton Heston. Such is the continuing dialogue in the television supertext.

REFERENCES

Allen, R. (1985). *Speaking of soap operas.* Chapel Hill: University of North Carolina Press.

Ang, I. (1985) *Watching Dallas.* London: Methuen.

Bakhtin, M. M. (1981). *The dialogic imagination* (M. Holquist & C. Emerson, Eds. and Trans.). Austin: University of Texas.

Browne, N. (1984, Summer). The political economy of the television (super) text. *Quarterly Review of Film Studies,* pp. 174-182.

de Lauretis, T. (1985). *Alice doesn't.* Bloomington: Indiana University Press.

Eco, U. (1980). Towards a semiotic inquiry into the TV message. In J. Corner & J. Hawthorne (Eds.), *Communication studies: An introductory reader.* London: Arnold.

Eco, U. (1986, Winter). Innovation and repetition: Between modern and post-modern aesthetics. *Daedalus,* pp. 161-184.

Ellis, J. (1982). *Visible fictions.* London: Routledge & Kegan Paul.

Fiske, J. (1986). Television: Polysemy and popularity. *Critical Studies in Mass Communication, 3*(4), 391-405.

Fiske, J., & Hartley, J. (1978). *Reading television.* London: Methuen.

Gitlin, T. (1983). *Inside prime time.* New York: Pantheon.

Gitlin, T. (1987). Car commercials and MTV: "We build excitement." In Todd Gitlin (Ed.), *Watching television* (pp. 136-161). New York: Pantheon.

Hall, S. (1980). Encoding/decoding. In S. Hall et al. (Eds.), *Culture, media, language.* London: Hutchinson.

Hall, S. et al. (Eds.). (1980). *Culture, media, language.* London: Hutchinson.

Hartley, J. (1984). Encouraging signs: Television and the power of dirt, speech and scandalous categories. In W. Rowland & B. Watkins (Eds.), *Interpreting television: Current research perspectives* (pp. 119-141). Newbury Park, CA: Sage.

Himmelstein, H. (1984). *Television myth and the American mind.* New York: Praeger.

Jameson, F. (1979). Reification and utopia in mass culture. *Social Text, 1,* 130-148.

Katz, E., & Liebes, T. (1984). Once upon a time in Dallas. *Intermedia, 12*(3), 28-32.

Liebes, T. (1984). Ethnocriticism: Israelis of Moroccan ethnicity negotiate the meaning of Dallas. *Studies in Visual Communication.*

Morley, D. (1980). *The nationwide audience: Structure and decoding.* London: BFI.

Newcomb, H. (1984). On the dialogic aspects of mass communication. *Critical Studies in Mass Communication, 1*(1), 34-50.

Newcomb, H., & Alley, R. (1983). *The producer's medium: Conversations with America's leading television producers.* New York: Oxford.

Newcomb, H., & Hirsch, P. (1983, Summer). Television as a cultural forum: Implications for research. *Quarterly Review of Film Studies.*

Radway, J. (1984). *Reading the romance: Feminism and the representation of women in popular culture.* Chapel Hill: University of North Carolina Press.

Rowland, W., & Watkins, B. (Eds.). (1984). *Interpreting television: Current research perspectives.* Newbury Park, CA: Sage.

Silverstone, R. (1981). *The message of television: Myth and narrative in contemporary culture.* London: Heinemann.

Thorburn, D. (1976). Television melodrama. In R. Adler & D. Cater (Eds.), *Television as a cultural force.* New York: Praeger.

Wolf, M., Meyer, T., & White, C. (1982). A rules-based study of television's role in the construction of reality. *Journal of Broadcasting, 26*(4), 813-829.

Chapter 5

DALLAS AND GENESIS[1]
Primordiality and Seriality in Popular Culture

Tamar Liebes and Elihu Katz

WE HAVE BEEN STUDYING THE WAYS in which members of different ethnic groups decode the worldwide hit program *Dallas*. Our interest in this problem arose, originally, from the question of how such a quintessentially American cultural product crosses cultural and linguistic frontiers so easily. Despite the universal popularity of American films and television, and the allegations of cultural imperialism that accompany their diffusion, almost nobody has bothered to find out how they are decoded or indeed whether they are understood at all. Our subjects are persons of some secondary schooling drawn from four ethnic communities in Israel—Arabs, newly arrived Russian Jews, Moroccan Jews, and kibbutz members—and nonethnic Americans in Los Angeles. Groups of six persons—three couples, all friends, meeting in the home of one of them—are asked to discuss an episode of *Dallas* immediately after seeing it on the air. We have begun to conduct a parallel study in Japan—one of the few countries in which *Dallas* failed—but have only preliminary results so far.

Obviously, this is not the research design that will lead to a conclusive answer to the secret of the popularity of American television overseas. We chose to study one such program, as a start, in order to observe the mechanisms through which people understand, interpret, and evaluate a program, and to compare such understandings across cultures. As a result, we now have some good ideas about how people do these things, or, more generally, how these programs manage to engage and enter the lives of widely different kinds of viewers.

Before we summarize these findings, we wish to dismiss the widely held view that the success of programs like *Dallas* can be explained in terms of their simplemindedness or in terms of their rich visual appearance. The fact is that the program is not simple at all—one must learn the complex relationships among the large number of characters, and one must learn how to make a coherent story out of the "staccato" series of scenes and subplots that are presented to the viewer without benefit of narration. Moreover, the pretty pictures are by no means sufficient to an understanding of the narrative. One cannot decode the story without its words, and in Israel, for example, these words appear in subtitles in two languages, Hebrew and Arabic.

We think, rather, that the secret of *Dallas* is in the ways in which it offers viewers at different levels and in different cultures something they can understand from within themselves.

We are not referring here to the superficial problem of understanding; in fact, we find that all of the groups we studied have an elementary understanding of the story as a drama of human relationships (whether this is true of the whole world, we cannot yet say, but we assume that it is). What we do wish to do here is to distinguish, first of all, among different types of understanding. Then we wish to show that these types of understanding are related to different types of involvement. Finally, we will argue that programs like *Dallas* invite these multiple levels of understanding and involvement, offering a wide variety of different projects and games to different types of viewers.

ON VIEWER
UNDERSTANDING AND INVOLVEMENT

It is often remarked that *Dallas* provokes conversation. An essay on *Dallas* in Algeria, for example (Stolz, 1983), argues that the program replaced the conversation following grandmothers' story-telling around the fireside. Our study documents this phenomenon extensively. A kibbutz member says that the secretariat of the kibbutz is occupied with talk of *Dallas* on the day after the program. A new immigrant from Russia says that *Dallas* is compulsory viewing for anybody who wants to be part of Israeli society!

What we want to say is that to view *Dallas* overseas—perhaps even in America—is to view a *program,* and not—as certain critics think—to view moving wallpaper. It is, in fact, more than viewing a program: it is becoming engaged with a narrative psychologically, socially, and aesthetically, depending on the background of the viewer. Programs like *Dallas* appear to be able to activate very different kinds of viewers.

To analyze these different types of understanding and involvements, we distinguish, first, between the referential and the metalinguistic. In answer to our question, "Why all the fuss about babies?" some viewers refer to real life and explain that families, especially rich ones, need heirs.[2] Others, using a metalinguistic frame, say that babies are good material for conflict, and the narrative of soap opera needs conflict to keep going. Within the referential, we distinguish between real and ludic keyings. The one makes serious equations between the story and life, the other treats the program more playfully, subjunctively, and interactively—turning the group discussion into a kind of psychodrama. Making a further distinction within the referential, some viewers key the program normatively, judging messages and characters moralistically; others treat the program as observers and withhold value judgments. The moralizing statements tend to be couched in the language of "we": "Their women are immoral; our Arab women would not behave that way." Less moralizing statements come either in the language of "they"—for those who generalize from the program to the universals of life—and in the language of "I" and "You" for those who treat program and life more playfully.

Applying these distinctions to viewers of different education and different ethnicity reveals how understanding and involvement may vary among groups. While all groups make many more referential than metalinguistic statements, the better-educated viewers use the metalinguistic frame much more. Better-educated viewers decode the program at two levels—referential and metalinguistic—thus involving themselves not only in the narrative but in its construction.

Patterns of involvement vary by ethnicity as well. The more traditional groups—Moroccan Jews and Arabs—do not stray far from the referential. Even the well-educated among them make comparatively few metalinguistic statements. They accept the program as real, and deal seriously with its relationship to their own lives. The Arabs in particular discuss the program moralistically, and in terms of "them" and "us." This pattern of relating to the program is at once involving and defensive: the program is discussed referentially and seriously, but, at the same time, it is rejected as a message for "us." Even if this rejection serves as a buffer against the influence of the program, it nevertheless reflects a high level of engagement.

The American and kibbutz groups show an altogether different pattern of involvement. The rate of their metalinguistic statements is high, and their use of the referential is often in the ludic mode. Some of their dialogue reminds one of fantasy games.

Like the Americans and kibbutzniks, the Russians also have a high proportion of metalinguistic statements—the highest proportion, in fact. They are critical not only of the aesthetics of the story (comparing it unfavorably to Tolstoy and other literary sagas) but about the message, which they regard as an ideological manipulation. Beware, say the Russians, of the false message of the program. They tell us that the rich are unhappy because that's what they want us to think!

Note the difference between these forms of criticism and those of the traditional groups. The Arabs, as we have said, criticize the seeming real-life behavior of the characters as immoral but believe the surface message of the narrative that the rich are unhappy. This decoding is precisely what the Russian criticism warns against.

Curiously, however, when the Russians use the referential frame, they seem to set aside their ideological suspicions and treat the program, as the Arabs and Moroccans do, as if it were a documentary. Going even further than the traditional groups—who accept the program as the truth about Americans but reject the program as a portrayal of themselves—the Russians seem to be saying that entire classes of people—women, businessmen, and so on—behave as their *Dallas* counterparts do. The seriousness of their sweeping universal generalizations from the program to life are altogether different from the ludic keyings of the Americans and kibbutzniks.

Thus we see at least three different patterns of involvement in these decodings. The more traditional viewers remain in the realm of the real (and the serious), and mobilize values to defend themselves against the program. The more Western groups—the Americans and the kibbutzniks—are relatively more aware of, and involved in, the construction of the program, and deal with its reality more playfully. The Russians are also metalinguistic—most of all, in fact—but they show more awareness of the message of the program than of its structure. This concern seems to go together with the seriousness with which the Russians enter the referential just as the more constructionist concerns of the other Western groups go hand in hand with their more playful keyings of the referential.

It is evident that each pattern of involvement includes a mechanism of defense. The Arabs, accepting the program's reality, reject the values of the characters. The Russians reject the values of the producers. The Americans and kibbutzniks reject the idea that the values—either of characters or producers—are to be taken seriously.

We cannot answer the question whether these forms of distancing—any one or all—reduce the extent of viewer vulnerability. While it may appear, at first glance, that ludic keyings and metalinguistic framings are more resistant to influence, we are by no means certain that this is so. The ludic may be seductive in the sense that fantasy and subjectivity invite one to be carried away. Similarly, constructionist concerns distract attention from the ideological message. Even ideological decodings are vulnerable to influence in the sense that the decoders believe that their oppositional reading is the truth!

Whatever the answer to this question, the fact that the program invites very different—educationally and ethnically—kinds of viewers to become involved in their several ways is the concern of this chapter. We turn, therefore, to the next question, namely, what it is about a program like *Dallas*—or perhaps, what is it about the soap opera genre to which it is related—that makes this kind of multidimensional participation possible?

In attempting to answer this question, we are led by the viewers to two dimensions of the *Dallas* genre, the semantic dimension, which draws so heavily on primordial themes of human relations, and the syntactic dimension of seriality, which regularly combines and recombines this set of basic relational elements to tell endless variations of the same story. In other words, we are suggesting that these two dimensions of the genre constitute invitations to the viewer to invest his or her emotions, empathy, and expertise as a card-carrying member of a kinship group and to invest his or her imagination and puzzle-solving predilections in the game of how they are going to do it this week.

We cannot claim to be discovering more than our colleagues have, and cannot prove that we were first. In fact, the idea of the universal appeal of soap opera as a drama of kinship in which we are all connoisseurs has been stated by others, both in general (McCormack, 1982) and with respect to programs like *Dallas* (Morgan & Spanish, 1984; Tracey, 1985). And the idea of seriality as a form of aesthetic pleasure has also been stated, most recently by Umberto Eco (1985). What we can say is that our point of departure does not proceed from content analysis of the text to some imagined reader supposedly constructed by the text, but inductively, from real readers—and the variations in their readings—to those aspects of the text that invite different levels of decoding and different forms of involvement. Thus we can show that Eco's two readers—the "naive" and the "smart," which ostensibly correspond to semantic and syntactic decodings, may, in reality, be the same person. To show that these two model readers can coexist in the same minds and hearts is one of the advantages of our method.

ON HOW *DALLAS*
INVITES INVOLVEMENT

Primordiality: Dallas is a primordial tale echoing the most fundamental mythologies. Consider the parallels *mutatis mutandis* between *Dallas* and Genesis. Just as our forefathers were the giants of their time, dividing the world among themselves, so the characters in *Dallas* fill the whole of the frame dwarfing governments and shutting out any aspect of the real world that they do not control. Gradually, readers of the story come to believe that the dynasty *is* the world, at least the world from which will emerge a nation and its rulers. This is obvious in the case of Genesis, but in *Dallas* too, both the professional critics and the American viewers in our study make allusions to the Kennedy clan.[3]

The Biblical entanglement of business and family predates the modern separation of the two. But Dallas is modern, and it reverts, nevertheless, to the primordial model. The two institutions are inexorably intertwined, each invades the other, and the same rules apply to both. Family is as instrumental as business and business is as affective as family. Marriages are power alliances and the elemental passions—rather than the rules of the game—govern business. Thus, J. R. buys up all the oil wells in Texas in order to bring home his estranged spouse, as Jacob worked for 14 years in order to buy his chosen wife.

Dynasty is the major preoccupation of the first book of Bible. Marriage between a favored son and his father's or mother's brother's daughter or granddaughter functions to keep property within the family and to enhance the family's power.

Altogether, one might say that the Genesis story is about "the social construction of family," or, alternatively, about God's intervention in the planning of unusual births and deaths and "in reversals of the iron law of primogeniture" (Alter, 1981).[4] Consider how closely *Dallas* fits Alter's analysis of Genesis as the repeated election of a younger son to carry on the line "through some devious twist of destiny" (p. 6). The brothers in *Dallas*—J. R. and Bobby—are simply variations on Cain and Abel, Isaac and Ishmael, Jacob and Esau. The brothers compete for their parents' blessing; each brother seeks to be named the official heir; each brother tries to outdo the other in the instrumental (not moral) tests that will prove his qualifications; the parents conspire, each with his favorite, and manipulate each other on behalf of their favorite; brothers and parents divide in their inclinations toward nature and culture, excess and moderation, wildness and domesticity.

In Canaan as in *Dallas*, the key women have problems with fertility; they repeatedly fail in the mission to produce an heir; they are forced to acquiesce in the acquisition of other women's children; they have to endure the tension of the presence of these other women, who are, often enough, their own sisters or predecessors. Both in Canaan and in *Dallas*, there is concern for the continuity of the "house" (Lévi-Strauss, 1983). In Canaan, this means seeking out alliances with distant kin in order not to assimilate locally; in *Dallas*, it involves making alliances with rival dynasties to subvert them from within.

A striking difference between the two texts is that the women in Canaan have a lot more influence on their husbands, both directly and indirectly, than the women in *Dallas*, who are basically victims. Another difference, we think, is that the Bible prefers the sedentary home lovers—the studious, the dream-decoders, and the "dwellers in tents"—to the hunters and the Dionysians of *Dallas*. We refrain from pronouncing *Dallas* more archaic than Genesis, but that would seem to be the case. Unlike the rest of soap opera, the hero of *Dallas* is a villain or trickster whom Fiedler (1982), for one, would find compatible with his theory that the best of popular culture—including media culture—is subversive of the bourgeois order, although the message is regressive rather than progressive.

Even without explicit mention of sources, the mythic reverberations figure in many of the group discussions. For example, Ayad, in one of the Arab groups (group 40), tells the *Dallas* story as follows:

> It's about a rich family who have a large inheritance. They have oil, and two sons. The older son is a cheat. He wanted to grab control of all the wealth of his father and mother. The younger one tried to share in the property but the older one schemed and plotted to get the money. And the two brothers quarreled.

Notice how this quote omits the name of the characters in favor of their primordial roles, and how familiar it all sounds to teller and listener.

A more sophisticated version of this same kind of telling is Eitan's in one of the kibbutz groups (group 80): "He was the elder son, and it's as if he was constantly trying to prove his worth to his parents. There was another (a third) brother whom the mother loved, and baby Bobby was loved by the father."

A Japanese viewer also recognizes the primordial quality of these relationships but makes clear that these are better forgotten: "It certainly reminds us of the Japanese before the war. Elements such as inheritance, relationship between bride and mother-in-law and powerful eldest son—these are points we want to forget."

There are different levels of sophistication, different theories that are invoked in telling, attributing motivation, and interpreting, and a different selection of issues that are focused upon. But sophisticated or not, mythic or not, we all are connoisseurs of these human relations and the psychology, sociology, and politics that define them. In other words, all viewers—each at his own level of sophistication and embedded in his own culture—will find familiar the narrative of the embroilments of kinship, and can become involved in how these characters are organizing their lives by comparison with all of the other kinship texts we know— our own, our neighbors, and our forefathers. It is likely that these kinship stories become so engrossing that the rest of social and political reality are shut out and not missed. This clearly has a political consequence.

Seriality: Our involvement in these characters and their stories not only reflects their enactment of human texts that are familiar to us but reflects no less our week-to-week familarity with them. We are connoisseurs not just of the situation but of these very people. The familiarity that results from these weekly visits leads, for one thing, to what is known as parasocial interaction (Horton & Wohl, 1956) whereby people talk back to the characters approvingly or disapprov- ingly, wishing them well or ill, urging them on, warning them of danger, worrying about the shame they will bring upon themselves. Indeed, seriality at the referential level often puts the viewer in a position where he knows more about a character than the character knows about himself, thus increasing the viewer's sense of control over the goings-on.

The Bible is a serial-story too; it is written as such, and read as such. If repetitiveness is essential to seriality, one may say that *Dallas* reenacts the same story with the same characters (they marry, unmarry, remarry continually; they die and are resurrected; and so on) while Genesis repeats the same stories in successive generations (Alter, 1981). If installments in the telling are essential to seriality, the weekly portions of the Bible read throughout Jewish and Christian worlds easily qualify. Moreover, Jewish synagogues have been "rerunning" the Old Testament for 2000 years.

The open-minded nature of the family serial, of course, distinguishes it from some of the formulaic constraints of the series in which each story is self-contained and has to be resolved within 50 minutes

(Newcomb, 1974). The serial allows for greater character development, more ambiguity, and more complexity. In a word, soap opera *is* more like reality, and it is no wonder that the stories enter into the realm of gossip. Moreover, the incomplete nature of each episode that leaves us hanging on a cliff is reminiscent of the Zeigarnik effect, which posits that interrupted tasks are better remembered than completed ones. This is yet a further dimension to help explain the active nature of reader involvement in serial narratives, as literary theorists (Iser, 1978) have already noted.

Seriality as an invitation to viewer involvement operates not just at the referential level but also at the metalinguistic level. At this level, viewers can name the genre and compare it to others: they can define its attributes and dramatic conventions such as its division into subplots woven around characters and the staccato succession of two- and three-person dialogues. While the Americans compare the dynamics of *Dallas* to those of other television dramas, the Russians use the classic novel much to the detriment of *Dallas*. From our study, it is clear that television viewers are much better critics than they are usually given credit for. They become quite involved in these analyses and comparisons, which are often emotionally loaded. Indeed, some viewers show considerable sophistication about the constraints that operate on producers. Thus certain kinds of viewers can identify the elements out of which the story is constructed and the characters created. In other words, viewers in the metalinguistic frame can do what they do not do in the referential frame, namely, to put the pieces together—to combine and recombine them—as the writers do, while managing, nevertheless, to switch back and forth from the referential to the metalinguistic.

The key to viewer involvement at this level is in the realization that the story is like a contest in which the outcomes can repeatedly change or like a game in which the pieces can be put together in different ways. For long periods of time, the pieces are the characters as given—in number, gender, personality, and kinship roles. These characters can be rotated through an elementary series of changing problems and relationships that are necessary to keep the story going. Viewers who relate to the program at this level become interested in how the characters will next confront a problem or each other. Consider Deanne (American group 9), who says, "Now it seems that Katherine has got her eye on Bobbie, and in this one episode there is just a little bit of hint she will have her way." Continuing her thought, Jill says, "This will snap Pam out of her depression fast enough." And Deanna adds, "Or put her into a worse one."

Another viewer, Greg (American group 3) sees a seesaw domination and subordination at work. He says it's like a wrestling match.

> The bad guys keep squashing the good guys using all the dirty tricks and then every once in a while some good guys will resort to the bad guy's tricks and, you know, stomp on the bad guys for a while, and all the crowd will go yeah yeah yeah and then the next week the bad guys are on top again squashing the good guys.

Greg's involvement is in his intellectual perception of the program as contest, and not in the emotions of soap opera. In the longer run, the character of the characters also changes, and viewers get the idea that the true building blocks, or pieces, of the puzzle may not be the characters as given once and for all but structural attributes that are redivided among the characters. Thus the good and the bad guys may not only struggle for domination but actually exchange roles. This kind of jigsaw puzzle or Lego set or computer game invites the metalinguistic viewer to anticipate the combinatorial possibilities and to stay with the program to prove him- or herself right. This is quite different, obviously, from the linear model of Proppian narrative (1968).[5]

CONCLUSIONS

In conclusion, we would like to review the argument of the chapter and to point out some theoretical implications and certain problems that remain unsolved.

To begin with, we should remind ourselves, perhaps, that we are here trying to explain the near-universal popularity of programs like *Dallas*. We are not dealing at all with the question of effect. Our argument, then, is as follows:

(1) People talk about *Dallas*; the program seems to provoke conversation. We have evidence of this from research in a number of cultures (Algeria, Denmark, Germany). It is also a basis for talk across cultures, of which this chapter is itself an example.

(2) We have tried to stimulate this talk in group discussions among viewers in different ethnic contexts. Analyzing these discussions, we distinguish between statements that connect the program to real life, often to the viewer's own life, and those that see the program as a narrative, discerning themes and story-telling formulas. We call the former referential framing, and the latter metalinguistic.

(3) Examining these statements in an attempt to identify what in the story motivates conversation and involvement, we identify two major

clues: the one we call primordiality, the other seriality. Primordiality evokes in the viewer an echo of the human experience and makes him an instant connoisseur of the *Dallas* variations on the elementary forms of kinship and interpersonal relations. Seriality is an obvious invitation to involvement in the regular visits of familiar characters, in the gossip of anticipation, and in discovering the rules of the producer's game.

(4) It is wrong to assume, however, that the referential deals only with the primordial and the metalinguistic only with the serial. Rather, the viewer may frame both the primordial and the serial either referentially or metalinguistically. Thus a referential framing of the primordial would recognize the similarity of sibling rivalry in *Dallas* and in Genesis, where the Biblical characters are also perceived as real. The metalinguistic framing would perceive the literary paradigm that guides the writers of both stories. Seriality may also be framed in either way. The referential framing of seriality attributes reality to the characters whose lives go on even between episodes (Booth, 1982) while the metalinguistic framing of seriality is concerned with the art of construction of syntagmatic combinations.[6]

(5) While Eco's distinction between the mythic and the strategic seems to correspond to our primordial and serial, we find ourselves in disagreement with his exclusive attribution of the mythic to the "naive" reader and of the syntactic to the "smart" reader. For better or worse, real readers insist on behaving more ambiguously than the roles that theory assigns them. This is the point at which to recall that we have two kinds of readers—those who remain almost exclusively in the referential frame and those who move between the referential and the metalinguistic. What we are now saying is that the primordial content of *Dallas* makes the referential reader more involved in reality, but so does its serial structure. That is, referential readers treat the characters as real not only because of semantics but because of syntactics. For those readers who move to the metalinguistic, we are suggesting that the serial structure gives them ample material for syntactic games but also that the primordial content allows them to play Lévi-Straussian games.[7]

(6) We cannot here presume to solve the aesthetic problem of how this movement is possible, that is, how viewers can be involved at once in the reality of the narrative and in the strategies of its construction. One suggestion, however, arising from the present study calls attention to the compatibility of the family saga and the serial form. The naturalness of this fit would explain why the referential readers are so little disturbed by the ostensible artificiality of the construction. It may also explain why the movers find it possible to move from the referential to the metalinguistic and back. The kinship story, obviously, repeats itself in

reality and we become aware of the structure of sameness and variation in real-life repetitions. It is an easy step from this reflexive position to thoughts of combining and recombining. It is another easy step from these thoughts to the awareness that the serial form is doing exactly this.[8]

(7) Returning, finally, to the question of global programs, this analysis suggests that both content and form of *Dallas*, and the relationship between them, are invitations to viewers of very different backgrounds to act as connoisseurs of life, or stories, or both. By cross-tabulating referential and metalinguistic frames with the primordial-semantic and serial-syntactic, we have illustrated four ways of relating to the story.

NOTES

1. The Hebrew *lehavdil* (to differentiate) deserves to be invoked here, connoting "if you will forgive the comparison." The word is used, traditionally as well as in common parlance, to qualify an otherwise valid analogy between something sacred and important and something profane or trivial. The study on which this paper is based was supported by grants from the Trustees of the Annenberg Schools, Inc. and the Hoso Bunka Foundation. An earlier version appears in the proceedings of a 1985 conference, in Paris, in Lucien Sfez, (Ed.), *Nouveaux Programmes et Communication Audiovisuelle: Actes du Colloque CNCA,* Paris: Mission TV-Cable and Centre Georges Pompidou, 1986.

2. The quantitative analysis of these data (Liebes, 1986; Liebes & Katz, 1986) emphasizes *self*-referential statements in which viewers relate the program to their *own* lives. In the present chapter, however, we treat all statements about the reality of the program as referential.

3. The producers help, too, by choosing names like John and Bobby.

4. Professor Arnold Band of UCLA points out that the God of Genesis intervenes subtly (gynecologically, says Daniel Dayan), while the God of Exodus intervenes thunderously. These types of intervention remind one, in turn, of Leo Braudy's distinction between "soap opera time" and "catastrophic time"!

5. The classical fairy tale, according to Propp, begins with a problem ("lack") and ends with a coronation or a wedding. The typical serial episode—having to end in suspense ("lack") typically moves from harmony to tension rather than vice versa (Liebes, 1986).

6. This also explains the well-known problem of serial actors who cannot play any other role because they are so heavily identified (even by themselves) with their characters. Thus an American group member, even while insisting that she is not the kind of referential viewer who writes letters to soap opera characters, says, nevertheless, that she would slap Larry Hagman if she met him at the airport.

7. There are two points here: (1) that real readers often play both of Eco's roles, the smart and the naive; and (2) that even readers who remain in the referential are influenced in their referentiality not only by the mythic but by the strategic, that is, both the primordial and the serial influence referential and metalinguistic readings.

8. The case of *Dallas* may be even a better fit for the serial structure than the soap opera itself if Michael Arlen (1980) is correct in distinguishing between the strict morality

of classical soap opera and the improvisatory morality of *Dallas*. Obviously, improvisation and flexible personalities and values makes the story even more never ending.

REFERENCES

Alter, R. (1981). *The art of biblical narrative*. Berkeley: University of California Press.

Arlen, M. (1980). Smooth pebbles at Southfork. In *Camera age: Essays on TV* (pp. 38-50). New York: Farrar, Strauss and Giroux.

Booth, W. (1982, Fall). The company we keep: Self making in imaginative art old and new. *Daedalus, 4.*

Braudy, L. (1981-82). Popular culture and personal time. *Yale Review, 71*(41), 481-488.

Eco, U. (1975, Fall). Innovation and repetition: Between modern and post-modern aesthetics. *Daedalus.*

Fiedler, L. (1982). *What was literature? Mass culture and mass society.* New York: Simon & Schuster.

Goffman, E. (1974). *Frame analysis*. New York: Harper & Row.

Horton, D., & Wohl, R. R. (1956). Mass communication and parasocial interaction. *Psychiatry, 19.*

Iser, W. (1978). *The act of reading: A theory of aesthetic response.* London: Henley, Routledge & Kegan Paul.

Jakobson, R. (1972). Linguistics and poetics. In De George & De George (Eds.), *The structuralists: From Marx to Lévi-Strauss.* New York: Anchor Books.

Lévi-Strauss, C. (1983). Historie et ethnology. *Annales, 38.*

Liebes, T. (1986, June). Cultural differences in the retelling of TV fiction. Paper presented at the ICA Conference, Chicago.

Liebes, T., & Katz, E. (1986). Patterns of involvement in television fiction: A comparative study. *European Journal of Communication, 1.*

McCormack, T. (1982). *Studies in communication* (Vol. 1). London: JAI Press.

Morgan, D., & Spanish, M. (1984). *Focus groups and the study of social cognition: A new tool for qualitative research.* Unpublished manuscript, University of California, Riverside, Department of Sociology.

Newcomb, H. (1974). *TV, the most popular art.* New York: Anchor.

Propp, V. (1968). *Morphology of the folk tale.* Austin: University of Texas Press.

Stolz, J. (1983). Les Algeriens regardent "Dallas." In *Les nouvelles chaines,* Paris: Presse Universitaire de France, and Université d'études du developpement, Geneve.

Tracey, M. (1985, Fall). The poisoned chalice? International television and the idea of dominance. *Daedalus.*

Chapter 6

THE *MARY TYLER MOORE SHOW* AND THE TRANSFORMATION OF SITUATION COMEDY

Thomas H. Zynda

THE SITUATION COMEDY I am concerned with here, the *Mary Tyler Moore Show* (1970-1977), is one of a trio, along with *All in the Family* (1971-1983) and *M*A*S*H* (1972-1983), that hold an honored place in our view of television's cultural history. Because of these shows, the period from September 1970 to September 1972, during which they premiered, is seen as *the* watershed in American television. Viewed as an event, this period was a revolution in programming that divides television history into before and after halves.

In this view of television history, the first half, from 1948 to 1970, begins with the golden age of the 1950s, which brought us lively variety shows, engrossing live drama, and the delightful early situation comedies. Television experimented with the form it was to take and with its relation to American life. The golden age ends with the entrance of the major movie studios into program production. Production moved from New York to the West Coast, and was rationalized in the form of the series, which, as the fundamental unit of television, gave programming the consistency and uniformity of any mass-market product. The business values of the major studios suppressed creativity and real-life themes; program content became domesticated, unpolitical, and often juvenile. Live drama, which reflected the confrontational political and personal style of New York, gave way to vapid westerns and mindless situation comedies. By the end of the 1950s, television had become an economic and organizational combine of the networks, the major studios, and the major advertisers, for whom ideal television was ideologically somewhere between *Ozzie and Harriet* (1952-1966) and the *Donna Reed Show* (1958-1966).

The first period of television history, then, is the story of takeover of a medium of great creative potential by the dominant economic forces of the society. Under their regime, television became a stable, culturally conservative money-making machine of only occasional value as popular art.

In the transformation, which is seen to take place with increasing velocity over the two-year period, small independent producers made an end run around the majors by showing the networks how the television game should really be played. These new producers brought into television young scriptwriters, actors, and directors whose social concern, independent spirits, and confidence resembled their own. They turned the series genres, especially the situation comedy, into vehicles for representing the important issues in American life—those ideological, cultural, social, and demographic struggles reflected in the turmoil of the late 1960s and early 1970s. These producers thus created television that appealed to the first generation to have grown up with it, the young adult audience of the 1970s. From this rebirth grew the second half of television history, today's television, which is unafraid of treating controversial issues of politics, power, or sexuality in an adult manner.

As a general view, there is a good deal of truth in this, and also much that misleads. I am more concerned, however, with its structure as a mythology and its uses in interpreting the shows of the transformation. It is not, of course, how we detail programming history when we study it, because even popular histories with little analysis portray the immense complexity and variety of programming. Most programming, moreover, simply has not yet been critically analyzed. It seems to me, though, that the view I have outlined is how we characterize programming's history in a general way so as to have an orderly approach to individual shows. Its central theme as a history is the issue of how television can be made to serve the purposes of a liberal society. This is a central issue for a medium that was potentially of great ideological power, yet was installed in society as a profit-making enterprise.

Because I will consider the *Mary Tyler Moore Show* both within this perspective and also from a revisionist one, it seems to me useful to describe the position we assign to it in the transformation, along with *All in the Family* and *M*A*S*H*. I wish to bring into relief the differences among these series to highlight the distinctiveness of the *Mary Tyler Moore Show*.

THE SITUATION
COMEDY OF THE TRANSFORMATION

Todd Gitlin observes that "sometimes [1970s] network television seemed to succeed in packaging images that drew on unresolved tensions in the society. . . . These shows demonstrated that television could be popular by . . . squeezing some version of some truth into the conventions of an already established form" (Gitlin, 1983, p. 12). This packaging of some truth about the experience of the times made these series breakthroughs. Although each relied upon the established situation comedy form, each revealed a different strategy for approaching the issues of the time.

Norman Lear's *All in the Family* innovated the explicit address of alarming issues, such as birth control, rape, bigotry, homosexuality, and abortion, along with realistic vocabulary such as "spic," "spade," and "wop," and like epithets. The abusive language, coupled with the characters' shouting, created an atmosphere of psychic violence that certainly made it one of the most bone-jarring of shows. This loudness in itself was revolutionary in years when the situation comedy aesthetic required seamless editing and pleasant, light repartee.

In these traits, *All in the Family* reveals its roots not in the British series *Till Death Do Us Part* (1966-1968) that inspired it, but in an American example from the golden age, *The Honeymooners* (1952-1957). *All in the Family* did not imitate *The Honeymooners,* but in it Lear resurrected the underside of American society, the working class. Like the gangster of the 1930s movies, Ralph Kramden and Archie Bunker were characters precisely because they insulted the whole idea of what an American was supposed to be. Lear's genius lay in shifting the cause of the comic catastrophe from Ralph's penury to Archie's equivalently mean spirit. As time and politics passed, though, *All in the Family*, like a Bernard Shaw play, overwhelmed character with its explicit issues; it dated quickly and, by the end of the decade, converted Archie into a small businessman in *Archie Bunker's Place* (1979-1983).

Almost equally important as its topicality, *All in the Family* headlined a distinct studio style. The show's spin-offs, *Maude* (1972-1978) and *The Jeffersons* (1975-1985), along with other Lear shows such as *Good Times* (1974-1979) and *One Day at a Time* (1975-1984), carried on the Tandem studio signature: the comic exposure of social issues via characters whose definite class identities give them comic qualities.

M*A*S*H has received curiously little critical attention, despite its extreme popularity among both critics and audiences. One reason for the lack of critical analysis is that *M*A*S*H* is only technically a sitcom and, like Shakespeare's problem plays, difficult to define critically. Through the analogy *M*A*S*H* established between its Korean War situation and the Vietnam war, the audience confronted the war that official policy, despite the nightly network reports from Highway One, tried to keep at a distance. For this reason, some critics consider *M*A*S*H* to be a unique form outside the usual categories of sitcom and drama (Hofeldt, 1982, p. 180; Newcomb, 1974, p. 228). Their judgment is supported by the fact that the show's distinct style did not establish a new studio style, as *All in the Family* and the *Mary Tyler Moore Show* did for Tandem and MTM, respectively. In part, this is due to the fact that, although Larry Gelbart originated it, it was produced by a major studio, 20th Century-Fox. The larger explanation, however, is that *M*A*S*H*'s content, themes, and style formed a single unique piece. While some *M*A*S*H* characters carried on in *Trapper John, M.D.* (1979-1985) and *AfterMASH* (1983-1985), the aesthetics of these were indistinguishable from other, non-*M*A*S*H* series.

Despite its lack of stylistic progeny, *M*A*S*H* enjoys as much acclaim as *All in the Family*. Archie Bunker's chair is on display at the Smithsonian Institution, but its 1983 *M*A*S*H* exhibit was so popular that tickets had to be rationed. The exhibit emphasized *M*A*S*H*'s realism by displaying photographs and implements of actual Korean War battle hospitals alongside the sets and equipment used in the show. The Vietnam war context of the series was barely mentioned, but was instead tactfully suggested by the exhibit's title, *Binding up the Wounds* (Smithsonian Institution, 1983).

Unlike *All in the Family*, the message of which supported public policy on racism and sexism, *M*A*S*H* voiced the contradiction between government policy and the feelings of a large section of the audience, especially the baby boom generation of incipient Yuppies. In the face of a stonewalling government, *M*A*S*H* was the popular culture asserting its distrust of the government, its contempt for authority, and its rejection of the whole idea of necessary war.

In this respect, *M*A*S*H* was not only depictively realistic; it was understood by the public to be more realistic in its attitude toward the war than was the government itself. In November of 1982, the Vietnam Veterans Memorial in Washington had been finally dedicated, after nearly 10 years of government refusal to think about it or the war (when Saigon fell, President Gerald Ford called on Americans to forget about the war that had killed 57,000 U.S. troops). But the public had ritually recognized the war all along through M*A*S*H, which was the nation's first memorial of the war.

This appeal, and the appeal of Hawkeye and the other surrogates for the American character, survived the roller coaster political shifts of the 1970s and 1980s, through the Nixon, Ford, Carter, and Reagan administrations. Its final episode, in February 1983, a few months after the dedication of the Veterans Memorial and midway through the first Reagan administration, drew a 60 rating and a 77 share, making it the most viewed series telecast ever.

All in the Family and *M*A*S*H* intruded upon a television world that had slept through cultural change in sanitized domestic comedies from *Ozzie and Harriet* (1952-1966) to *My Three Sons* (1960-1972). The new comedies innovated by directly referring to central public issues, bringing the anxieties and conflicts of the larger society into the living room. *M*A*S*H* contained its reference in a dramatic metaphor, producing a comedy-drama that could stand by itself, as the continuing appeal of the show to young people demonstrates. *All in the Family* dated quickly because of its direct reference to the specific social problems of the 1970s. Yet both series were fundamentally didactic in character, especially as *M*A*S*H*, after its third season, turned from dramatizing issues to sermonizing in the voice of Alan Alda.

THE *MARY TYLER MOORE SHOW*

The third show of this group, the *Mary Tyler Moore Show*, was the earliest and, in many ways, the most different from earlier television. The difference is most noticeable now in the continued critical attention given to the show, especially to its "style." In the critical explanation that has developed around it, the *Mary Tyler Moore Show* heralded the studio formed to produced it, the distinct style of that studio, and, most important, the distinct life-style alleged to identify its audience. The MTM style, both in the sense of the organizational style of MTM and in the aesthetics of its products, is understood as the style of this generation of viewers.

The importance of establishing a signature style is not merely one of brand-naming; a studio that exerts its style across a set of series, whether comedies or dramas, provides the impression of having both authorship and vision. Authorship is communicated simply by the stylistic resemblance of one of the studio's series to another—say *Mary Tyler Moore* to *Rhoda* (1974-1978), *Phyllis* (1975-1977), and the *Betty White Show* (1977-1978). If such series place their characters in situations that imply sufficiently different kinds of life problems for the characters, the studio's style will be understood to imply an authorial "vision" that encompasses the wide variety of life itself. Its shows will be understood as a family of different surveys of society, as in the case of the MTM dramas *Hill Street Blues* (1981-1987), *St. Elsewhere* (1982-), *Bay City Blues* (1983), and *L. A. Law* (1986-).

Jane Feuer (1984) identifies MTM's style with "quality" in television. This "quality" appears in a number of guises in her analysis, but in her most significant use of the term, it denotes a complex of studio-program-theme. It refers to MTM as a particularly attractive corporate author: an organization characterized by a large degree of freedom for its creative staff, who thus were able to develop the "quality" program style that identifies the *Mary Tyler Moore Show* and its spin-offs (Feuer, 1984, p. 33). This style, or "image," as the term may be applied to the studio, provides a producer identity in the overall flow of mundane television.

I would draw an analogy here to corporate style in manufactured products as, for example, the GM style evident throughout its different brands of cars, or the Black and Decker design style that identifies its tools. In such design schemes, consistent design characteristics identify the producer without the need for a designer label—a primary marketing advantage, because the product's form instantly evokes its producer's reputation—for durability, cleverness, or other quality relevant to its purpose. In television, as Feuer points out, a studio's style "serves to differentiate its programs from the anonymous flow of television's discourse and to classify its texts as a unified body of work" (Feuer, 1984, p. 33). Distinguishing its products against the generic flow of all sitcoms, a studio's style elevates its series to special, nongeneric, "quality" status, just as a BMW makes other vehicles more similar than different from each other, relegating them to mere utilitarian value.

The *Mary Tyler Moore Show* was the first of the new breed of shows designed to do more than get the audience from A to B or from 9:30 to 10:00 p.m. How the show and, with it, the MTM style, were born is a matter both revealed and shrouded in the recollections of its creators. Unlike literary researchers, students of television have no diaries, notebooks, memos, and early drafts of writers, editors, producers, directors, and programming executives. We have only their recollections, as voiced to interviewers, about their creative roles and those of their collaborators, and the specific sources of their inspiration are unknown in the case of most shows.

We do know, however, that the *Mary Tyler Moore Show* resulted from a collaboration among Grant Tinker, James L. Brooks, and Allan Burns. In 1969, Tinker left one major studio, Universal Enterprises, and moved to another, 20th Century-Fox, where he met Brooks and Burns.

"In early 1970, Tinker began exploring with the two men, separately, the possibility of a new show as a vehicle for his wife, Mary Tyler Moore." According to Burns, he and Brooks were sent to CBS to try out the concept of the new show, "which dealt with the efforts of a recently divorced woman to create a new life for herself by moving away from her home" (Newcomb & Alley, 1983, p. 198). The meeting with CBS was a near disaster. The network objected to, among other things, identifying Mary Richards as a divorcée, because it would seem like she'd divorced Dick Van Dyke, her television husband in the *Dick Van Dyke Show* (1961-1966). CBS's concern may seem less foolish if we recall that Moore and Van Dyke, although married only in the show, were regarded as one of television's most glamorous couples in the mid-1960s, just a few seasons before Brooks and Burns proposed making her a divorcée. Brooks and Burns were faced, then, with providing Moore's character with a clean break from her previous, and extremely popular, role.

Oddly enough, CBS agreed to their redesigned proposal, which retained the same Mary Richards but characterized her as having previously lived with a man (Gitlin, 1983, p. 214; Newcomb & Alley, 1983, pp. 199-200). Apparently this background was more acceptable than divorce because it evaded the question of how an attractive woman of 30 had never been married, yet it did not involve breaking sacred vows (Gitlin, 1983, p. 214). Thus some of the show's innovative reflections of the culture of the time were actually the inadvertent result of CBS's extreme conservatism.

Otherwise, the shape of the show—its style—came from Brooks and Burns's collaborative imagination. Burns reports that "we wanted to do something that seemed like it was in the real world," and hence "we came up with the newsroom concept" (Newcomb & Alley, 1983, p. 200). This shows them taking a well-worn route to their goal of realism, for the newsroom has traditionally been the setting for films of ultrarealistic exposés of society. With Moore and Arthur Price, Tinker formed MTM Enterprises to produce the show, and gave as complete creative freedom as possible to Burns and Brooks while he ran interference for them with CBS (Newcomb & Alley, 1983, pp. 200, 224-227).

The story of the combination—of Tinker, the writers, MTM Enterprises, and the *Mary Tyler Moore Show*—illustrates the value of corporate innovation, which was to become an obsession in the business culture of the 1980s. There are other stories, such as those of Steven Jobs and Apple computer or An Wang and Wang Laboratories, in this 1980s mythology. Such organizations, in the popular discourse on the entrepreneurial society that emerged after 1980 (with encouragement from the highest levels of government), were allegedly to characterize the service society of the baby-boomers grown into Yuppies. The *Mary Tyler Moore Show* itself, in its humane newsroom where work was familial fun, anticipated the rose-colored descriptions of the future workplace featured in Alvin Toffler's *The Third Wave* (1980) and John Naisbitt's *Megatrends* (1982). Tinker's celebrated qualities as a television executive make him a forerunner of the new kind of managers called for in recent business advice books. Many of these, such as Thomas J. Peters' *A Search For Excellence* (1985), emphasize top executives' sensitivity to the feelings of other executives and employees as the secret of their organizations' success.

And MTM was extraordinarily successful—the Honda of television. Its the *Mary Tyler Moore Show* was the first model of a series that would include such shows as the *Bob Newhart Show* (1972-1978), *Rhoda* (1974-1978), *Phyllis* (1975-1977), and *WKRP in Cincinnati* (1978-1982). In the recollections of Brooks and Burns and in the view of many critics, MTM Enterprises, the *Mary Tyler Moore Show*, and its viewers form a complete society—management, television, and audience—as distinct from the general run of American business as the MTM show was from mundane television.

MTM's shows got on and stayed on network schedules because they coincided with what David Marc describes as the "broad shift in American marketing from the building of mass audiences to the cultivating of class target groups," which is to say, people with plenty of disposable income and a yen to spend it. Among the output of all studios in the 1970s, MTM's comedies were "distinguished by their ability to capture the interest of well-educated people" (Marc, 1984, p. 113). In giving this audience what it wanted, MTM earned allegiance from it and established its comedy aesthetic among the networks as a trademark of success. As Feuer summarizes the situation, "MTM [was] in the business of exchanging 'quality TV' for 'quality demographics' " (Feuer, 1984, p. 34). Thus the MTM story is one of enlightened capitalism finally delivering the cultural promise of television.

In this respect, the celebration of Tinker as a corporate hero, of MTM Enterprises, and of the *Mary Tyler Moore Show* and its audience partakes of a major shift in American social and political imagery. After 1980, it was the Yuppies who counted. *Yuppy* does not describe an actual group but a profile assembled of qualities highly valued in marketing—youth, potential for rising income, higher education, urbanity, and acquisitiveness. As the new generation, it was with them that any marketer would have a future and, therefore, that television had a future. The situation was similar for political parties and candidates. The lower middle class that had built television in the 1950s and 1960s, and had its dreams of social mobility served up in the ads for cars and the decor of *Ozzie and Harriet* and the *Dick Van Dyke Show*, fell into permanent marginal employability and was likewise discarded by the consumer marketplace and television. Indeed, Norman Lear's *All in the Family,* pillorying the working class as the barrier to the liberal paradise, was television's first directly political expression of this shift.

The work of Norman Lear, Larry Gelbart, and, especially, Grant Tinker's MTM transformed the situation comedy into a reality-oriented form to fit the young audience that demanded expansion of the genre on which it had been raised. MTM's special contribution was what Horace Newcomb calls the domestic comedy. In contrast to the situation comedy, domestic comedy has "less slapstick, less hysterical laughter ... more warmth and a deeper sense of humanity ... a richer variety of event, a consequent deepening of character, and a sense of seriousness" (Newcomb, 1974, p. 43). It is closer to drama, with the muted laughter reflecting an appreciation of the characters' humanity. The comic devices, moreover, "produce the laughter of recognition, an identification that is especially acute for the 'sophisticated' audience" (Feuer, 1984, p. 41).

Domestic comedy also places the characters and the audience in a new relationship. The characters themselves are more developed than those of the earlier sitcoms. They do not have much more depth, but even as flat characters, they are rounder, developed in a number of dimensions of personality. Almost all previous situation comedy characters, of which Lucy Ricardo of *I Love Lucy* (1951-1957) is the prime illustration, were confined simply to repeating a single dominant trait, much like their historical prototypes in the seventeenth-century Comedy of Humors.

The *Mary Tyler Moore Show* also pioneered in the ensemble of characters. Mary, Lou, Murray, Rhoda, Phyllis, and Ted formed a family structure. They solved problems therapeutically within the family, as in the light dramas of Earl Hamner (*The Waltons*, 1972-1981) or Michael Landon (*Little House on the Prairie*, 1974-1983). Indeed, the family structure made the *Mary Tyler Moore Show* a kind of *My Three Sons* for adults.

In the *Mary Tyler Moore Show*, the workplace family and its resolution of conflicts were highly idealized. The workers in the show get along with each other with far less conflict than most actual families, not to mention actual workplace colleagues. As Marc notes, "true hate, as one can find in almost any modern office, remained an emotion beyond the purview of the sitcom" (Marc, 1984, p. 115).

Critics consider this familial frame to be the show's major contribution. It meant "bridging the distance between . . . concerns for tradition and innovation, family and individuality" and "the creation of a genuine surrogate family in the newsroom setting." Here "the relations among Lou, Murray, Ted, and Mary progressed from narrowly defined professional interactions to deeply felt emotional ties" (Newcomb & Alley, 1983, p. 206).

The emphasis on family served as the show's farewell message in the final episode. In it, WMJ is purchased by another company that fires everyone except Ted. Mary makes a speech in which she tells her former workmates that they are her family, "people who make you feel less alone and really loved."

With this destruction of the family by financial power, the *Mary Tyler Moore Show* confessed its own naive idealism. Interestingly, this confession is not unique; Michael Landon's *Little House on the Prairie* (1974-1983) ended similarly. In this case, a land company evicts the townspeople, who then dynamite all the homes, putting a strangely violent, "adult" end to the *Little House* fantasy.

However much the *Mary Tyler Moore Show* idealized the workplace, this depiction had a basis in reality, in Brooks and Burns's membership in the "quality" organization that MTM was in the days it produced Moore's show. Looking back on it, Brooks has commented that

> television is great. It is warm and when it's working that surrogate family . . . is not only on the screen, it's part of your life. There is something about coming in for five or six years and doing good work with the same people day in and day out—it's a terrific environment—it's like an idealized company town. (Newcomb & Alley, 1983, p. 223)

Brooks's description reveals the degree to which, for the producers of new American visions, the corporation had come to seem the only haven for community in a conflict-ridden society. The *Mary Tyler Moore Show* itself lends validity to Brooks's view, for the collaborative approach he describes gave birth to the new comic sensibility of the MTM studio. Richard Corliss defines this style by contrasting it to Lear's: against Lear's ego, aggression, overacting, and big issues, the MTM shows emphasized superego, camaraderie, repression, smiles, underacting, and little dilemmas (Corliss, 1982, p. 67).

Because these are the social graces of middle-class moderation and decorum, it is not surprising that the *Mary Tyler Moore Show*'s writers deny its political content. Burns claims that "The *Mary* show couldn't be accused of having a political bias" (Newcomb & Alley, 1983, p. 218), and that, in general, he and Brooks tried to avoid issues in favor of character development. "Lear deals with controversy," he explains, "we are subtler about it"; "we were content to take on small issues, the day-to-day issues of living . . . of interpersonal relationships and heartbreak and hopes" (Newcomb & Alley, 1983, p. 215).

Yet, in its emphasis on problems such as Mary's independence, labor-management relations, Mary's relations with men, and her confrontations with Lou Grant's power, the *Mary Tyler Moore Show* was always dealing with issues. They were dramatized in the naturalized relations of the ensemble of characters, however. The problems are not only implicit rather than explicit as in Lear's shows, but miniaturized and engulfed by the reassuring workplace family. Because Mary's problems were solved within her primary social group, they appeared not to be "political." This is directly relevant to the show's unrealistic depiction of the workplace as a locale of family, for it reveals the family structure to be a strategy for depoliticizing the issues that were the show's claim to realism. Even the potentially controversial issue of the "liberated woman" was cushioned by cautious characterization of Mary as somewhat girlish and cutely awkward in moments of conflict.

The family structure, the warmth of the relationships among the coworkers, and the absorption of issues by character produced a show that evaded the seriousness of the issues. In this sense, the *Mary Tyler Moore Show* was a reactive response to its time, in which *everything* was political, and particularly the relationships of power, money, and independence with which Mary is supposed to be grappling.

This very lack of verisimilitude, however, has its advantages. It means that, while not showing us reality, television shows us "ideal solutions to mythicized versions of real problems." The *Mary Tyler Moore Show* and MTM's later workplace comedies show us that "vision of love and work that Freud said was the ideal of mental health, and that many would also see as the ideal of political health." They show us this ideal "over and over again in what in reality are the most oppressive institutional contexts: the hospital, the police precinct, the TV station" (Feuer, 1984, p. 58). In short, in such shows, reality is sanitized in the interest of inspiration toward a better world.

SOCIALIST AND
CAPITALIST REALISM

If the *Mary Tyler Moore Show* is not realistic in the usual sense of the term, how can we understand the claim of its producers, its audiences, and of television critics that it was realistic? This question has to do with how television is able to present us with symbolic depictions that govern our interpretation of experience in times of cultural change.

Most television is approached through analysis of narrative structure. While such analysis can be extremely fruitful for drama, it is not very revealing when applied to situation comedies, which are not narrative but static visual and dramatic forms. The general characteristics of such images have been outlined by Susanne Langer:

> Visual forms—lines, colors, proportions, etc.—are just as capable of *articulation*, i.e. of complex combination, as words. But the laws that govern this sort of articulation are altogether different from the laws of syntax that govern language. The most radical difference is that *visual forms are not discursive*. They do not present their constituents successively, but simultaneously, so the relations determining a visual structure are grasped in one act of vision. (Langer, 1957, p. 93; emphasis in original)

The individual symbolic elements in visual images "are understood only through the meaning of the whole" (Langer, 1957, p. 93). Such images are "presentational wholes," "the *Gestalten* or fundamental perceptual forms which invite us to construe the pandemonium of sheer impression into a world of things and occasions" (Langer, 1957, p. 98, emphasis in original).

Situation comedies embody meaning and are perceived by us in the terms Langer describes. They less resemble narrative forms than they do cartoon strips or paintings. For example, while they take place in time, like any series, their repetitive ensemble of the same situation and story makes the experience of following a sitcom comparable to that of repeated viewings of a painting. This effect is most noticeable in viewing the *Mary Tyler Moore Show* as it is often shown in syndication, as a five-day-a-week strip. Moreover, such repeated viewing of the same text, at whatever frequency, is implied by the production of a series of nearly identical episodes, as it is implied in painting by exhibiting paintings in public halls for ritual viewing and reproducing them as prints to be hung at home. This comparison may be underscored by the fact that cultural texts identified as centrally evocative, such as Edward Hopper's *Nighthawks* and the *Mary Tyler Moore Show,* occupy equivalently high status ranks, although one in high art and the other in popular art.

Finally, the rigidity of the situation comedy form mimics the frozen form of a painting. Sitcoms usually take place in one or two settings, such as the WMJ newsroom and Mary's apartment; other settings that occasionally appear (restaurants, for example) we understand to be incidental to the main situation that has the primary claim upon the characters. The emblem of the *Mary Tyler Moore Show* is Mary Richards in the newsroom. Likewise, Alice Hyatt of *Alice* (1976-1985) cannot escape the routine environment of her apartment and Mel's Diner; when we see her in a restaurant, we know that she is on an excursion into a world she will never really join. Each episode of such comedy series brings us the same paradigm of setting, characters, typical plot actions, lines of dialogue and gestures, and facial expressions, while the trivial differences in the specific plots of episodes emphasize the rigidity of the situation. The individual episodes, moreover, do not stand by themselves, but only as examples of the whole. The whole, also, is not a story but a static image, and requires a different kind of analysis than narrative.

The coherence of a static visual form—a painting or a situation comedy—lies in its aesthetic rather than its narrative logic. Given this, it is the particular aesthetic of the *Mary Tyler Moore Show* that I wish to focus upon in discussing its "realism."

We have as yet no catalog of television aesthetic genres, such as we have of film, for which categories such as film noir or the western denote styles of depiction as much as content of scene, character, and event. Art aesthetics, however, offers a fruitful means of understanding television's static forms. For the *Mary Tyler Moore Show* and for other socially conscious situation comedies such as the *Cosby Show*, we find an appropriate aesthetic in Socialist Realism in painting, especially as it developed in the Soviet Union.

Socialist Realism may seem a farfetched comparison, and certainly I do not intend to tie the MTM aesthetic to the ideological system of Soviet Socialist Realism. Rather, I am concerned with it as a depictive technique and strategy in popular art. It has had little exposure in the United States for a number of reasons, some of aesthetic preference and others of politics. Indeed, even American realism, the 1930s movement equivalent to Socialist Realism, is not widely admired. There have been few academic studies of Socialist Realist paintings in this country, and Americans usually regard them as propaganda rather than art. Derogated under such labels as "tractor art" for their scenes of young lovers on collective farms or similar clumsy encouragements to productive effort, they seem to illustrate the backwardness and falsity of Soviet official culture.

However common such hackneyed scenes in Socialist Realism, it actually has considerable variety and vitality, and as well as genuine roots in Russian culture. Though its origins are too complex to go into here (see Bowlt, 1977; Higgens, 1971; James, 1973; Valkenier, 1977), a sketch of its theory and of the qualities of its paintings can indicate its relevance.

Formal development of the Theory of Socialist Realism dates from proclamations by Maxim Gorky and Andrei Zhdanov at the First Congress of Soviet Writers in 1934 (James, 1973, pp. 75-83). They explained it as an artistic method that presents "a true, historically concrete depiction of reality in its revolutionary development [for] the task of ideologically transforming and educating the workers in the spirit of Socialism" (Bowlt, 1972, p. 104).

The theory prescribed specific types of content, such as the use of labor heroes and an emphasis on the typical rather than the individualistic in scenes and figures (Bowlt, 1972, p. 104, 1977, p. 13). It required that artists use subjects and a depictive technique readily comprehensible to all, particularly uneducated workers and peasants. Hence the theory mandated that objects and figures be represented as they appeared superficially and in normal perspective; this was the basis of the aesthetic's claim to realism. This aesthetic was aimed both at developing a popular art and at employing it for didactic purposes, for educating the masses in social awareness and inspiring them to work to build Socialism (James, 1973, pp. 84-88). With this intent, the Socialist Realism aesthetic was finally required of all Soviet artists in the Stalin years (James, 1973, pp. 67-83).

As a consequence of its political role, Socialist Realism painting is highly idealistic in theme and technique, rather than literally faithful in the Western sense of "realism." As one art historian explains, it "was a visual rhetoric" that "strove to transmit the idea of the imminent fulfillment of a utopian dream through the lyrical distortion of reality" (Bowlt, 1977, p. 13).

While a verbal explanation can only hint at the qualities of these paintings, it can at least suggest their appeal. Finally, though, as in the case of a television series, one must view them, at least as reprinted as plates (American Heritage, 1970; Bowlt, 1972; James, 1973). Also, I am here emphasizing Socialist Realism practice of the 1950s, which is but one of its several varieties, but the one that most clearly expresses the aesthetic theory.

An American seeing Socialist Realist paintings for the first time is astounded. To begin with, they are very large, from four by six feet to the size of a living room wall, thus compelling attention, as effective popular art must. Rendered in a pastel palette, they seem to be filled with light, bearing a startling resemblance to television, which actually *is* filled with light.

The depiction is very often a work scene, on a farm or in a factory, or the city (usually identified as Moscow) in a state of construction. In such depictions, figures of playfulness—lovers or young girls—may be shown enjoying themselves among the construction, oblivious to the context of socialism a-building, which, because it forms the setting, we understand as making their pleasure possible.

The figures themselves are clearly social types and, with the pastel palette, flooded with uniform light reminiscent of the flat lighting of situation comedy. No shadows suggest complexity or inwardness of character—reality is entirely superficial and objectively rendered. The figures are formed with regular, simplified features, smiling or firmly expressing purpose; they illustrate the attributes of the positive hero. The depiction is an idealized version of actual work, workers, and the workplace; a depiction of the world as the ideology promises it to be rather than as it is experienced by actual people.

The artistic motive this aesthetic reveals we usually call propagandistic. We detect what one Russian critic of Socialist Realism calls its domination by "Purpose," or didactic motive, rather than by the reality to be conveyed (Tertz, 1960).

This intuition of propaganda is a worthwhile one. To Americans, propaganda is the equivalent of a departure from reality that yet claims to be true. In Socialist Realism, it is often the use of a literal or "realistic" style to depict something that is not actual, in the interest of convincing the audience that it is a "true" rendering. Socialist Realism, in short, depicts the potential future as though it were the present. Consequently, it is often the case that the reality of "oppressive . . . contexts" such as the farm and the factory is idealized. But this is also the case with the world that Mary Richards inhabits.

The workplace of the *Mary Tyler Moore Show* is the major element of this comparison. Mary Richards has her primary relationships and finds her primary identity in the workplace. Her whole identity as a single woman living alone, as economically independent, as a professional, and as a symbol of the new, nonsexist society turns on her primary membership in the workplace.

The scriptwriters' vision of a workplace as her primary setting is, as I have suggested, a vision of work in a corporate context as the main activity of building a new society. Also, their choice of the newsroom as the workplace followed from their intent to achieve a realistic picture of social change. This followed the tradition of newsroom movies, but also reflected the sorts of professions that, in the early 1970s, were understood as building the new, postindustrial society of fulfilling, nonsexist, and socially constructive work. In her adoption of such constructive work as the means to her fulfillment and independence, Mary is a socially positive heroine.

Mary's workmates are social types—Murray, the work buddy; Ted, the office pain in the neck; Lou, the boss—who fulfill family roles as well. The technique of depiction is third-person objective, but their characterization is through Mary's eyes. Lou's comically explosive temper, his role as disciplinarian, and his softheartedness reflect Mary's little-girl view of him as a father figure, for example. In other words, the characters are typified in terms of both psychological and occupational roles.

Their typicality is reinforced by the fact that they cannot change— Ted will be the egotist looking at his photographs of himself on the wall no matter how many lessons in proper values he learns. Thus the characters afford us the opportunity to see, over and over again, what those lessons are. Visually, the idealization of the workplace is accomplished by its simplification and its balanced, symmetrical composition on the television screen. No real newsroom was ever as neat and orderly as Mary Richards's, which includes just enough props and details to make it recognizable as a newsroom.

The colors are not actually pastels, but they appear so because of the fullness and uniform brightness of the lighting. The lighting affects characterization as well, rendering it superficial by presenting all there is to know of the figures visually, and allowing no shadow—which would suggest interior, unseen dimensions of personality—to break their seamless visual surface. Moore's face is thus simplified, reduced to the basic elements required for recognition: her wide mouth and large eyes. Created in this way as an icon, her face expresses what critics have often noted as a unique combination of innocence and sophistication.

This iconography was not merely a matter of the television's objective representation. Moore's films, from *A Thoroughly Modern Millie* (1967) to *Just Between Friends* (1985), reveal the variety and depth of expression she is capable of fitting to character. Moore's Richards face is a visage tailored to the motive of the *Mary Tyler Moore Show* as popular art. It is a face that represented the moment of America's shift from the culture of marriage, family, and regimented work to one of liberated individual lives, and of liberated television. Moore's Richards visage thus became the visual center of the show, the icon of its cultural significance, and, eventually, the totem of MTM Enterprises, its "quality" television, and its "quality" audience. The "realism" of the show is the vision of the future represented by Mary Richards as an icon.

In the terms of Jacques Ellul's analysis of propaganda as vertical/agitative and horizontal/integrative (Ellul, 1965, pp. 61-90), such depictions are considered vertical propaganda, that is, attempts to encourage an audience to change its attitudes and behavior to achieve some future state more in line with national values and aspirations. By contrast, horizontal/integrative propaganda depicts what does exist, as a means of maintaining social adherence to existing attitudes, values, and behaviors.

Given their aesthetic technique, however, Socialist Realist paintings and the *Mary Tyler Moore Show* are a crossbreed form: they are cases of vertical/agitative propaganda representing itself as horizontal/integrative progaganda, in effect disguising its persuasive motive. Rhetorically speaking, such depictions convince their audiences (and their producers) of their "realism" by the aesthetic strategy of presenting the possible and desired as the actual. In this strategy lies the pleasure of viewing them.

This appeal of the *Mary Tyler Moore Show* can be seen more clearly when we consider it in contrast to Moore's most recent show, *Mary*, which premiered in December 1986. In this show, Moore contradicted the role of Mary Richards and what she signified. She moved from wholesome Minneapolis to tough Chicago and was reincarnated as Mary Brennan, a divorced executive for *Women's Digest* magazine. The opening moments of the first episode echo the destruction of the WMJ family and establish the political milieu of the show, as the publisher closes the magazine and fires the staff. This is a hard blow for Mary for, as she tells a friend, the job was the only thing that kept her sane through her divorce. But here her coworkers are no family; they simply shout "good bye!" as they rush out carrying whatever potted plants they can grab, leaving her alone. The ideal of the workplace family has failed.

There follows a brief but effective depiction of Mary's exhausting and fruitless job hunt. Finally, despairing of finding respectable work, she takes a job at a trashy tabloid.

The humor in *Mary* is pervasively cynical, in keeping with the tough characters that populate its unglamorous newsroom. Prostitutes, gangsters, and a demented murderer appear for laughs. When Mary first walks into the tabloid office, a hard-bitten woman staffer takes her for a prostitute because of what she calls Mary's "All-American" appearance. In a particularly bitter bit of humor that demolishes the milieu of the *Mary Tyler Moore Show*, a prostitute is in fact expected—to be interviewed for a feature on working women.

In *Mary*, Moore herself has clearly aged, as well as matured, especially in the way her face is presented. Her exhaustion during the job hunt is no matter of comic exaggeration, but a neutral representation of the faces one sees on city streets; the simplified visage of Mary Richards now bears the lines of experience. *Mary* drew extremely poor ratings, and was canceled—"put on hiatus," in MTM's euphemism—after just three months.

PURPOSEFUL COMEDY

One of television's peculiarities is that its stars become identified with the characters they play, actually losing their public identities to their roles. Among Moore's distinctions is that she is one of the very few actors who have successfully moved from one very popular character (Laura Petrie, in the *Dick Van Dyke Show*) to another, Mary Richards. She has not, however, been able to escape Mary Richards. The public's rejection of Mary Brenner, Moore's attempt at a character "realistic" for the 1980s, indicates the continuing strong appeal of Mary Richards and the ideal she signifies.

The difference in the public reception of the two characters is suggestive of the relationship between situation comedy and its audience since the transformation period. Ordinary realism, as a depictive strategy, operates at a level of awareness quite different from that of comedy. Such realism, of the type we associate with, for example, John Updike's novels, intends to establish something like a neutral affect level to convey an impression of objectivity.

Comedy, on the other hand, establishes a distance from the actuality, to achieve order and balance in a disrupted situation. In comedy, the pressing and disturbing facts of social conflict or personal aberration are shown to be constrained by some larger order. This overall order may be some type of universal view, as in seventeenth- and eighteenth-century English stage comedy, or it may be that of a specific social ideology, like the liberalism of the *Mary Tyler Moore Show*. This perspective embodies the dominant cultural values; it is what makes the characters—who are deviant from it—comic.

Thus all three of these transformational series approached issues indirectly, through a perspective that made them less threatening by promising to absorb and contain them in its order. Each of these series accomplished this in a different way. The *Mary Tyler Moore Show* viewed its characters and their issues from the perspective of a promised future, *All in the Family* via a liberal vantage on the working class, and *M*A*S*H* in a more complex way. *M*A*S*H* managed a tragic-comic perspective, not by looking at the war from a vantage point in the future, but by presenting an analogous past war in what, for that war, was the future, which was the *audience's* present. This technique implied that the current war was equally gainless and equally tragicomic, and hence resolvable by means other than arms. These comedies thus reduced the anxiety of social conflict by showing the issues resolved within an overarching liberal politics, which, they imply, represents dominant cultural values.

Quite in contrast to the attitudes of Lear and Gelbart toward their own shows, the creators of the *Mary Tyler Moore Show* felt that it was not "political." As I have tried to show, this apparent contradiction may be understood in terms of the dramatic structure of the show. It also has much to do with Moore's qualities as a star. For stars to appear in a society, as Francesco Alberoni explains, "certain systems of action [must be] institutionally considered as *unimportant from a political point of view* (Alberoni, 1972, p. 76; emphasis in original). Stars belong to a "powerless elite," for they do not hold positions of decision making for society (Alberoni, 1972, p. 75). They are understood by the public to instead represent a sphere of action outside that of politics.

The significance demanded by the public of stars is closely related to the ideology of the Western democracies, then, particularly the United States, in representing this apolitical sphere. Stars, as Alberoni explains, "bear witness, by their existence, to the large possibilities for social mobility" in the society (Alberoni, 1972, p. 90). Moore's own career as a star represents such mobility. Even more, however, her Mary Richards in the newsroom combined the testimony of her own stardom with that of a character who represented the same social mobility. The Mary Brenner of *Mary*, though, testified to the impossibility of social mobility, unless it was downward, and so represented a clearly political accusation, something highly threatening even in comedy.

All three of these transformational comedies were conceived of as didactic television, aimed at bringing about change. In one way or another, all have lasted. Each does well in syndication. Archie's chair is in the Smithsonian Institution, although Lear's aggressive style of comedy has almost disappeared from television. Alan Alda, made a star by *M*A*S*H* has done little television since, but has become a live spokesman on various issues and, as a member of the board of the Museum of Broadcasting, a spokesman for television itself ("Alda Stars," 1986). Mary Tyler Moore/Mary Richards, though, lives on as an icon. Of the three series, only the *Mary Tyler Moore Show* convincingly promised its audience a future more desirable than the present. Its star character lives on as an icon because, far from being "realistic" to either the 1970s or the 1980s, she is understood to illustrate the promise of American life.

REFERENCES

Alberoni, F. (1972). The powerless "elite": Theory and sociological research on the phenomenon of the stars. In D. Mcquail (Ed.), *Sociology of mass communications* (pp. 75-98). Harmondsworth: Penguin.

Alda stars in televised *M*A*S*H* seminar. (1986, October 18). *New York Times*, p. 12.

American Heritage. (1970a). Pointing the way. In *The horizon book of the arts of Russia* (pp. 352-353). New York: Author.

American Heritage. (1970b). The popular imperative: The arts under the Soviets. In *The horizon book of the arts of Russia* (pp. 339-343). New York: Author.

Bowlt, J. R. (1972). The virtues of Soviet realism. *Art in America, 60*(6), 100-107.

Bowlt, J. R. (1977). Foreword: Between east and west. In *Russian and Soviet painting* (pp. 11-13). New York: Metropolitan Museum of Art/Rizzoli.

Corliss, R. (1982). Happy days are here again. In H. Newcomb (Ed.), *Television: The critical view* (pp. 64-76). New York: Oxford.

Ellul, J. (1965). *Propaganda* (K. Kellen & J. Lerner, Trans.). New York: Knopf.

Feuer, J. (1984). The MTM style. In J. Feuer, P. Kerr, & T. Vahimagi (Eds.), *MTM: "Quality television"* (pp. 32-60). London: British Film Institute.

Gitlin, T. (1983). *Inside prime time.* New York: Pantheon.

Higgens, A. (1971, April). The development of the theory of socialist realism in Russia, 1917 to 1932. *Studio International, 181*(932), 155-159.

Hofeldt, R. (1982). Cultural bias in *M*A*S*H.* In H. Newcomb (Ed.), *Television: The critical view* (pp. 158-166). New York: Oxford.

James, C. V. (1973). *Soviet socialist realism.* London: Macmillan.

Langer, S. K. (1957). *Philosophy in a new key.* Cambridge, MA: Harvard University Press.

Marc, D. (1984, November). MTM's past and future. *Atlantic, 254*(5), 113-120.

Naisbitt, J. (1982). *Megatrends.* New York: Warner.

Newcomb, H. (1974). *TV: The most popular art.* Garden City, NY: Doubleday Anchor.

Newcomb, H. (1982). *Television: The critical view.* New York: Oxford.

Newcomb, H., & Alley, R. S. (1983). *The producer's medium.* New York: Oxford.

Peters, T. J. (1985). *In search of excellence.* New York: Harper & Row.

Smithsonian Institution. (1983). *M*A*S*H: Binding up the wounds* (Exhibition Guide). New York: George Fenmore Associates.

Tertz, A. [pseudonym for Andrei Donatevich Siniavskii] (1960). *On socialist realism* (G. Dennis, Trans.). New York: Pantheon.

Toffler, A. (1980). *The third wave.* New York: William Morrow.

Valkenier, E. (1977). *Russian realist art. The state and society: The Peredvizhniki and their tradition.* Ann Arbor: Ardis.

Chapter 7

TELEVISION STARDOM
A Ritual of Social
Typification and Individualization

Jimmie L. Reeves

IN MAPPING OUT CENTRAL PREMISES and concerns of a *cultural view of stardom*, it's instructive to compare media star studies to inquiry in an entirely different discipline that also treats "stars" as objects worthy of rigorous investigation: that discipline is astronomy. On a clear night, most of us may recognize the Milky Way, or even a prominent constellation like Orion, but generally, only a few of those million distant suns are distinct to the naive eye. Being content to let a star be a star be a star allows us to swim in the pristine beauty of a starry night, sustaining a kind of mystical pleasure—but unfortunately, it can never generate much knowledge or understanding. Those minds taking on the monumental task of making sense of that starry night abstain from naive pleasure and develop a different relationship to the cosmos. By seeking that infinite sea of light as an area of scientific examination rather than a source of aesthetic delight, this cult of sophisticated stargazers has succeeded in mapping what to the rest of us seems unchartable. But to attain an enlightened sense of the universe, early astronomers had to work around many widely held misconceptions that thwarted even the most valiant attempts to grasp key relationships governing the existence of the earth, moon, planets and stars: situating a flat earth at the center of all creation fostered pseudoknowledge that severely limited man's ability to comprehend the grand celestial scheme.

Similarly, in media star studies, historically determined conditions at work in the academy have championed misconceptions that pervert our understanding of the phenomenon of stardom: One fashionable misconception has resulted in mainstream star studies being distorted by the institutional context of the star system; another misconception has channeled scholarly inquiry toward a governing model that privileges the peculiarities of the cinematic actor/performer/star. On the one hand, studies reducing the phenomenon of stardom to the star system tend to treat the star as a commodity, pure and simple; and in this reduction, stardom is narrowly understood as a mere function of media exposure and industrial manipulation.[1] On the other hand, treating stardom as supremely a cinematic phenomenon tends to privilege the movie star as the only "true" form of stardom while placing noncinematic stars in some other category—typically, that of the "celebrity" or "personality."[2]

Rejecting both of these widely held presuppositions, a cultural approach focuses on *meanings* triggered by star discourse: an orientation that can expand the intellectual horizons of media star studies in the same way that placing the sun at the center of the solar system led to a quantum leap in humanity's understanding of the natural universe. Taking what James Carey terms a *"ritual view of communication,"* a cultural approach to stardom addresses issues related to how media stardom assists in the production, repair, and transformation of social reality: put another way, it addresses how stardom contributes to "the maintenance of society in time" (Carey, 1975, p. 6).[3] By framing stardom in a larger cultural context, this orientation on meaning liberates star studies from the constraints of both the star system and the cinema: a liberation that allows us to acknowledge the star's dual status as both commodity and communication; a liberation that allows us to conceive of stardom as a force that cuts across media boundaries.

Indeed, only from this larger perspective can we begin to account for TV's diverse host of stars as they spangle the expanse of the medium—for *television explodes the cinematic model of stardom.* Just as placing the sun at the center of the solar system illuminated relationships between earth and its sibling planets, placing meaning at the center of a cultural approach illuminates relationships between various orbits in media stardom: With a cultural approach to stardom, we can finally recognize the hero celebrated *in* the news, the news anchor, the talk show host, the sports star, the movie star, and the popular series character as being *different forms of the same complex phenomenon.*

The astronomy comparison also illustrates a cultural view's relation to critical approaches that mystify the star performance. Just as astrology's celebration of the signs of the Zodiac has no legitimate place in astronomy, critical concerns associated with questions of authorship or the aesthetics of screen acting are not relevant to a cultural view of stardom. Rather than assume an evaluative approach to the star performance, a cultural view adopts an *interpretive* stance—a stance that attempts to make sense of the star performance as the projection and embodiment of what Carey calls "community ideals" (1975, p. 6). Having much in common with cultural anthropologists, communication scholars adopting a ritual view of communication are actively engaged in the *interpretation* of culture: a critical endeavor that departs from the imposing of formal standards associated with key traditions in literary, theatrical, and film criticism.

THE STAR AS
COMMUNICATION AND COMMODITY

As a complex, multifaceted phenomenon with social, textual, and institutional dimensions, stardom occupies a central position in all of America's information and entertainment industries. Taking an interpretive stance toward stardom means that a cultural approach embraces the complexity of the star's dual status as commodity and communication: in other words, orienting our analysis around meaning does *not* mean that we must be blind to industrial manipulation at work in the star system.

To account for stardom's social, textual, and institutional dimensions, stardom is perhaps best understood in terms of a societal transaction involving a kind of informal, provisional election—a thesis borrowed from Francesco Alberoni. In Alberoni's word's, "The star system . . . never creates the star, but it proposes the candidates for 'election,' and helps retain the favor of the 'electors' " (1972, p. 93). Inspired by the profit motive, producers, casting directors, and even network news chiefs constantly act as *interpreters of the culture* when screening and selecting potential stars. In the interpretive role, they take their place beside advertising agents and fashion designers as what Marshall Sahlins calls "hucksters of the symbol." In Sahlins's words:

> In the nervous system of the American economy, theirs is the synaptic function. It is their role to be sensitive to the latent correspondences in the cultural order whose conjunction in a product symbol may spell mercantile success. (1976, p. 217)

We can, then, accommodate the star's status as communication without taking the untenable position that there's no manipulation at work in the star system: For there is industrial manipulation—the star system is vitally concerned with manipulating meaning systems alive in our culture in hopes of constructing and exploiting a "product symbol [that] may spell mercantile success." That manipulation encounters resistance from the audience, however, as evidenced by the number of shows canceled at midseason and the number of new faces introduced only to be quickly discarded. By expanding the horizons of star studies beyond the narrow context of the star system, this industrial manipulation becomes only one major moment in a grand cultural process—a process that includes interpretation on the part of the industry and validation on the part of the audience.

A RITUAL OF SOCIAL
TYPIFICATION AND INDIVIDUALIZATION

As communication, the star commodity contributes to the production, maintenance, repair, and transformation of social reality by animating a ritual of social typification and individualization. But grasping the significance of this ritual requires that we first understand how important social typification is to modes of apprehending and dealing with others in everyday social encounters. These encounters are governed by a taken-for-granted sense of the world—the shared intellectual space called "common sense," According to Berger and Luckmann, common sense privileges *recipe knowledge*, or "knowledge limited to pragmatic competence in routine performances." And this recipe knowledge is not so much concerned with "the truth" as it is with "the appropriate." Channeled more toward the "how" of everyday life than the "why," *typificatory schemes* constitute a major part of a culture's social stock of recipe knowledge. In Berger and Luckmann's words:

> The social stock of knowledge further supplies me with typificatory schemes required for the major routines of everyday life, not only the typification of others . . . but typification of all sorts of events and experiences, both social and natural. (1967, pp. 19-46)

Anthropologist Clifford Geertz also describes social typification as being a major "orientational necessity" of the world of everyday life:

> Peoples everywhere have developed symbolic structures in terms of which persons are perceived not baldly as such, as mere unadorned members of the human race, but as representatives of certain distinct categories of persons, specific sorts of individuals. . . . The everyday world in which the

members of any community move, their taken-for-granted field of social action, is populated not by any bodies, faceless men without qualities, but somebodies, concrete classes of determinate persons positively characterized and appropriately labeled. And the symbol systems which define these classes are not given in the nature of things—they are historically constructed, socially maintained and individually applied. (1973, pp. 363-364)

As a ritual of social typification, stardom has evolved into a "symbol system" that defines and maintains "appropriate" modes of being in American society: The stars, in representing community ideals associated with what it means to be a person in America, are experienced as *individualized social types*—a mode of being that reconciles personal identity with social identity, and individualism with conformity. The dynamic behind star-audience identification is, in fact, central to this ritual "function" of stardom. Identification results from a fundamental paradox: The star is at once ordinary and extraordinary; the star, in other words, is typical enough to be accessible and recognizable, yet individuated enough to be experienced as unique and interesting. As Richard Dyer suggests, social types available in the culture at large form the symbolic background from which the stars emerge as strong figures of audience identification. In his words: "What is abundantly clear is that stars are supremely figures of identification . . . and this identification is achieved principally through a star's relation to social type" (1979, p. 111). Star-audience identification, then, involves a ritual interplay between living social relations at work in the commonsense world and the mediated human representations of those relations.

According to Dyer, stars achieve individualization by maximizing, inflecting, or resisting social typification (1979, p. 111-113). TV stars representing the maximization of social types include Archie Bunker (the incarnation of blue-collar bigotry) and Joan "Alexis" Collins (the supreme "rich bitch"). Don Johnson, Tom Selleck, James Garner, and Peter Falk, all have enjoyed TV stardom by virtue of their unique inflections of the basic detective type. And Muhammad Ali stands a prime example of a TV star gaining notoriety by resistance to type when, while a champion of the most combative of professional sports, he declared his conscientious objection to the Vietnam war. But, at the same time, Ali's stardom demonstrates the fuzziness of Dyer's categories: Ali also represents a maximized type—the ultimate boxer (as opposed to slugger); and many have condemned Ali as an inflection on a negative racial stereotype (the "uppity nigger").

Therefore, Dyer's relational categories are far from being mutually exclusive structures. A Grand Dragon of the Ku Klux Klan, an antiwar activist, a boxing fan, a Black Muslim, all will assign different shades of meaning to Ali's performance in an insecticide commercial. Although there may be a correspondence to the meanings associated with Ali's performance, that correspondence will be inflected by the relevance structures and social agendas that stratify the world of everyday life. If we are to comprehend the importance of a star representing an individualized social type, then we must adopt an interpretive strategy that accounts for multiple and shifting meanings being available in the appearance and performance of a star like Muhammad Ali: We need an interpretive approach that conceives of social interaction as a constant negotiation and interplay between contradictory and, in many cases, competing meaning systems—a theoretical framework that can account for change by emphasizing living process instead of frozen system.

INTERPRETING THE STAR RITUAL

Although many well-known studies employ *semiotics* in the interpretation of meanings associated with the appearance and performance of the media star, this study will, instead, adopt the *translinguistics* of M. M. Bakhtin. In contrast to the mechanistic outlook of semiotics, translinguistics gives us, in Horace Newcomb's words, "a theory of language and theory of text that offer[s] a processual, dynamic, dialogic perspective on communication without sacrificing an understanding of the struggle for dominance central to that process" (1984, p. 37). Just as *semiotics* is the "science of signs," *translinguistics* is the "science of discourse": Where semiotics scrutinizes the structuring of signifiers, paradigms and syntagms, translinguistics investigates the dynamics of enunciation, intonation and dialogue.[4]

Conceiving of language as an ongoing social production, ever in the "process of becoming," Bakhtin saw the meaning-making process as animated by a dialectical clash of two opposing social forces: the centrifugal forces of social stratification and diversification; and the centripetal forces that tend toward social unification and systemization. Michael Holquist describes the unifying forces' relation to the centrifugal forces as "akin to the interworkings that anthropologists nominate as the activity of culture in modeling a completely different order called nature" (Bakhtin, 1981, p. xix). *Heteroglossia*, the concept at the heart of Bakhtin's philosophy of language, is, according to Holquist, "as close a conceptualization as is possible of that locus where centripetal and centrifugal forces collide; as such, it is that which systematic linguistics [including semiotics] must always suppress" (Bakhtin, 1981, p. 428).

For Bakhtin, heteroglossia was "the base condition governing the operation of meaning in any utterance" considering that

> at any given moment in its historical existence, language is heteroglot from top to bottom: it represents the coexistence of socio-ideological contradictions between the present and the past, between the differing epochs of the past, between different socio-ideological groups in the present, between tendencies, schools, circles and so forth, all given bodily form. These "languages" of heteroglossia intersect each other in a variety of ways, forming new socially typifying "languages." (1981, p. 428)

Just as Berger and Luckmann conceive of the social stock of knowledge as being "socially distributed, that is, possessed differently by different individuals and types of individuals" (1966, p. 46), Bakhtin understood language as being socially inflected, or "possessed differently," by different social types in the stratified heteroglot.

Bakhtin's analysis of the "speaking person in the novel" demonstrates how the concept of heteroglossia can be applied to interpreting the star ritual. He argued that the speaking person is not the image of "a man in his own right [in other words, a real person], but a man who is precisely *the image of a language*. But in order that language become an artistic image, it must become speech from speaking lips, conjoined with the image of a speaking person" (1981, p. 336). Then, after much elaboration, Bakhtin concluded that

> in a word, the novelistic plot serves to represent speaking persons and their ideological worlds. What is realized in the novel is the process of coming to know one's own language as it is perceived in someone else's language, coming to know one's own belief system in someone else's system. (1981, p. 365)

By conceiving of stars as *representations of socially typifying* language operating within a conflicted national language, we can better accommodate the complexity, the temporality, the "humanness" of the star ritual. Rather than treat the star as a structurally static *sign* conforming to Saussure's privileging of the abstract language system (*langue*) over the speech act (*parole*), translinguistics allows us to conceive of the star performance as dynamically open-ended *discourse*—discourse that can trigger a multiplicity of meanings in the culture. In embracing the complexity of star communication, this interpretive strategy foregrounds the fundamentally *intertextual*, or *dialogic*, nature of media stardom: for as discourse, the star breaks traditional critical boundaries—narrative boundaries, generic boundaries, media boundaries—and weaves through diverse media texts, linking them, inflecting them, and refracting their meaning.

In the concept of heteroglossia, translinguistics also provides a powerful cultural model for coming to terms with the relationships between the social, textual, and institutional dimensions of stardom.[5] If thought of in terms of heteroglossia, the institutional web constituting the star system can be treated as a centripetal force in the dynamic of stardom: a unifying force, sustained by the profit motive, which tries to interpret, contain, organize, and manipulate the social heteroglot. Stardom as social phenomenon, then, might best be conceived of as the grand cultural dialogue that arises from the collision of media institutions and their stratified, heterogeneous audience. In this scheme, stardom as media discourse becomes the individualized articulation of relevant, strategic social types that represent culturally significant ways of speaking, of seeing, of being.

Individualized by maximization, inflection, or resistance to social type, the star makes the typical strange, the ordinary extraordinary. And in making the typical strange, the star, like the speaking person in the novel, allows us access to our "own language as it is perceived in someone else's language," thereby allowing us to know our "own belief system in someone else's system." In representing language images, then, stars also represent worldviews—ideological stances in the stratified culture. Therefore, as participants in a complex ritual of social typification and individualization, stars like Muhammad Ali activate a clash of conflicting meaning systems: For in making sense of the worldview projected in Ali's performance, we are forced to make sense of our own views of race relations, of foreign policy, of religion and so forth; in other words, Ali's ritual discourse only takes on meaning when placed *in dialogue* with our own views of the world. And that is what is meant by the dialogic nature of human communication, in general, and the star performance, in particular. It is the dialogic collision of worldviews activated by the stardom ritual that a cultural view should seek to interpret, understand, and explain.

ANALYSIS:
THE LAYMAN, THE EXPERT, AND THE
WELL-INFORMED VIA TV

In elaborating the central premises and concerns of a cultural view of stardom, we have finally arrived at a definition to guide interpretation of the stardom ritual: A star is the *discourse* of an *individualized social type*—and as such, the star represents a *strategic socioideological worldview*. This definition is flexible enough to apply throughout the television medium. Whether the star be a movie actor, news anchor, or professional wrestler, it's the star's individualizing relationship to social type that charges his or her performance with cultural meanings beyond the typical and makes the star the subject of audience identification/ recognition/ desire.[6] With this definition, we can now embark on a concrete analysis of how the stardom ritual contributes to the maintenance of society in time by expressing relationships between three grand modes of being central to life in modern cultures: the layman, the expert, and the well-informed.

According to Alfred Schutz and Thomas Luckmann, the progressive division of labor in modern, technological societies has complicated the social distribution of knowledge:

> An important consequence of the progressive division of labor is a shift in the proportions of general and special knowledge within the social stock of knowledge. With the expansion of special knowledge, the importance of being a specialist increases as a dimension of the typification of self and others. (1973, p. 328)

Residing on what Roger Silverstone (1981, p. 5) identifies as the forward horizon of common sense—the horizon of "the particular sciences and arts (with their own horizons of the new and the unknown)," the expansion of these special realms of knowledge has resulted, ultimately, in "the growing gap between expertness and the lack of it, and the growing, almost continuous dependency of the layman on the expert." According to Schutz and Luckmann, "in subjective experience, this state of affairs is reflected in a multileveled union . . . of lack of knowledge, half-knowledge, and knowledge of 'power' and dependence." In other words, in societies with a complex social distribution of knowledge, the layman, the practitioner of common sense, is conscious of the fact that he or she doesn't know all that is known—and, further, realizes that the possession of "all knowledge" is "typically impossible." Schutz and Luckmann suggest that, in this situation, "everyone is at the same time a layman and an expert and is thus given the chance to grasp consciously the gap between expertness and the lack of it" (1973, p. 331).

Of course, this knowledge of "the gap between expertness and the lack of it" disturbs the tranquility of everyday life. As Silverstone (1981, p. 5) observes, it is the unknown and the unthought we fear the most— and in complex societies, we are constantly reminded of gaps in our individual stock of knowledge. According to Schutz and Luckmann, "a strong impulse arises" in this unsettling state of affairs "to diminish the dependence on experts in areas where one is a layman, but which reach decisively into daily life" (1973, p. 331).

One consequence of this reaction against dependency on experts is the emergence of a social type particular to modern societies. Calling this new social being the "well-informed," Schutz and Luckmann contrast this type with both layman types and expert types:

> This type is differentiated from the layman above all by the fact that he is not ready unreflectively to accept dependence on the judgment of the expert; on the other hand he is differentiated from the expert by the absence of specific explicit knowledge in the area in question.

Possessing knowledge of the "'perspectives,' the main methods, and the basic presuppositions" of special realms of knowledge, the well-informed inhabit a strategic position in the commonsense world between "expertness and the lack of it." Put another way, the well-informed maintain horizons between common sense and special realms of knowledge. And, according to Schutz and Luckmann, this strategic positioning enables the well-informed "to turn to the 'correct' experts, to form a judgement concerning contradictory experts, and to make more or less well-founded decisions for one's own actions" (1973, p. 331).

Ultimately, Schutz and Luckmann conclude that

> in complex social distributions of knowledge, the subjective orientation in the total social reality can thus be apprehended ideally-typically by means of three types: the layman, the well-informed, and the expert, where expertise includes further socially defined degrees of competence. The concrete relation of these types to one another, and the consequences of this relation for apprehending oneself and others, are determined by means of the social structure and the social stock of knowledge. (1973, p. 331)

In giving bodily form to relevant, strategic modes of being in our culture, stardom via TV is a key ritual that represents "appropriate" relations between the layman, the expert, and the well-informed—and in this ritual operation, stardom contributes to the production, maintenance, and repair of the social stock of knowledge.

Unlike the cinema, which tends to privilege heroic expert types, the most strategic star positions in the flow of television are occupied by the well-informed. Walter Cronkite, Johnny Carson, David Letterman, Howard Cosell, Barbara Walters, and Phil Donahue, as moderators of the medium, all operate on horizons between the commonsense world of the layman and the specialized realms of science, politics, sports, art, and show business. Some, like Howard Cosell, represent "authoritative language" by bending the well-informed type in the direction of expert knowledge; others, like Johnny Carson, represent the sensibility of the layman by channeling the well-informed type in the direction of common sense; all participate in the maintenance of cultural horizons because all translate the new, the unknown, and the unknowable into terms that are accessible and forms that are familiar to the stratified audience.

Where TV stars representing well-informed types generally act as unifying forces in the flow of television, stars representing layman and expert types often express social stratification and diversity—that is, they act as centrifugal forces in television discourse. In discussing stardom associated with expert types, we will also consider a type of star that usually attains cultural prominence via television's news arena:[7] the "star personality."[8] By virtue of the relevance of their social existence *outside the flow of television*, star personalities become the site of conflicted discourse *within the flow of television*. Although many stars in television's fictional programming represent heroic expert types— that is, they project appropriate and valued modes of being—expert star personalities appearing in the TV news often give voice to the darker side of expertise and power. Charles Manson, for example, as an expert in drugs, mind control, and murder, gave bodily form to a demonic version of the inappropriate "hippie" type. Perhaps only the discourse of cult leader Jim Jones surpasses Manson's as stardom emerging in the news arena that traumatized the culture by threatening the commonsense world with chaos and disorder. And outside the news arena, the star discourses of both Manson and Jones received commodification in the form of highly rated docudramas exploiting fears alive in the culture. Indeed, demarcating the inappropriate with villainous discourse is as vital to the star ritual as celebrating the appropriate with heroic discourse. Expert criminal types emerging from the shadows of the commonsense world have long commanded a certain attraction and fascination in the American culture: From Billy the Kid through John Dillinger to Gary Gillmore, outlaw discourse has often resulted in a notorious kind of stardom.

Star discourse associated with the layman is perhaps best illustrated with a figure from TV's series arena. As a "star character," Archie Bunker animated a clash of conflicting meaning systems by giving bodily form to what was intended to be interpreted as the maximization of a foolish layman type. The early episodes of *All in the Family* were, in fact, overtly involved with the complicated task of "fool-making."[9]

Producer Norman Lear depicted Bunker's pompous bigotry, blind patriotism, and male chauvinism as inappropriate socioideological stances—marks of ignorance and stupidity. Audience response to Lear's overt fool-making, however, was far from uniform. Even though the episodes were structured so Bunker almost always came out on the short end of ideological confrontations, a study by N. Vidmar and M. Rokeach (1974) determined that viewers sharing Bunker's attitudes and beliefs were immune to Lear's didactic overtures. According to the study, "prejudiced" viewers applauded Bunker's bravura in the face of cynical liberalism and dismissed, or "selectively perceived," the many resolutions casting Bunker as an absurd, villainous fool. Although Vidmar and Rokeach's study assumes a "transmission view of communication," their findings support our cultural view of stardom. Lear's artistic intentions, his attempts at fool-making, encountered resistance from the stratified heteroglot: just as a Grand Dragon of the Ku Klux Klan and a Black Muslim assign different shades of meaning to Muhammad Ali's star discourse, the meanings assigned to Archie Bunker's foolish actions and attitudes are inflected by relevance structures and social agendas that stratify the world of common sense. As Brooks and Marsh put it:

> By the summer of 1971, *All in the Family* had become a controversial hit, and the number-one program on television—a position it retained for five years. Part of its appeal was based on the fact that it could be interpreted in several different ways. Liberals and intellectuals could cite it as an example of the absurdities of prejudice, while another large segment of the audience could agree with Archie's attitudes and enjoy him as their kind of guy. Like *The Honeymooners*' Ralph Kramden in the 1950s, the loud-mouthed yet vulnerable Archie Bunker was a man for all audiences. (1980, p. 938)

As the individualization of a layman type, Archie Bunker was marked as *both* an inappropriate *and* a relevant socioideological being. And it was the paradoxical nature of this inappropriate relevance that made Archie Bunker one of television's most familiar, controversial, powerful, and enduring star characters. Rather than explain the multiple meanings associated with Bunker's star discourse in terms of selective perception, a cultural view of stardom explains it in terms of heteroglossia: *for meaning is not inscribed on the text and transmitted to a passive audience; instead, meaning arises in the dialogic collision of a value-laden text and an active audience stratified by conflicting worldviews.*

To an astronomer, a star is a red giant, or a yellow dwarf, or a pulsar—it's never *just* a star. If we are to develop a similar sophistication in media star studies, we must also not be content to let a star be a star be a star. In interpreting stardom's ritual of social typification and individualization, we must guard against arriving at narrow, obvious truths. For instance, that the star ritual tends to "reinforce" the *status quo* is one such obvious, and not too remarkable, truth. Although questions of how stardom may enforce a dominant ideology are certainly relevant to a cultural view, star studies must also embrace even more complex questions regarding how the star ritual can challenge, alter, and even transform the world of everyday life. Cultural views of stardom adopting Bakhtin's model of heteroglossia are uniquely equipped to address questions concerning both the struggle for dominance and the struggle for freedom expressed in the star's dual status as commodity and ritual communication.[10]

NOTES

1. Boorstin's famous "pseudoevent" thesis has set the tone for most analyses of stardom's institutional dimension, and has also been responsible for delaying and inhibiting serious critical inquiry into the phenomenon of stardom. According to Boorstin (1964), the star is well-known simply for his or her "well-knownness"; thus the star is void of any real significance and not worthy of study except as a phenomenon of media marketing. An elitist vision of art, nostalgia for the fixed, stable social relations of an idealized past, and a romanticized conception of heroism form the bases of Boorstin's opinion. For a critique of Boorstin's view of heroism, see Rollin (1983).

2. For instance, Ellis treats prominent cinematic performers as stars, while invoking Boorstin in dismissing prominent figures on television as "personalities"—"someone who is famous for being famous, and is famous only insofar as he or she makes frequent television appearances" (1982, pp. 106-107). Ellis supports his position by arguing that television operates in a "narrative regime" that is "qualitatively different" from the cinematic experience: while in the cinema, the "photo effect" presents an absent presence working in what Ellis characterizes as "the impossible mode of 'this is was,'" television generally "presents itself as an immediate presence"—a "this is now" transmission mode. According to Ellis, because the photo effect is lacking in television, there is a diminished sense of the extraordinary with regard to its performers: the immediacy of the television performer reduces his or her status as a paradoxical figure of attraction and identification (pp. 99-106). Clearly, Ellis makes too much of the photo effect. Although the photo effect may amplify the "extraordinary/ordinary" paradox at the heart of the audience identification dynamic, it is most certainly *not* a necessary condition for identification with a mediated human figure. See Dyer (1979, p. 108) for a discussion of how literary and dramatic characters also become figures of audience identification by this same extraordinary/ordinary paradox.

3. Carey uses the term *ritual* in a particularly broad sense. While the archetypal case is the "sacred ceremony which draws people together in fellowship and commonality," Carey stretches the concept of ritual to include projections "of community ideals and their embodiment in material form—dance, plays, architecture, news stories, strings of speech" (1975, p. 6). This study is obviously informed by Carey's expanded sense of ritual.

4. Much of Bakhtin's work was published under friends' names (most notably V. N. Voloshinov and P. N. Medvedev). In an early work attributed to Voloshinov, Bakhtin challenged the very foundations of semiotics (which he labeled "abstract objectivism") by disputing Saussure's privileging of the abstract language system: For Bakhtin, Saussure's central error was taking "the system of language and regarding it as the entire crux of linguistic phenomenon . . . [while rejecting] the speech act—the utterance—as something individual" (Voloshinov, 1973, p. 62). For an elaborate discussion of translinguistics' relation to linguistics, see Todorov (1984). And for discussions of the intrigue surrounding the authorship of many of Bakhtin's early works, see both Todorov (1984) and Clark and Holquist (1984). Although there's overwhelming evidence establishing Bakhtin's authorship of *Marxism and the Philosophy of Language*, to aid research, the book appears in the reference section under Voloshinov's name.

5. These relationships are often understood in terms of another powerful cultural model: Gramsci's hegemonic model. Certainly, Bakhtin's model casts these relationships in a different light: where Gramsci's formulation emphasizes unifying social forces, Bakhtin's stresses the centrifugal forces; where Gramsci sees ideological domination by those in control of the means of production, Bakhtin sees ongoing ideological struggle, stratification, and diversity; ultimately, where Gramsci sees systematic repression, Bakhtin sees the possibility of freedom.

6. This definition is also discriminate enough to separate the stars from the other human figures appearing on television. The other human figures represent social types, but they are not sufficiently individuated to be perceived as extraordinary and unique figures of audience identification: they articulate the typical without making the typical strange. For a discussion of how social typification can rob these figures of their individuality, see Fiske and Hartley's excellent analysis of a television news story covering the action of "typical" British soldiers in Belfast (1978, pp. 41-44).

7. In my dissertation, I develop a framework for organizing the stars on television. In this framework, I tentatively break down television programming into six major discourse arenas: (1) news; (2) sports; (3) variety; (4) advertising; (5) nonseries stories; (6) series stories. In the daily flow of television, these arenas both intersect and interact: TV's turbulent climate of signification has resulted in their constant collision and, in many cases, their synthesis. Consequently, I offer these arenas knowing that their boundaries are at best fuzzy, and at times overlapping (Reeves, 1984, pp. 70-76).

8. I also propose a taxonomy categorizing TV stars: *star presenters, star personalities, star performers, star characters,* and *star constellations.* Just as a star can develop more than one relationship to social type, a star can straddle two or more of these categories. Even so, they do allow for a considerable amount of analytic precision (Reeves, 1984, pp. 77-100).

9. According to Klapp, fool-making is a "propaganda device of special significance":

There is a tendency to dramatize social forces as a conflict of heroes and villains. In this human drama, the fool also plays a part. Whereas the hero represents the victory of good over evil, the fool represents values which are rejected by the group: causes that are lost, incompetence, failure, and fiasco. So that, in a sense, fool-making might be called a process of history. (1971, p. 6)

10. Clark and Holquist even describe Bakhtin as a "philosopher of freedom":

In his work on the play of values as they energize and are constrained by social forces, [Bakhtin] attempts to think through the conditions of possibility for greater degrees of personal and political liberty. Liberty for him is grounded not in the will of the monologic God, the inevitable course of history, or the desire of men, but rather in the dialogic nature of language and society. Through his translinguistics Bakhtin seeks to give both individual selves and social ensembles their full due. His attempts to bridge the age-old gap between system and performance by finding connections for both in extrapersonal, but not transcendent, social energies has the effect of putting new movement and possibility for exchange into the dichotomy of self and other. (1984, p. 11)

REFERENCES

Alberoni, F. (1972). The powerless elite: Theory and sociological research on the phenomenon of stars. In D. McQuail (Ed.), *Sociology of mass communication* (pp. 75-99). London: Penguin.

Bakhtin, M. M. (1981). *The dialogic imagination: Four essays* (M. Holquist, Ed., C. Emerson & M. Holquist, Trans.). Austin: University of Texas Press.

Barthes, R. (1972). Mythologies (A. Lavers & C. Smith, Trans.). New York: Hill and Wang.

Berger, P., & Luckmann, T. (1966). *The social construction of reality: A treatise in the sociology of knowledge.* Garden City, NY: Doubleday.

Boorstin, D. (1964). *The image: A guide to pseudo-events in America.* New York: Harper & Row.

Brooks, T., & Marsh, E. (1980). *The complete directory to prime time network TV shows: 1946-present.* New York: Ballantine.

Carey, J. (1975). A cultural approach to communication. *Communication, 2,* 1-22.

Clark, K., & Holquist, M. (1984). *Mikhail Bakhtin.* Cambridge, MA: Belknap Press of Harvard University Press.

Dyer, R. (1979). *Stars.* London: British Film Institute.

Ellis, J. (1982). *Visible fictions.* London: Routledge & Kegan Paul.

Geertz, C. (1973). Person, time and conduct in Bali. In *The interpretation of cultures: Selected essays.* New York: Basic Books.

Klapp, O. (1971). *Social types: Process, structure and ethos.* San Diego: Aegis.

Newcomb, H. M. (1984). On the dialogic aspects of mass communication. *Critical Studies in Mass Communication, 1*(1), 34-50.

Reeves, J. (1984). *Star discourse and television: A critical approach.* Ph.D. dissertation, University of Texas at Austin.

Rollin, R. (1983). The Lone Ranger and Lenny Skutnik: The hero as popular culture. In R. Browne & M. Fishwick (Eds.), *The hero in transition* (pp. 14-45). Bowling Green, OH: Bowling Green University Popular Press.

Sahlins, M. (1976). *Culture and practical reason.* Chicago: University of Chicago Press.

Schutz, A., & Luckmann, T. (1973). *The structures of the life-world* (R. Zaner & H. Engelhardt, Trans.). Evanston: Northwestern University Press.

Silverstone, R. (1961). *The message of television: Myth and narrative in contemporary culture.* London: Heinemann.

Todorov, T. (1984). *Mikhail Bakhtin: The dialogical principle.* Minneapolis: University of Minnesota Press.

Vidmar, V., & Rokeach, M. (1974). Archie Bunker's bigotry: A study in selective perception. *Journal of Communication, 24*(1), 36-47.

Voloshinov, V. N. (1973). *Marxism and the philosophy of language* (L. Matejka & I. R. Titunik, Trans.). New York: Seminar Press.

Chapter 8

TELEVISION MYTH AND RITUAL
The Role of Substantive
Meaning and Spatiality

Stewart M. Hoover

A NEW PHENOMENON HAS RISEN to prominence in the past decade that has significant implications for our understanding of how contemporary media serve to undergird the experience of meaning (both transcendent and sociocultural) by their audiences. Large, prominent, and seemingly successful religious broadcasting organizations (most often referred to, collectively, as the "electronic church") have emerged, which may have the potential to undermine the institutional strength and significance of both "the church" and "the secular media." At a time when the communication research community has been rediscovering "meaning" as an object of human activity, these developments have provided an occasion for consideration of a communication event that claims to be substantively meaningful at its base.

Religion has not been a comfortable field for communication research in recent decades. Social science, in general, and communication research, in particular, has seen religion either (through the eyes of positivism) as a fading concern of residual sectors of industrial society, or as a phenomenon easily accounted for by social measurement of the behaviors assumed to constitute it (church attendance, self-reported religiosity, "traditionalist" social attitudes, and so on). Equally common has been the perspective of the dominant sectors of the so-called "critical" school, for whom religion's major significance is as a powerful tool of social hegemony. That religion might be a powerful or vibrant social force exercising any major, independent, social or cultural influence was not obvious until the much-publicized resurgence of conservative evangelicalism in the 1970s. A central element of this evangelicalism has been evangelical media, broadcast and otherwise, which places this phenomenon squarely on the agenda of media research.

It is not surprising that these developments have left communication researchers searching for tools of measurement, analysis, and theory-building. Among the most relevant directions have been those of the cultural analysts who, following Carey's (1975) influential thought, have begun to look at mass communicational phenomena in a new, radically sociocultural way. Basic to this cultural approach has been an openness, theoretically and methodologically, to consideration of data that are not easily measurable or readily quantifiable.

The development of the "electronic church" quickly stimulated public and scientific debate over its major "effects" and implications. Producers of these programs have been thought to have both theological or ecclesiastical power, and considerable political influence, rivaling both "conventional church" and "conventional television" in unique ways.

The existence of such a phenomenon, where presumably large numbers of viewers[1] are being drawn to an alternative source of entertainment and identification, one which claims at its base to be "religious," is an important test of the significance of both religion and television as contemporary cultural institutions with competing claims to social and cultural ascendancy. It is additionally intriguing to consider the fact that the presumed (and largely empirically confirmed) audience for these programs is made up of conservative, "traditionalist," fundamentalist Americans, who should be attracted to symbolic expression of a conservative, antimodernist sort. Yet, they seem to be participating, by their viewing, in a ritual based in the metropolitan centers of society, one that is shaped and cultivated by the same "modernist" values of the postindustrial age that they find so disturbing in the political sphere. Is the typical viewer of the typical religious television program aware or conscious of the cosmopolitan origins of television (even religious television)? Is this disquieting for them? Can the presumed power of television give to religious broadcasting an ability to overwhelm the conventional (and largely "local") churches? Is religious television an "alternative" medium to conventional television, a competitor for audiences and salience, or are such comparisons simply irrelevant?

PREVIOUS RESEARCH

Many questions, such as who watches such programs, their easily measured functional impacts, how big the audiences actually are, their potential political "effects," and so on, are amenable to survey measurement. A certain amount of such research has already been done. (See, in particular, Buddenbaum, 1981; Clark & Virts, 1985; Gaddy & Pritchard, 1985; Johnstone, 1971; Parker et al., 1954). A vexing problem, however, has been that overall audience size for religious programs is not large, and has not changed appreciably in spite of the best efforts of these new "commercialized" religious programs (Hoover, 1987). As a result, it is difficult to locate samples of sufficient size to carry out careful analyses. In addition, what polling data have been available have been suspect due to the inordinately high numbers of respondents who claim to view religious television. Such polls regularly report that over 40% of American claim to watch religious television regularly, when the ratings and other measures do not justify such high estimates.

More recently, a major study undertaken by the Annenberg School of Communications and the Gallup Organization (Gerbner et al., 1984) sought to answer some of the questions using a database of much higher quality than previously available. Using a sample of viewers obtained from the ratings diary archives of the Arbitron corporation, the Gerbner et al. team was able to reinterview samples of respondents who had actually viewed some religious television during the time they participated in the ratings "sweeps."

The result was an exceptionally reliable estimate of total viewing, of programs viewed, and of a variety of social and cultural measures. The Annenberg-Gallup study confirmed, for instance, that the audience for religious television is rather small, and that duplicated viewing (viewing of more than one religious program per week) leads to misleading overestimates of total religious audience when ratings for individual programs are simply "added" to achieve a weekly figure (something that has been typically done by the proponents of this *genre*). They found that these programs, in spite of the claims that their "new formats" of music, entertainment, interviews, and so on are capturing an increasing audience of younger, more liberal, more educated viewers, are actually attracting pretty much the same audience that has always been there for religious broadcasting. They found that the viewers, being already "heavily religious" by conventional measures of functional religiosity, tend also to be heavy attenders and contributors to conventional churches, so that feared negative effects on those bodies seem not to be justified. There were other, more interesting, but more "minor" findings, including that *conventional* television viewing is far more negatively associated with measures of religiosity than is *religious* television, so that if "the church" were to wish to look for a threat from the world of electronic media, it might best be looking in that direction, rather than at the "electronic church" (Gerbner et al., 1984; Hoover, 1987; Hoover et al., 1987).

The issues are, of course, far more complex than can be stated in such a summary. We still know nothing, for instance, about the *causality* or *directionality* of these relationships. We assume, of course, that "heavy viewers" of religious television who are also "frequent attenders" at local churches were the latter first. Actual attendance, the interpersonal ritual, seems on a *prima facie* basis to be logically prior to something like religious television viewing, but cross-sectional data cannot confirm this. We also lack information about the actual *substantive* nature of the ritual of religious viewing. Peter Berger (1974) has pointed out that social research has always had a bias toward the *functional* attributes of religiosity, and has tended to ignore the fact that religion is (or claims to be) *substantively* different from other cultural phenomena. It reserves for itself a special place "beyond" the tangible and material. For this reason alone, it must be considered in a different way than are other areas of meaning and belief.

A QUALITATIVE APPROACH

The extension of this survey research has been an in-depth study of 20 families who are members of one of the best-known of these religious programs, the "700 Club." The methodology has been one of *elaboration* of the earlier, quantitative findings. Taking the major associations discovered there, interview agendas have been pursued with these families that are intended to reveal issues of primacy and recency, depth of meaning, social and cultural associations, sources of belief, and class and ideological determinants of their involvement in religious broadcasting, and their overall place in contemporary American life. Are they, as we have assumed, "traditionalists" struck on the "fringe" of a modernist world that is leaving them behind? Are they the vanguard of a new political, social (or media) majority that will prove to be a check on rampant secularism? Are they viewing these programs only for social, ideological, or religious "comfort," happy to find some glint of "their" *weltanschauung* in an otherwise secularized and dangerous medium? Are they the passive "pawns" of these "electronic church" preachers, gradually being molded into a political and social force for theocratic purposes? Such questions cannot be answered without a coherent fusion of what we know, reliably, from large-sample data, and what we can learn anecdotally and qualitatively from small samples whom we consider in some depth.

Religion, particularly "substantive" aspects of religiosity, is a particularly apt field for such qualitative analysis. Religious consciousness develops through a complex interplay of social, cultural, and individual forces. Belief in a transcendent reality (one way of defining religion) holds out an intangible referent for cultural and social practice. Anthropologists such as Clifford Geertz (1974) and Victor Turner have demonstrated that only through "thick description" of religiously based social systems can we come to basic theoretical understandings of how meaning is constructed, whether in so-called "traditional" or in "modern" societies.

This research is methodologically based in the tradition of ethnography, and is focused on the objective of learning as much as possible about the role that mediated communication plays in the developing consciousness of these families. It assumes that these issues are, at their base, substantive ones, and thus have been "open" to learnings about them, not closed to data that are "ataxanomic." It further assumes that these questions are relevant to the issue of "meaning," even "substantive meaning," in the context of mediated processes that are not self-consciously described as "religious." Cultural meaning can, of course, be transcendent in a way, and can be as deep and foundational as meaning we connote to religion. Television is the arena of American "civic piety," or "civil religion," and, as such, must play a role in the establishment of its meanings.

This issue of the "substantive" nature of meanings is important to our understanding of the social and cultural value of television. If viewing of television is to be conceived of as anything other than an ephemeral, trivial aspect of contemporary life, its relationship to foundational elements of contemporary consciousness must be charted. Purely on methodological grounds, if not on other grounds, it is essential to make a connection between research in this area and more foundational theoretical work available to us from fields of social psychology and anthropology.

MEANING, MYTH, AND RITUAL IN TURNER'S SYSTEM

The work of Victor Turner has been particularly useful to a number of theoretical approaches to the relationship between contemporary media and contemporary meaning. Martin (1981) has used Turner's concept of *liminality* to explain contemporary cultural change and development. Newcomb and Alley (1983) have been interested in television as a central cultural ritual of liminal suspension. Dayan, Katz, and Kerns (1984) have looked at television "media events" such as papal journeys, as "pilgrimages" for their viewers, evoking Turner's *liminality* and *communitas* through suspension of television's own forms of discourse.

Turner is, indeed, a fertile source of theoretical understanding of processes of cultural and social signification, meaning, ritual, and formation. He has identified, within the ritual processes of "traditional" cultures, a process of development of individual consciousness that he calls "liminality." This term, derived from the Latin, is taken to mean a "threshold" experience, where the individual is suspended between "two worlds of meaning"—a functionalist, structured, hidebound world of everyday existence (which he has come to call *societas*), and an unstructured, voluntary, emotive, compelling, and substantive world "full of possibility" (which he calls *communitas*). Through ritual suspension of everyday structures of culture, class, family, work, and so on, the individual is led to "see forward" into the possibility that a broad community, a *substantive* community, can exist (Turner, 1969).

For my purposes here, the fact that the individual must be aware of *both* the profane, secular, and functionalist *societas* and the sacred, evolving, and substantive *communitas* is of utmost importance. The *interplay* between these two levels of consciousness (or between these two realizations) is the source of the dynamic salience of these processes. For Turner's "ritual process" to work, the individual must have an awareness of both levels of structure. It is obvious that the well-known and often-observed characteristic of "the media" to bring widely scattered people into "social linkage" through simultaneous experiences over great distances (social *and* physical) could play a role in a system of consciousness based on individual awareness of such differences and similarities.

KEY FINDINGS FROM THE
QUALITATIVE STUDY

My findings so far have been meaningful largely on a methodological level. The elaboration of previous large-sample data has revealed a number of ways in which past assumptions about these relationships have been too narrow (at best) or misleading (at worst) both in the specific case of "religious broadcasting" and in the broader area of "meaning" in conventional broadcasting.

TELEVISION AND "TRADITIONALIST" ATTITUDES

Both television and religious television are most heavily viewed by conservative, politically and socially, "traditionalist" viewers. The viewers of religious television are unique from the broader group in that they are *more* conservative, and (not surprisingly) *more* religious, but only in certain ways. All television viewers are more likely than nonviewers to believe in God and hold fundamentalist Christian attitudes about the Bible. Conventional viewers do not pray as frequently or actually read the Bible as frequently as viewers of religion, however (Gerbner et al., 1984).

Largely confirming findings of an earlier study by Bourgault (1985), it further seems that the conservative and traditionalist viewers of religious television actually are *less* so if they are heavily involved in the religious medium (Hoover, 1985). This is consistent with a tendency in conventional television audiences described as "mainstreaming" by Gerbner and his associates. It is also consistent with conscious intents of the purveyors of these programs. Sources at the Christian Broadcasting Network (CBN), the producer of the "700 Club," make it clear that there has been a careful process of "watering down" of the most unique and potentially controversial elements of the Pentecostal roots of that program, so as to not offend the large, public, and heterogeneous audience they see to be their target (Hoover, 1982).[2] The fact that these programs, seen to be ultraconservative (and justifiably so) by many observers, can be said to represent relatively *moderate* attitudes compared to certain of their audience's attitudes is significant of the extreme conservative and traditionalist elements that exist in the American political landscape.

RELIGION AS A
SPECIAL PROBLEM FOR
COMMUNICATION THEORY

Mass communication theory has proposed a variety of ways of explaining the relationship between religion and mass communication. Many of these have followed the lead of Gerbner (Gerbner & Connoly, 1978) in seeing this interaction in the context of the sociocultural preeminence of the church in Reformation-era Europe supplanted in contemporary society by the preeminence of the mass media, particularly television. What happens to religion as an institution in an age where some of its major functions have been assumed by television can thus become a critical test of the sociocultural roles of both institutions. How religion accommodates to the media age begins to outline other basic theoretical issues in communication, as well.

In fact, a hypothesis that portrays television and religion as competing institutions on the contemporary American scene, and looks to formal, denominational religion as its referent, is too simplistic. While it has been shown (Gerbner et al., 1984) that television in general can be said to undermine some basic proprietary values of formal, institutional religion, when we look at the "electronic church" with its social, religious, and political implications, we are left with a serious question still unanswered. In terms of the battle for "turf" between television and religion, is the "electronic church" *television* or is it *religion*?

The major finding of my work (Hoover, 1985) is that there is a *third* institution or setting involved. It is not a question of "church" versus "media." Instead, I have found it most helpful to conceptualize an entirely new institutional setting in which these struggles occur: the "parachurch."

"PARACHURCH" RELIGIOSITY

The United States is a remarkably "religious" country, at least measured through traditional, "functional" means. Church attendance and membership are very high. The majority of Americans claim to believe in God. Even a significant portion of the Jews agree that "Jesus was the Son of God," when so queried by opinion polls. The self-consciously "religious" essence of the American mind-set is signified by the ubiquitous prayers before sporting events and at political rallies. A religiosity is a material part of the *urgeschichte* of the collective American consciousness.

The capitalist economic system has been ready to serve this cultural task. Dating back to at least the "Great Awakenings" of the nineteenth century, there has been an active industry in the marketing of religious paraphernalia, religious "revivals," religious media (print and nonprint), and religious experiences. The age of new electronic gadgetry has exacerbated this process so that, today, there are an enormous variety of religious television and radio programs, videotapes, magazines, newsletters, record labels, traveling revivalist-entertainers, consulting agencies, advertising firms, production companies, and manufacturers targeting the "Christian marketplace." In addition, there are hundreds of national "ministries," some quasi-commercial, others more "conventional," offering prison chaplaincy, counseling, education, training, "mission opportunities," Holy Land pilgrimages, musical programs, and a host of other opportunities to a potential market of religiously motivated Americans.

These commercial organizations link up with a broad network of nondenominational, "independent" churches around the country to form a loose "noninstitutional" institution of what I have called "parachurch religiosity" (Hoover, 1985). By this I mean that individuals can find, through its networks, opportunities to "be religious" and have access to religious experiences beyond those they get from their local, conventional churches. Religious broadcasting is significant, in this view, not so much in terms of its impacts on, or relationship to, *conventional* religious groups, but because it is so firmly rooted in this area of the "parachurch."

All religions are, of course, communicative systems. What is unique and interesting about this "parachurch" area is that such a large measure of its activities are mechanically mediated communicational ones (print and nonprint); and the extent to which such mediated communication actually forms the core of its expression, institutional maintenance, and teaching. The significance of a differentiated "parachurch" realm falls into place when consideration of viewers' experiences from a "cultural" or "qualitative" perspective shows that some basic assumptions about the meaning of "electronic church" broadcasting were not justified (Bourgault, 1985; Hoover, 1985).

First, viewing of these programs is less of a direct challenge to the formal religious establishment than is often assumed. Not only do viewers express little interest in the traditional sectarian controversies between the faiths (exemplified by the *moderation* of attitudes among the viewers I interviewed), qualitative data have confirmed that religious television viewers are also among the most heavily involved members of "conventional" churches (Gerbner et al., 1984). The typical heavily involved viewer or member of the "700 Club," then, is a highly religious person who, nonetheless, cares little for the institutional controversies that have typified "establishment" churches.

Second, this "antiestablishment" bias and quasi-universalist openness masks a deeper dimension, that of the so-called two parties of American Protestantism. The liberal or mainline churches, in particular, have come to be a field of controversy between the "social" concerns of the liberal, "social gospel" movements and individuals, and the "spiritual" concerns of the conservative, fundamentalist churches and individuals. This division has been shown to form the basis of much tension, conflict, and controversy *within* individual churches, particularly in the mainline denominations (Hoge, Perry, & Klever, 1978). This has proven, quite understandably, to be threatening to those churches, and a major basis of concern over the emergence of "electronic church" broadcasting. Among those I interviewed, viewers who represented this "two-party" split (typically, conservatives who happened to belong to more liberal churches) perceive that their church has "grown away" from them, but they do not leave it, often preferring instead to devote time and attention to "parachurch" religious activities (Hoover, 1985).

A third component of this "parachurch" religiosity seems to be its sophistication and institutional depth. The array of organizations and involvements that are available outside the formal confines of a church allows viewers to live in two separate religious-institutional worlds, one defined by their church membership and other formal identities, and another by their involvement in informal and "parachurch" activities.

The existence of this elaborate parachurch context is significant when we begin to consider the conditions under which substantive meaning may be engendered through nontraditional mediated means. The mythic and symbolic world accessible to the individual is quite simply more broadly based and potentially more pervasive than that defined by either the institution of "the church" or the institution of formally constructed "media" such as television. Viewers thus interact with more "texts" than those manifestly and formally constructed by cultural centers traditionally thought to be the *loci* of religious or substantive meaning and ritual. Individuals have access to a variety of "parallel texts," of which, in the case of conservative Protestantism, the "parachurch" realm is a dominant source.

Regardless of whether we consider television, religious television, or a more diffuse parachurch reality to be the foundation of a certain process of meaning construction, we still must elaborate mechanisms by which such texts serve to support such processes for audiences. Mediated communication is the context with which we have been most concerned, and the special qualities of mediated communication imply certain things about how such processes might take place. Transportation has always been a particularly attractive metaphor for mediated communication. Descriptions of "armchair travel" have consistently been applied to the vicarious experiences available to the viewer through television. Anthropology has provided a model for understanding meaning formation in the area of religious or transcendent consciousness, which is also a transportation model—that of religious pilgrimage.

THE POSSIBILITY OF "ARMCHAIR PILGRIMAGE"

Victor Turner's more recent work concentrated on the process of liminal ritual in more advanced societies (Turner, 1978). He became convinced that it was through religious pilgrimage that the more modern societies of the Third World could experience the stylized and ritualized processes of "structure" and "antistructure."

> I myself tend to see pilgrimage as that form of institutionalized or "symbolic" "antistructure" (or perhaps "metastructure") which succeeds the major initiation rites of puberty in tribal societies as the dominant historical form. It is the ordered anti-structure of the patrimonial-feudal systems. (Turner, 1978, p. 203)

Whereas in a "primitive" setting, the structure-antistructure dialectic is realized by religious ritual on a designated feast day, involving incantations, drama, specific rites and actions, in the modern era, pilgrimage has given the individual the opportunity to do the same things through travel. The suspension or transcendence of structure is realized by the travel itself. The pilgrim experiences the travels of the journey, travels far from the familiar turf of home and family, and encounters many people from different places. As he or she nears the pilgrimage center, more and more of those encountered are going the same place. At the center itself, there is the realization that everyone is there for the same purpose, and a sense of *communitas* is derived from the suspension of class and geographic boundaries. People from many places, speaking many languages, representative of many classes all come together, and, for the individual, a sense of *communitas* ensues.

Can such a thing occur vicariously? Dayan et al. (1984) made an argument for papal visits and other "media events" serving such a function through the liminality of television's *own* abilities to suspend its normal form and textural structure to accommodate them. In my work, I see another possibility, the possibility that the *self-consciousness* I have spoken of might undergird a kind of social-structural experience of liminality and pilgrimage for certain viewers.

The respondents in my study are very much aware of sociostructural and cultural *space* and *distance*. Robert Redfield (1972) has suggested that there is, within the individual's consciousness of local community, a consciousness that the community exists within a context of other communities. A community does not exist in isolation (even in the most primitive, untouched, isolated locations). It is, instead, a "community within communities."

The religious viewers with whom I spoke were very much aware of this, as would be any viewer of the cosmopolitan medium of television anywhere in the world. I have called this dimension of their relationship to the "700 Club" *"localism* and *translocalism,"* the awareness that their own local "communities of reference" exist within a wider framework, and that in terms of their religious consciousness, the program is significant as it represents the wider, *translocal* realm. Therefore, there is a sense in which they, as they view, "travel" metaphorically from their home community to one further away.

One of them described a physical pilgrimage that he had taken to the CBN headquarters in Virginia. Very class-conscious in his descriptions of others (he constantly referred to "people with [academic] degrees . . . *top* people"), he was moved by the physical and class-oriented mobility he achieved through his visit to CBN.

> We went down [to CBN] and stayed for three or four days. I was excited to meet a man [Robertson] face-to-face who has the education, and degrees, who is so pleasant, and humble, he's a servant of the Lord, not a "somebody" to show off his abilities or anything like that. (Hoover, 1985)

The respondent and his wife then went on to give an account of their visit that evokes Turner's sense of pilgrimage based on *communitas*.

> And the thing that shocked me, but I expected it, *every* person loving you, hugged you . . . they'd say "praise the Lord," and it's not that they were fanatical, these were people who had college degrees and whatever, and had been in manufacturing . . . for some reason as you got into conversation, they were people who could express themselves . . . and for the first time I said to myself, "this is a taste of heaven," *every* person, *loving* you, smiling, you felt free, you felt like flying around. Occasionally, I'd pick out people who had just met, and I'd overhear, and they were talking about Jesus, about how great he is . . . and there was this sense of "melting to Christ." . . . this whole thing was so organized, and yet the Holy Spirit was in control . . . everything was done top-notch. Nothing was left to chance, from the entertainment, the food, the service, you stayed in the best hotel, you really felt like you were "king's kin." We especially enjoyed touring, going into the buildings.

The pilgrimagelike associations in this viewer's experience of the program itself (and of other respondents as well) was equally tantalizing. It is difficult to claim at this stage that a television program could entail the profound and foundational consequences for religious consciousness that a real, physical pilgrimage might, particularly in a less-developed culture than our modern cosmopolitan one.

There are senses, however, in which the experience of the program could accommodate such associations for its viewers. First, the "moderation" of the content of the program, making it attractive to a more "centrist" audience, leads to a religious "universalism" of a kind, where a wide variety of religions and religious viewpoints are tolerated by the program and by its audience. The Catholic viewers of this Protestant program said, when queried about whether they ever felt that the program was not open to their particular faith, "We're all Christians, aren't we?" The Jewish viewer responded, "We all worship the same God, don't we?" This universalistic tolerance is both striking when seen against the backdrop of intolerance that has typified the Fundamentalist roots of these viewers and the program itself, *and* perfectly consistent with the idea that the program enforces a type of "communitas" in Turner's sense.

Second, these viewers are well aware of the space and distance, both physical and sociocultural, that separates them from the "700 Club" and its host, Pat Robertson. They identify him (in a particular way) with the feared and mistrusted metropolis, the source of the secularized threats against their local ways of living and thinking, and yet he has overcome and conquered those centers, even conquering their most important forum for expression—television itself. One viewer said,

> Pat Robertson is about *power* . . . he's into radical incursions into the centers of power, he's on a different plane. There's no way that the local pastor in Timbuktu, Iowa, can compete with that.

Yet, at the "center," the program itself, they see reaffirmed the basic values of family, God, home, and country they themselves hold dear. Convinced that a "revival" is overtaking America, they are able to participate in a viewing ritual that reaffirms for them that this revival is striking far away places, both local communities such as their own (confirmed through the program's "testimonies" from ordinary people) and translocal meta-communities (through the program's many film stories on politics and national and international affairs).

Third, television itself thus entails both the window on these developments—the "route" of the journey, as it were—and a potential source of peril of its own. The very secularism and cosmopolitanism that typifies the dangers and threats these viewers see from wider society, comes to them through the same medium. Television is, in a word, potentially dangerous and threatening itself. The ability of Pat Robertson and Jerry Falwell to "capture it for good" is a powerful reaffirmation of an evolving national "communitas" centered on these programs (at least potentially).

I am certainly not prepared to claim any of this as empirically demonstrated beyond doubt by my interviews. Rather, I am sketching out the possibilities that have emerged from my elaboration of the large-sample quantitative work that preceded my own. It is too simplistic to say that religious television is "only" an alternative form of television. It is far more than that, not least because it has profound substantive claims to be "religious." Neither can it be said, it seems to me, that television's cultural significance lies only in its manifest "messages" or "symbol systems." Television, religious or not, must necessarily entail consciousness of space and distance on the part of its viewers. The fact that it is difficult to state that "religion" or "substantive meaning" are clearly separate means that in this sense all of television can be and is "religious" in a profound way. Belief, the basis of religion, can and does undergird *both* the consciously religious *and* the adamantly secular. Consciousness of community, of distance, of local versus translocal values, of contrasts between the "merely" *social* (*societas*, to Turner) and the transcendentally *meaningful* (*communitas*) is basic to all consciousness beyond the mundane and routine. Television surely undergirds this broader picture, whether it claims to be "religious" or "secular."

THE SIGNIFICANCE OF
SPACE AND DISTANCE

There is a broad and diverse literature that addresses the cultural meaning of television in the American context. Gerbner and his associates have engaged in a long-term study of television as a "cultural indicator," using a combination of institutional, context, and audience analyses. Early work by Adorno and others in the field of ideological studies has as its objective a charting of the process of cultural belief and meaning. The fields of cultural studies, literary analysis and criticism, and anthropology have contributed to a growing understanding of these issues. Critical studies have addressed themselves to the role of mediated communication in the formation of modern ideologies.

Carey (1975) has called for (and stimulated) a radically "cultural" approach to the study of mass communication. More recently, Newcomb and his associates have applied techniques of both literary and cultural criticism to American television (Newcomb & Alley, 1983). Much of this analysis has been remarkably silent on the subject of *spatiality* or *distance* as dimensions of these processes, however.

Two recent efforts are typical of this. Byars (1986) proposes that television must be seen as essentially "polysemic," a complex symphony between viewer and text in which "alternative readings" of the television text are not only possible but, in fact, the reality of viewing as it is actually experienced. In the process, viewers participate in the celebration of foundational images, types, roles, and power, which each viewer may experience in a different way. Power may be what television is all about (as Gerbner has said), but the power resides in the construction of meaning by the viewer in dialogue with the text, not in an instrumental "message" of power, or "exercise" of power by the medium itself.

Newcomb (1986) applies a close textual analysis to a typical evening of prime-time entertainment programming. Noting that a variety of "readings" of individual "texts" within prime-time entertainment are possible, he outlines a variety of "paths" viewers could take through an evening of television, each path encompassing a different "text" of its own, seen in its own particular sequence. He is very interested, obviously, in viewing as an *individual* process, an *individual* experience. His observation that "television must be seen as dynamic rather than static, as processual rather than merely as product, as a fissured and contradictory rather than monolithic ideology, as polysemy rather than univocality" is well taken, and describes the viewing experiences of respondents in my study rather well. In their experiences of all television, but religious television in particular, they exhibited just the sort of "subversive" readings of even the "700 Club's" texts that are so tantalizing to cultural analysts.

Viewing takes place in a social and cultural *context*, however. The dynamism of viewing as a cultural activity derives not from the consciousness of individuals as atomized beings but from the accumulated cultural heritage in which they live and grow. The logical outgrowth of analyses that focus on individual "power" in the viewing process is *either* the inference that the process is highly complex, and thus a great deal is known about an individual in particular, but not much of everyone in general, *or* that some inference should be made from individual readings *to* the general level (something the "cultural" view seems to eschew at the outset).

I see the need for a "middle level" of analysis, one that understands and builds on what can be known about the aggregate content of the medium, *and* that accepts the reality that the process is not instrumental, but rather devolves from the establishment of meaning by an audience in its encounter with mediated texts through which a variety of readings are possible. My middle level of analysis would begin with the simple proposition that not all viewers are the same in social or cultural terms. Not only are there sociocultural dimensions of the audience that can be said to be systematic, and thus (ultimately) quantitatively verifiable, there are also—and this is the critical point—dimensions that help *define* the cultural meaning they derive from television texts.

Space and distance are examples of this. If conventional television entails readings that relate to consciousness of social and cultural power and ascendancy, then systematic readings must result from similarly situated cultural groups. "Traditionalist" Protestants, for instance, identify television as the forum of secularized, profane, "East" and "West Coast" values. Their encounters with television's texts derive an additional measure of momentum from this consciousness. Indeed, in the case of religious broadcasting, it is possible that this profane nature of television as a "medium from outside" their own local frames of reference may serve to make the programming more salient for them in that it represents the capture of the profane context by the sacred.

Can the same dimensions be active in "conventional" television? Surely they must. Viewers live and learn in specific local contexts. They understand that their local communities exist within other communities. A Turnerian analysis of television—religious or "secular"—as a culturally significant experience, must rely on the individual's understanding that he or she is not an individual member of a "national audience," but rather a member of a local community. Further, for "liminality" to result in the consciousness of wider community, the individual must be conscious of other communities and of a wider society of which all are a part.

Simply put, consciousness of cultural "place," which can be understood in terms of geography, distance, class, society, ethnicity, religion, politics, or belief, is at the base of the evolution of consciousness of "meaning." I would content that for most previous research, such dimensions have been *tacit*—assumed by researchers and their critics. The "middle range" of analyses, those that would look at cultural and social context and consciousness as a dimension of the viewing experience, are essential next steps in our growing understanding of how individuals interact with, and achieve meaning from, their television viewing.

NOTES

1. See Hoover (1987) for a complete discussion of this issue.
2. It is not at all clear that this public audience is the actual audience for the program, however. It is equally likely that viewers, who are themselves "already religious," simply support the program being on "for someone else" who "really needs it." Many of my interviewees, including the heaviest donors, did not view the program regularly.

REFERENCES

Abelman, R., & Neuendorf, K. (1985, Winter). How religious is religious television programming? *Journal of Communication, 35*(1).

Berger, P. (1974, Fall). Some second thoughts on substantive versus functional definitions of religion. *Journal for the Scientific Study of Religion.*

Bourgault, L. (1980). *An ethnographic study of the "Praise the Lord Club."* Unpublished Ph.D. dissertation, Ohio University.

Bourgault, L. (1985, Winter). The "PTL Club" and Protestant viewers: An ethnographic study. *Journal of Communication, 35*(1).

Buddenbaum, J. M. (1981, Summer). Characteristics of media-related needs of the audience for religious TV. *Journalism Quarterly, 58.*

Byars, J. (1986). *Polysemy and power.* Paper delivered at the annual conference, the International Communication Association, Chicago.

Carey, J. (1975, April). Communication and culture. *Communication Research.*

Clark, D., & Virts, P. (1985). *Religious television audience: A new development in measuring audience size.* Paper presented at the Society for the Scientific Study of Religion, Savannah, GA.

Dayan, D., Katz, E., & Kerns, P. (1984). *Armchair pilgrimages.* Paper presented at the annual conference of the American Sociological Association, San Antonio.

Engel, J. (1984, June). Caution: Findings subject to interpretation. *Religious Broadcasting.*

Fore, W. F. (1980, October 23). *The electronic church: Pro and con.* Colloquium Presentation, the Annenberg School of Communications, Philadelphia.

Gaddy, G., & Pritchard, D. (1985, Winter). When watching religious TV is like attending church. *Journal of Communication, 35*(1).

Geertz, C. (1974). *The interpretation of cultures.* New York: Basic Books.

Geertz, C. (1982, May 27). Conjuring with Islam [Review article]. *New York Review of Books.*

Gerbner, G., & Connoly, K. (1978, April/May). Television as new religion. *New Catholic World.*

Gerbner, G., Gross, L., Hoover, S., Morgan, M., Signorielli, N., Wuthnow, R., & Cotungo, H. (1984). *Religion on television and in the lives of viewers.* New York: Committee on Electronic Church Research.

Hadden, J., & Swann, C. (1981). *Prime time preachers.* Reading, MA: Addison-Wesley.

Hoge, D., Perry, E., & Klever, G. (1978, Winter). Theology as a source of disagreement about Protestant church goals and priorities. *Review of Religious Research, 19*(2).

Hoover, S. M. (1982a). *The electronic giant.* Elgin, IL: Brethren Press.

Hoover, S. M. (1982b). *Religious group use and avoidance of television: A study of reasons and effects.* Unpublished M. S. thesis, University of Pennsylvania, Annenberg School of Communications.

Hoover, S. M. (1985). *The "700 Club" as religion and as television: A study of reasons and effects.* Ph.D. dissertation, University of Pennsylvania.

Hoover, S. M. (1987, Spring). The religious television audience: A matter of significance, or size? *Review of Religious Research.*

Hoover, S. M. (1988). *Mass media religion: The social sources of the electronic church.* Newbury Park, CA: Sage.

Hoover, S. M., Gerbner, G., Gross, L., Morgan, M., & Signorielli, N. (1987). *The contribution of cable television to religious audience size.* Unpublished manuscript, University of Pennsylvania, Annenberg School of Communications.

Horsfield, P. (1984). *Religious television: The American experience.* New York: Longman.

Johnstone, R. L. (1971, Winter). Who listens to religious radio broadcasts anymore? *Journal of Broadcasting, 16.*

Lerner, D. (1958). *The passing of traditional society.* New York: Free Press.

Martin, B. (1981). *A sociology of contemporary cultural change.* London: Basil Blackwell.

Marty, M. (1969). *The modern schism.* New York: Harper & Row.

Newcomb, H. (1986). *One night of prime time: An analysis of television's multiple voices.* Paper delivered at the annual conference, the International Communication Association, Chicago.

Newcomb, H., & Alley, R. (1983). *Television: The producer's medium.* New York: Oxford.

Parker, E., Barry, D., & Smythe, D. (1954). *The radio-television audience and religion.* New York: Harper.

Redfield, R. (1972). *The little community.* New York: Free Press.

Robertson, P. (1972). *Shout it from the housetops.* Plainfield, NJ: Logos.

Schultze, Q. (1985, Fall). Vindicating the electronic church? An assessment of the Annenberg-Gallup Study. *Critical Studies in Mass Communication.*

Teheranian, M. (1982, September). *Communication technology and fundamentalist revival.* Paper presented at the International Association for Mass Communication Research, Paris.

Thomas, S. (1985, Winter). The route to redemption: Religion and social class. *Journal of Communication, 35*(1).

Turner, V. (1969). *The ritual process: Structure and anti-structure.* Ithaca: Cornell University Press.

Turner, V. (1978). The center out there: Pilgrim's goal. *History of Religions, 12*(4).

Weber, M. (1963). *The sociology of religion.* Boston: Beacon.

PART III

THE PRESS

Chapter 9

THE WATERGATE AUDIENCE
Parsing the Powers of the Press[1]

Michael Cornfield

THE DEBATE OVER
PRESS/MEDIA POWER

A great news story is one in which the fact of coverage alters the course of history. Great news stories seem to mark peaks in the powers of the press, who gather and arrange the news, and in the powers of the media, especially television, through which the news is conveyed. In exploring the question of what makes a news story great, there is no better place to start than Watergate. Surely there has been no greater news story in recent times than Watergate, when press and media operations figured so dramatically in the fall of the Nixon administration, and the government's resolution of the tapes dispute occurred so baldly in public view.

In the decade since Watergate, prominent politicians, scholars, and journalists have criticized the press and media for arbitrary exercises of powers seen as increasing at the expense of other political institutions (Politicians: Carter, 1982; Cutler, 1984; Scholars: Lichter et al. 1986; Ranney, 1983; Journalists: Kraft, 1981; O'Neill, 1982; White, 1982, chap. 6). The plausibility of imperious behavior by a de facto fourth branch of government arises, for instance, if we ask why Watergate was a greater news story than Koreagate, Lancegate, and Iran (or Contra-) gate, to cite a few national scandals whose names evoke inferior historic parallels. One explanation, centering on press bias, might be that reporters and editors didn't hate Jimmy Carter and Ronald Reagan the way they hated Richard Nixon. Another explanation, focusing on the news media penchant for sensationalized news, might proceed from the assumption that no story could ever top Watergate for shock value, because the most that another scandal or disastrous policy could lead to would be the *second* resignation of a president in U.S. history. Both lines of reasoning would fault journalists for blowing Watergate out of proportion, with disastrous consequences for the Nixon administration and the presidency as well.

When journalists defend themselves against charges of bias, sensationalism, and imperiousness, they often cite the nature of the news itself. Koreagate and Lancegate, they might say, were not "big news" as Watergate was; smaller issues and fewer top officials were directly involved. And while the latest "gate" may be bigger news than its prototype, it hasn't proven as "good" in the telling—that is, the story hasn't stirred the wide and obsessive interest in detail that the events of 1972-1974 generated.[2] Appeals to news "bigness" and "goodness" deflect antipress and media charges by attributing the power of judgment to the audience, whose assessments of the story news media decision makers merely reflect. From this angle, the general population was largely responsible for the nation's anti-Nixon tilt and the lurid fascination with the final days of his administration. This position exonerates journalists from political capriciousness, but it strips away their heroic and professional image.

How can we gauge the effect of *Washington Post* reporters Robert Woodward and Carl Bernstein and other Watergate reporters upon American history? I side with the minimalist interpretations of press and media power in Watergate. I will argue in this essay that for a news story to become *great*, it must encompass both what elite readers regard as a *big* political controversy and what mass viewers consider to be the stuff of a *good* story. Because these audience perceptions have bases outside of journalism, the press and the media are not nearly as influential as they seem when a great news story grips the nation. What happens during a great news story is that the press and the media come to represent the audience—as agent and instrument, respectively—of narrative enforcement. They symbolize a cultural imperative to serve traditional expectations during the next round of news-making events. But it is the audience itself, and its fidelity to the values sustained in their favorite narrative forms, that inclines politicians to conform to the story as it should be told while it is being told.

WHAT MAKES A
NEWS STORY "GOOD"?

American journalists like to provide the news in narrative forms. By a *narrative*, I mean information about characters in action, arranged in a familiar sequence of beginning, middle, and end. Narratives make news more interesting, even compelling, through dramatic representation; narrative forms, as Kenneth Burke observed, arouse and then satisfy expectations. Consumers of political information prefer narratives over documents (too impersonal), arguments (too didactic), verse (too vague), and over the assortment of observations, releases, opinions, and labels that typifies news in its raw state. The vocation of journalism acknowledges the social preference for this kind of organization by calling a unit of journalism a *story*.

Journalists often use the word *story* interchangeably with the *news* itself. I am drawing a distinction with a difference: In this essay, *the story* refers to the entertaining and sequential context in which *the news* may appear to audiences. For example, the election of a president is news; the making of the president is the story that election news concludes. Similarly, the explosion of the space shuttle is news, while the investigation of its causes is the story thus begun.

By publishing news in story forms, journals can rely on narrative principles to augment both their technological reach and the intrinsic fascination of the information they have to sell. The serial format ("Tomorrow: Part Seven") illustrates this logic; journalists use serial formats to hook news consumers into following their column or show for several editions. More generally, journalists organize their work around a set of appealing news topics that audiences can easily recognize. We may know a journal by the narratives it extends, by what it covers. Readers attracted to the news in one edition come to understand that, if they purchase the next edition, or better still, subscribe to the journal, they will continue to find, at the least, a convenient update and summary of the story to date ("There was no word today from the House Rules Committee regarding the tax reform bill."), and eventually, word of anticipated developments ("After years of discussion and months of debate, the House of Representatives today finally began floor consideration of a sweeping tax reform bill.")

To be sure, the reportorial commitment to fresh facts, quickly communicated, puts a strain on journalistic story-telling. News often surfaces in fragments, and on disparate topics, as a look at any front page or evening news show discloses. This can make it difficult to perceive a story line relating today to yesterday and tomorrow. What, then, are the (literally) telltale signs of a news story, news written so as to captivate readers and viewers? And how can we identify a good news story, one that has caught on with enough news consumers to form an audience awaiting its resolution?

A good story is essentially a matter of taste; but popular conceptions of good stories are cultural phenomena that have recurring features.

Literary critics have developed a vocabulary for the identification of story genres, and they have designated certain genres as traditionally popular within a particular culture (or of universal interest to humanity). I have chosen to concentrate on six rudimentary elements of a story: the narrative frame, theme, set scenes, plot, characters, and point of view. As for popular American genres, I have drawn on my own socialization as an American and discursive reading of the critical literature. A good news story thus consists of journalism that evokes, in generic combination, the six elements typical of a popular American genre.

It seems perfectly obvious, for instance, that Americans adore "success" or "Horatio Alger" stories. Typically, the principal characters are loners who win riches and fame through hard work, luck, and risk-taking. When we read, in an opening chapter of a novel, of a poor but spunky lad who sells newspapers in the streets of a big city, we have a pretty good idea of the sorts of characters he will meet, the troubles he will encounter, and the virtues that will prove crucial to his triumph in the end. To the extent a news story conforms to the elements of one of these hallowed genres, then, it seems reasonable to assume it will become good; that is, attract an audience and hold it until the story reaches an acceptable conclusion.

When journalists tell a story well, they expand the dimensions of the audience that will find the next news in the narrative form good. But audience size, duration, and level of devotion also depend on the realities being narrated—and on the quality and extent of artistic imitating that occurs in that reality. Persons who find themselves depicted as characters in a journalistic story help determine how good the story becomes. We may see this power to make a story good in American journalism's equivalent to the Alger success story. Such stories often hew to the form of a profile, which brings us up-to-date on the rise of the subject. A well-written profile can focus attention on a political figure. But a politician who acts like a celebrity, and (along with his agent) supplies the press with current information on how he bears the burdens of fame, can also command audience attention. And too much about any single success story can spark audience disenchantment. The power to captivate news media consumers through generic conformity is thus diffuse and two-edged.

THE GENRE

I think Watergate became, through journalism, a real-life tale of crime and detection. In this genre of American fiction, the central character is a detective, a solitary agent of truth and justice who enters a situation where a crime has occurred and departs having figured out who committed it. (Arrest, trial, and punishment come, if at all, as anticlimaxes.) Where the British tradition of crime-and-detection stories concludes with the suspects gathered in a room so the detective can reconstruct the crime for us, the American tradition is less rational and more existential. Literary critic Steven Marcus (1974) outlined the format in his introduction for a 1974 reissue (timely for Watergate) of seven stories by Dashiell Hammett, a seminal writer of the American style whodunit:

> What happens is that the Op (Continental Detective Agency Operative) almost invariably walks into a situation that has already been elaborately fabricated or framed. And his characteristic response to his sense that he is dealing with a series of deceptions or fictions is—to use the words that he uses himself repeatedly—"to stir things up" . . . to make the fictions of others visible as fictions, inventions, concealments, falsehoods, and mystifications.

The American detective ventures beyond the scene of the crime. He seeks the man who paid the butler to do it. The story typically concludes with the detective embarrassing prominent and powerful figures by disassembling the self-serving explanations they have fostered in the community. Justice and truth are served, if not consummated, by his freedom to operate in society.

THE FRAME

Journalists bind the news into narrative forms through framing devices that specify a time sequence (beginning, middle, end) and a space for the characters to interact (setting). Framing devices surface in chronological sidebars and charts, in such phrases as "questions remain" and "only time will tell," and in references to time spans outside the one automatically established by the journal's periodicity. We tune in to the evening news to learn what has happened during the workday; when reports recapitulate events of the past year, or apprise us of a meeting scheduled two weeks hence, we go beyond the news update to story considerations. For example, *Time* magazine (May 21, 1973, p. 16) helped its readers frame the Watergate story with these sentences:

> Perhaps weeks later will come the potentially explosive testimony of fired Counsel John Dean. . . . [But] That may not satisfy the angry legislators. [The] prosecutors and the courts got to the bottom of Watergate last January when seven insignificant men were convicted. A more

momentous and agonizing question remains: Will anyone now get to the top of it?

The crime story genre, with its discovery-to-reconstruction sequence, gives the audience a familiar idea as to when the current events began and when they might end. It also alerts them to what and whom they should be looking for as the middle proceeds. Time and space orientations are constantly needed in journalism, with its emphasis on recently disclosed occurrences. Thus journalists usually reiterate "basic questions" in each news installment.

THE THEME

The sounding of a theme throughout a story lends unity to the narrative. The crime story's signature theme is that the place under description is corrupt. Journalists rely on metaphors to elucidate a story theme, especially in titles, leads, and closers, where they can encapsulate the uncertainty of the news, and, together with the story frame, suggest desirable resolutions. A metaphor says "X is Y," and the incongruity of the equation invites the audience to consider both the sense in which the reality-representation correspondence is literal and the sense in which it is figurative. For example, the "Saturday Night Massacre" did occur on that day of the week, but no one was killed, as in gangland Chicago on St. Valentine's Day, or as in revolutionary Boston. Nevertheless, the metaphor asked the Watergate audience to regard the resignations and firings as an excessive use of force against undeserving people. It was a figurative massacre, because a legal inquiry into criminal activity had been squelched without warning by the top suspect and his cronies. The crime story metaphor thereby encouraged the audience to expect an explanation for the act (the mastermind revealed), and some sort of retribution (the detective triumphant).

The popularity of the "Saturday Night Massacre" as a name for events harmonizes with the first labels for Watergate as a "caper," and with the climactic social discovery of "the smoking gun." The crime story theme led journalists to doubt the veracity of everything the Nixon administration did; days after the massacre, *Newsweek* (November 5, 1973) suggested that a worldwide military alert ordered in response to a reported threat of Soviet troops on the move toward the war-torn Middle East was a diversionary tactic. Other commentators pondered whether everyone in America did what Nixon did, asking aloud whether the president's only real crime was in getting caught. The theme led, too, to research of previous administrations for evidence of wiretapping, public deception, and campaign tricks. And the cynical mood typical of crime stories ultimately fed into a "post-Watergate syndrome," wherein investigative reporters had higher social status than elected politicians.

SET SCENES

Journalism draws scenes by expanding coverage before and after a big news event, and by labeling the event as special. (The earlier preparations commence, of course, the more contrived the news at the scene will be.) Audiences sense a big scene when television and radio interrupt regularly scheduled programs, newspapers print extra sections, and magazines add to and mark off their center pages. Few details are left out during a news scene, because any one of them could prove significant, and all of them will presumably be consumed. Thus reporters vacuum up trivia surrounding the central action, including the self-referential actions of vacuuming itself, as performed by a press that comments as individuals, but depicts itself en masse, as a pack. A common by-product of the news scene is the gaffe, a comment by a character regarded as inadvertently, and thus authentically, revealing. For example, on November 17, 1973, during the live broadcast of a news conference with managing editors, President Nixon said:

> I want to say this to the television audience. . . . People have got to know whether or not their president is a crook. Well, I am not a crook. I have earned everything I have got.

Generic story construction enables news scenes to be set with greater precision. Press and audience know not only that impending action will be crucial, but also what details in particular to look for: those that echo the theme, turn the plot toward a happier or sadder ending, reveal the main character's obligations and/or essential worth. The major set pieces of Watergate were Presidential Counsel John Dean's testimony, the decision on *U.S. v. Nixon*, the impeachment votes, the resignation, and the pardon. In the first of these hugely awaited scenes, the turncoat implicated the boss; the next three constituted the denouement, one on each stage of government; the last designated an official ending. Only the last worked to Nixon's favor.

THE PLOT

Plots explain narratives in terms of causes and effects. Crime story "hows" and "whys" are typically convoluted, and crucial to the success of the narrative. Investigative reporters and editorial writers can thus distinguish themselves through plot exposition during the telling of a newsworthy scandal. The audience's sense that there was, indeed, a plot behind the seemingly aberrant burglary at the Democratic National Committee heightened story interest.

Watergate as news unfolded in accordance with (and may have suggested) Steven Marcus's generic outline. A criminal plot was uncovered and disassembled, creating chaos, which in turn exposed more evidence, which was then pieced together in a more convincing, but less than reliable, replacement plot. In the first year of Watergate, journalism linked Watergate to such outstanding public mysteries as the Kennedy assassination, the Bay of Pigs invasion, and the political shenanigans of Howard Hughes and I.T.T. (Epstein & Berendt, 1973). Press and media quickly latched onto a question by Senator Howard Baker as the touchstone of the plot: "What did the president know, and when did he know it?" The audience's desire to know the answer undoubtedly fueled the "Firestorm" of public protest that followed the Saturday Night Massacre, and sustained the enormous pressure on Nixon to release the tapes.[3] Finally, journalism helped replace the White House explanation (a combination of nuclear age exigency and presidential carelessness) with an audience-comforting plot that stressed the primacy of the constitutional order and the incumbent's warped character. The Memphis *Commercial Appeal* editorialized on August 9, 1974:

> There is an ethic in the American character, an ethic which runs like a strong thread through the Constitution, which reveres honesty and abhors the liar and the cheat.
>
> Everything about Nixon has run contrary to this ethic . . . there was no justification for Nixon's cynical mauling of the honor, the dignity, and the faith of the presidency. It was Nixon's complaint that too much was made of Watergate for too long. But it was the perseverance of our other institutions—Congress, the courts, and also the free press—that brought an end to Watergate. When we teach our children to look to our form of self-government and our Constitution for right and justice, the Watergate experience will be one more proof that this Union can survive in tempest and in fire.

THE CHARACTERS

Stereotyping persons in the news with characterizations helps audiences appreciate what literary critics call the "subtext" of a work, that is, what the actors are thinking about as they perform in public. Journalists delineate characters not so much through incident (as Henry James advised novelists) as through the discovery and circulation of nicknames and other labels, which they affix to persons occupying prominent government posts. Patrick Anderson has written about the title variations that accompany the role of "crony," or friend to the president:

A "court jester" is a funny crony,
An "intimate adviser" is a powerful crony,
A "favorite presidential companion" is a rich crony.
A "longtime political retainer" is a crony reporters like.
A "political hanger-on" is a crony reporters don't like. (Anderson, 1968, p. 310)

The design and history of political institutions advance the model traits for officials, the roles that persons will fill for better or worse depending on their character. A president, for example, ought to agonize about what shall best serve the national interest, and he understandably strives to reconcile that goal with his electoral imperative to maintain popularity. House members should develop expertise on an issue, while Senators should adopt a more general view and be more resistant to fashionable opinions.

Story genres supply additional role specifications, indicating character traits appropriate to the action sequence on display. We expect different qualities to emerge from the president at the bargaining table than on the campaign trail or in the war room. The generic indication of motives along a narrative often alleviates our ignorance about the battle before our eyes while heightening our anxiety over the outcome. The reason lies close to the essence of drama: the better we anticipate what it takes for a player to prevail in an imminent conflict, the more we wonder how well the person will fill the role—or, perhaps, transcend and remake it. Stories promise "crisis" situations, during which protagonists tempt the fate prescribed by the roles they inhabit, and reveal their truest selves in the ultimate test of their willpower.

For many members of the Watergate audience, the tapes mattered above all because they were thought to have recorded the true Richard Nixon, in the throes of his biggest crisis. Disclosure of their contents would allow journalistic resolution of the plot mystery, and permit readers to determine whether this man was an authentic president or an impostor. The tapes (along with the method of their release) confirmed the suspicion that President Nixon was crooked. U.S. presidents traditionally make a show of their humility; Nixon, to cobble the titles of two best-selling books by journalists, committed a "breach of faith," and installed "a palace guard" between himself and the people (Rather & Gates, 1974; White, 1975). When he was alone, it was because he chose to isolate himself, not because of the loneliness of power. Behind his self-imposed barriers, Nixon lied in character—that is, to save himself, not out of practical necessity, as presidents may be excused for doing. On August 9, 1974, columnist Haynes Johnson of the *Washington Post* summed up the Watergate story characterization of Nixon:

> His ambitions, his insecurities, his aloofness, his resentments, his humorlessness, his inability to inspire popular confidence, his misplaced trust in others, his taste for the second-rate, his penchant for secrecy, for maneuver, for deviousness—these were the attributes that ultimately destroyed him.

POINT OF VIEW

If Nixon was the chief villain, there were several heroes: Judge John J. Sirica, Special Prosecutor Archibald Cox, Senator Sam Ervin, Representative Peter Rodino, and, most interestingly for this essay, reporters Bob Woodward and Carl Bernstein. The reporters are doubly important because the crime story was most memorably told from their point of view. Indeed, the story that begins with the break-in and ends with the humiliation of the ringleader depended on the intrepid performance of these journalist-narrators. A standard moral of the detective genre, that Americans preserve their freedoms thanks to the efforts of unruly characters, justified the reporters' own improper—but, typically, confessed—conduct. In the book *All the President's Men*, Woodward and Bernstein admit to misuse of telephone company data and infringement upon the sanctity of the grand jury. But the crime story point of view imbues these acts with the sweet whiff of righteous desperation. The audience is therefore disposed to forgive these flaws, as they are ill-disposed to forgive Nixon.

The double standard raises questions about the legitimacy of press power, which will be considered ahead. The point here is that the audience identified with "the boys" instead of the characters whose jobs ironically stood for law enforcement. The capacity of the audience to adopt their perspective on the issues was enhanced, if not fully made possible, by the representation of Watergate as a crime story. Pulling for the underdogs made this most serious of constitutional crises a thrilling consumer experience.

The identification of a story genre in the news is fundamentally a matter of interpretation. No threshold criteria for this or that kind of story can be reliably formulated. More than one genre may subsume and integrate the same story material; for instance, Watergate was also told as the "seventh crisis" in Richard Nixon's personal success story. And, even in retrospect, the fit of one form to the news will have imperfections. No one filled the staple role of the female betrayer in the Watergate detective story.

Yet gradually, provisionally, and then obviously, much of Watergate fell into the narrative form of a crime thriller. The book and film *All the President's Men* epitomized this genre, refining the Watergate story and rendering it larger than life. Yet the crime-and-detection context had clicked into focus in most national journals by March of 1973. On March 23, in an open court session, Judge John J. Sirica read a letter by burglary defendant James McCord that cited pressures on him and his cohorts from unnamed superiors. The news was that the burglars' silence had been ordered. So had perjury. These disclosures brought the Watergate story into the present tense: a cover-up was occurring, just as the *Post* and other investigating journals had alleged since the fall of 1972. The fact of a cover-up implied that whoever had given the orders was still at large, and perhaps still in public office. That, in turn, meant Watergate could no longer be regarded as a partisan wrangle over the previous year's election. It was a matter for current public concern. Henceforth, journalism would supply the nation with the story of the cover-up's dissolution. "Saturation coverage" became standard throughout the U.S. news media.[4] The Gallup Poll, a major source of presidential news, commenced surveys on the topic. Newsstand sales swelled for *Time* magazine whenever a Watergate cover appeared (Halberstam, 1979, p. 688). An audience had come into being.

Americans accepted this genre as an appropriate interpretive framework for an extremely confusing array of news items. Indeed, because bewilderment is characteristic of detective stories, the more of Watergate one observed, the more ingratiating the genre became. In the spring of 1974, after America had learned that tapes existed, but before the tapes had been released, they could follow the news with an awareness that no fewer than seven versions of the story could feed into journalism and attract their attention: the one on the tapes, the White House statements, the testimony before the Ervin Committee, the testimony before the Rodino Committee, the case the prosecutors made to the Watergate Grand Jury, the F.B.I. files, and the C.I.A. files. None of these accounts fully represented the truth, and each of them squared with institutional interests. One journalist compared the effort of understanding Watergate to listening to a symphony by hearing the different instrumental parts in sequence (Schell, 1975, p. 42). The material made Continental Operators out of millions.

Cultural arguments falter for being atmospheric, for having to appeal, literally, to "common" sense. Still, an appreciation of story-telling and audiences is indispensable, I think, to the study of press and media power. People who grow up in a particular community maintain the popularity of a few narratives as the dominant contexts for understanding what happens among them. They embrace the mythic resonations of leaders and events as a way of reasserting their belonging to a resilient community. To the degree that the facts emerging in the news evoked shared and longstanding fictions, audience members could prepare for what might—and what ought to—happen next. This, in turn, could cue their recognition of civic responsibilities.

A political audience is different than an opinion public. Analysts of the public and its opinions suppose that citizens deliberate about the information placed before them and respond with support, apathy, or opposition. Audiences may deliberate and respond, but in the main they react. They consider the implications of the information placed before them for the values they hold dear, and express approval or scorn accordingly. If the appealing narrative qualities of Watergate transformed a significant portion of the decision-making elite and the mass populace into an audience, then what did their presence imply for the political conduct of those inside the narrative? I think the presence of a huge, intellectually adroit, and utterly enthralled audience for the story of Watergate per se accounts for some of Watergate's peculiarities as an exercise in American democracy. Before we can see the peculiar, however, we must identify the normal, and review the textbook state of institutionalized relationships in national politics before the story came about. Only if we examine the nonstory elements feeding into Watergate history, especially relations between president and press, and presidential usage of mass media, can we understand how Watergate news turned out to be as vital as it was enthralling.

WHAT MAKES NEWS "BIG"?

Big news may be defined independently of journalism in terms of financial, legal, and military significance. Much as story goodness may be assessed in terms of literary authority, momentous decisions and developments in these spheres of political activity may be construed as "big" even if they do not receive commensurate coverage by examining them through the alternative lenses of theory and history. In terms of theory and history, Watergate does not seem very big until its final stages. Nobody drowned, as conservative bumper stickers of the day proclaimed; there were no American sons on front lines, no ethnic traditions or intense ideological minorities to accommodate, a minuscule amount of per capita tax and spending dollars in the balance. Watergate sprawled across the main venues of American government while leaving the economy, society, polity, and world of nations largely untouched. This lends credence to the maximalist interpretation of Watergate as a news creation of the press and media.

Yet, if we ask—not what—but who turned Watergate into big news, in this alternative sense of who determined the direction and magnitude of the major disputes Watergate engendered, then the powers wielded by journalists diminish. President Nixon's intransigence and/or incompetence, as well as the actions of opponents to the doctrine of executive privilege that his administration put forward, placed Watergate on the national agenda, as it were. And the Watergate audience upset the president's normally overwhelming advantage in the resolution of the conflict.

Some brief and familiar history is pertinent here. Richard Nixon was, by temperament and by office, acutely susceptible to news stories. He was a prescient suitor of the personalized, supra-partisan brand of popular support that the mass media could furnish to politicians who knew how to maximize favorable publicity. He lacked the panache of his Kennedy archrivals, however, and the heroic stature of his patron, General Eisenhower. His laborious stabs at the art of courting reporters only made his comparative shortcomings in image more obvious, and his press relations more abrasive. Every politician ducks questions. The sweat and spite Richard Nixon displayed while evading his interlocutors become a motif of his public appearances. He was dubbed "Tricky Dick" even when he obtained the victories he sought.

Throughout his national career, Nixon's staff advanced his political messages in ways and formats adapted from corporate marketing, show business, and war propaganda. The strategy behind these media end runs around the press is, to use a favorite Nixonism, perfectly clear. If public relations could contrive the most prominent public descriptions of the president so that they would reflect his dual desire for democratic support and a weakened opposition, then he could propose laws, appoint and nominate federal personnel, and issue executive orders in a governing atmosphere charged positive by near-unanimous awareness that public opinion was flowing in his favor. As Nixon confided to H. R. Haldeman on April 14, 1973, he was "a proponent of the idea, buy a good headline for a day" (Lukas, 1976, p. 454). The logic that publicity facilitates governance, which every modern president has accepted and acted upon to some degree, led in Nixon's case to the compilation of an Enemies List heavily laden with media figures, the criminal activities of the Plumbers unit (established to plug information leaks), and the obfuscation of the war in Cambodia. The approach worked famously well until Watergate, which marks the historic spot where the Nixon PR machine backfired and then broke down. Only in the final year of Watergate did the Nixon publicity strategy and organization fail to compensate him politically for his bad press.

When on July 16, 1973, the nation learned of the tapes' existence, the public narrative took an incredible twist. The answers to the questions raised by this good story, were, potentially, on the confidential recordings: the proof, with a vengeance, of Nixon's devious character. These were the spoils that crystallized the political antagonisms between the Nixon administration and the Democrats and the press into an adjudicable conflict. Closure, in both the story and the nonstory senses, was now conceivable.

Public opinion polls show that the nation split into three groups, as though anticipating the differences among Special Prosecutor Archibald Cox, President Nixon, and Attorney General Elliot Richardson that would culminate in the Saturday Night Massacre. Slightly more than a third (35.5% in a September 1973 poll) saw Nixon as guilty of serious infractions of office, and wanted severe punishment. Slightly less than a third (30.4%) exonerated the president in their minds of any Watergate wrongdoing. But 33% were, in effect, keeping the crime story context and the legal conflict distinct. As a *Newsday* headline put it, they favored a verdict of "Guilty, With Three Years [the remainder of the second term] Probation" (Lang & Lang, 1983, p. 64; McGeever, 1974). This last trisection formed a swing group. Their allegiance would prove crucial to the strength of any official decisions, by any branch of government, with respect to Nixon's fate.

Meanwhile, the discovery of the taping system subverted Nixon's approach to public communications. The president now had to construct a legal argument that would withstand the strictest of scrutinies, and convince the judicial experts among the highly suspicious audience that the recordings properly belonged to him, that he retained the executive privilege of keeping them secret despite their relevance to criminal investigations. Worse, on the mass level, Nixon had to sell that argument as something other than a maneuver to hide the truth from the American people. The climax of this publicity effort, which *Newsweek* sardonically labeled "Operation Candor," occurred with the release of the tape transcripts.

The release of the transcripts is worth recounting in detail, because the events attest to the decisive role played by the audience with respect to the political fights over the tapes. The events also suggest that the influence of the press was mixed, at best, while the media industry facilitated the reaction of the audience. On April 11, 1974, the House Judiciary Committee voted 33-3 to subpoena 42 tapes—the first subpoena of a president by a House Committee in American history. Eighteen days later, Nixon spoke to a nationwide audience on live television for the 36th time in his presidency. Nixon wanted

> to tell you something about the actions I shall be taking tomorrow— about what I hope they will mean to you and about the very difficult choices that were presented to me.

Several of these actions involved publicity maneuvers. Only the Committee Chairman and ranking minority member would be permitted to listen to the tapes and state any objections to the president directly. The entire country would have the chance to read over 1300 pages of transcripts that

> include all the relevant portions of all of the subpoenaed conversations that were recorded, that is, all portions that relate to the question of what I knew about Watergate or the coverup and what I did about it.

And the press, who, along with other committee members, were in the best position to challenge Nixon's definition of "relevant portions," would receive the transcripts approximately two hours before the evening newscasts for April 30, along with a 50-page "summary statement" prepared by the president's lawyer, James St. Clair.

As Nixon spoke, viewers could see a stack of binders that contained the transcripts. The bulk of his talk provided a guide to their contents. The president reduced the questions at hand to whether John Dean's charges about his personal involvement in Watergate were true; all the rest, he said, was media rumor, insinuation, gossip, and wild accusation. (Special Prosecutor Leon Jaworski's subpoena for 64 tapes fell into this category by default.) Subsequently, Nixon answered his own question (the charges were false), referred to the personal difficulty of the move he was announcing (his own pain might spare the nation the ordeal of impeachment), described the move as an exception to the rule of executive privilege, and urged the nation to quit Watergate and return to the big political issues of the day.

Initial commentary by the national press corps bought President Nixon his desired day. Reputed members of the anti-Nixon conspiracy accepted (with conditions) the speech and the release of the transcripts as a valid response to the subpoena. R. W. Apple of the *New York Times*

and Howard K. Smith of ABC News praised Nixon's screen performance. The *Los Angeles Times* called the speech "a giant step . . . a
reasonable basis for compromise." James Reston of the *New York
Times* and the editors of the *Denver Post* deemed it reasonably effective;
if Nixon had not refuted John Dean's testimony, he yet might have
injected enough ambiguity into the record to save his second term.

But then a most unusual media event occurred: the print media
disseminated the entire 1300 pages in special newspaper supplements
and fastback books—so that millions of people could peruse the
tape/transcript contents at their convenience.[5] Led by the staunchly
Republican *Chicago Tribune*, 19 big city newspapers printed
supplements. Bantam, Dell, and Brentano's (not normally a publisher)
rushed three million paperback copies into print within a week of the
speech. (By comparison, 300,000 copies of the Tower Commission
Report were "fast-booked" at this pace during Irangate.) Consequently,
not only the press and the Congress, who could be expected to wade
through a government report, saw through Nixon's gambit, but much of
the American electorate did too, as part of the audience for the crime
story. The transcripts remained public currency well beyond Nixon's
television address, and they seemed to document all of the worse
judgments about the nature of Nixon's character. The president, or "P"
in the document, evinced much more concern for himself than for the
country, the law, or the truth. For many readers, privy to Oval Office
language for the first time, his raw calculations were shocking. The
Gallup Poll published on May 5, 1974, reported that transcript readers
came away with a less favorable opinion of Nixon by a 3:1 margin.

Nixon's support among loyal Republicans disintegrated. Representative Robert McClory, the second-ranking minority member of the
House Judiciary Committee, successfully proposed on May 2 that the
panel permit live television of its forthcoming impeachment proceedings.
This paved the way for the main spotlight of national attention to move
from the White House to Capitol Hill. On May 7, Nixon stalwart and
Senate Majority Leader Hugh Scott relayed his disapproval of White
House conduct. Two days later, the *Chicago Tribune* called upon Nixon
to resign. His character "could not stand that kind of scrutiny" that the
transcripts afforded his countrymen.

WHAT MAKES A
NEWS STORY "GREAT"?

We have ample reasons to believe that a crime story audience existed
in the minds of the president, the press, and other Washington

politicians who had information about or authority over Watergate. Both the "Firestorm" of protest after the firing of Special Prosecutor Archibald Cox in October 1973 and the tremendous popularity of the published White House tape transcripts in May of 1974 are incidental demonstrations of an audience presence. Unlike "normal" expressions of public opinion, these reactions were spontaneous, emotional, and incongruous to the party/gender/income sort of categories favored by political analysts. In the context of a received and running story, however, they made perfect sense: hisses and groans for the Saturday Night Massacre, a headlong rush for the latest and biggest installment when the transcripts appeared in store windows. As political feedback, these messages lacked the definition of election returns, poll data, campaign contributions, or even organized protest—but those involved in Watergate knew what had been said.

More generally, once substantial television ratings came in for the Ervin Committee hearings in the spring of 1973, national politicians and journalists had to assume that a Watergate story audience (generically attuned or not) existed. Because, as E. E. Schattschneider (1975, p. 244) formulated it, the extent of spectator involvement in a fight can swing its outcome from one side to the other, one's image within the story had the potential to change politics either by inspiring observers to enter the fray, and/or by discouraging participants into wavering or quitting. Audience reactions—and the lack of anticipated reactions—thus affected the morale and momentum of the contending forces. The concept of a political audience helps us understand why an American president would resign three days after the public discovery of a recorded passage of a private conversation he had had with an aide two years before. This passage was immediately and unanimously comprehended as "the smoking gun"; recognizing that sociopolitical fact left Nixon no alternatives aside from resignation or impeachment, and no additional time to stall. The story audience concept also sheds light on an unusual feature of Watergate noted by Gladys and Kurt Lang in *The Battle for Public Opinion*, the best social scientific study of the subject to date. Right after the resignation, the Langs wrote:

> Some fifteen months of apparent polarization suddenly ended without any serious political clashes or much visible dissent, without joyful demonstrations or dancing in the streets.

This "strangely muted public response" is bizarre, indeed, as a national reaction to a succession crisis. But it is the recognizable behavior of an audience to a conclusive display of shame, and of an antiaudience forced to face a painful truth. In such situations, people grow quiet, and then return to their regular affairs.

Looking at Watergate as a great news story provides us with an appreciation for the subtle contributions of the story and its audience to the conflicts that politicians attempt to calculate and manage. We need this audience awareness in order to guard against two flawed analogies underlying post-Watergate arguments that credit press and media for much of what transpired.

(1)The Watergate bookshelf is crammed with memoirs, narratives, and (videocassettes of) miniseries that either state or imply by their choice of topic that the Nixon presidency was won and lost primarily in the mass media, as a battle of publicity. Political history reduced to a contest among public relations teams and media figures sells well, in part, because of its self-referential logic. It is easy and fun to follow a description of a conflict that explains it in terms of manipulations by and of people consumers already recognize. These popular accounts appeal to a lazy cynicism, and to an American form of Schadenfreude; "Thank God I'm not merchandised, used, and discarded like a box of tissue paper."

Yet were public relations as orderly and decisive a tool of political influence as both its exponents' memoirs and its detractors' exposés can make it seem, President Nixon would have blunted the Watergate story with his release of the transcripts, his televised speech, and his proposed conditions for their consumption.[6] Instead, his failure points up an error in the analogy of political to commercial publicity. The assets publicity brings to mass communications—brand name saturation, financial muscle, and celebrity association—work in inverse proportion to the moral qualities of the product being sold. The less consumers care about the choice of product, the more susceptible they are to packaging and merchandising. Conversely, the more an audience perceives a message in terms of community values, the less likely they are to act like routine, snap-judgment consumers. And news stories, especially those continuing along the contours of a traditional genre, remind people of such values in the course of accentuating emotion.

Indeed, the sensibility associated with the detection story in particular encourages the audience to be on guard against salesmanship and hype. Sniffing out false moves is an integral satisfaction of the genre, and when political topics are implicated, resistance to publicity initiatives symbolizes personal freedom. No matter what Nixon contrived, then, his message would have been launched into an environment acutely hostile to contrivance.

(2) Quite distinct from the public relations industry, the medium of television has been cast as a *deus ex machina* in American history, used to explain such sea changes in public attitudes as the disenchantment with the Vietnam war and the hard right turn from Jimmy Carter to

Ronald Reagan. After Watergate, we read the following from leading popular historians and political scientists:

> If television gave the press a new power base, then it never showed so clearly as that night in Washington [of Nixon's resignation], when [CBS newsmen] Rather, Cronkite, and Sevareid were not so much like reporters covering a story as politicians wanting to get 51 percent of the vote. (Halberstam, 1979, p. 704)[7]

> Neither of the two great anchormen of the seventies—Walter Cronkite and John Chancellor—was entirely happy with the power that had fallen to them: the power to set up summit conferences between the Arabs and the Israelis, the power to place Watergate and Richard Nixon before the judgment of the people. (White, 1982, p. 182)

> Television is television—and television news is essentially television, too. Perhaps the one conclusion that should be drawn is that in a free society, the medium providing the major source of both news and entertainment must fundamentally influence the public, the government, and the relationship between them. (Robinson, 1977, p. 39)

> All of the ways in which the American way of government has changed since the end of World War II certainly cannot be blamed (or credited) solely or perhaps even mainly on the advent of television. But . . . the glare of television's attention has helped significantly to weaken the ability of presidents and congressmen to govern. It seems equally clear that television's relative inattention to bureaucratic politics has significantly helped the unelected officials . . . to fill the policy-making vacuum left by the declining power of the elected officials. (Ranney, 1983, p. 154-55)

The authors of these statements invest great significance in what "television" (and its personification, the network news anchorman) has done to American politics. The impulse to roll the forces of story traditions, news sources, clever publicity strategy, technological access, on-camera performance skills, and good relations with the press into one causal factor and call the whole thing "television" gathers credibility on the strength of an analogy of consumer to civic experience: surely, because everyone everywhere is seeing what I am seeing, the political implications are as uniform as the feed. But armchair interpretations of television's impact on politics can mislead. The text may be the same, but receptions may vary among members of different audiences and publics.

For instance, social science research has confirmed that the Ervin and Rodino Committee hearings, while televised extensively, did not change people's positions so much as it reinforced partisan and to some extent generational biases (Lang & Lang, 1983; McLeod et al., 1977; Robinson, 1974). These findings suggest that the political power attributed to television after Watergate rests on illusory underpinnings. And the data do not begin to account for audience perceptions, in the context of a crime story or any other suitable interpretive context.

For, as suggested above, the same Watergate information may be understood in the framework of another genre (Nixon's personal success) or a nonnarrative argument (Nixon's managerial short-comings). Other plausible and valuable contexts include

— *Sideshow.* The war in Vietnam fueled the battle over the tapes on both sides, with the Pentagon papers as the preliminary round, and the pardon of draft evaders as an answer to Nixon's pardon as the final round.

— *Carryover from the 1960s.* Hippies, new journalists, and sympathetic elders challenge established authority on principle, and Nixon responds in kind, so that what was once normal politics is now occasion for outrage.

— *Thermonuclear transference.* The cover-up grows out of emergency state or "national security" tactics, rationalized as a means to avoid atomic annihilation.

— *The imperial presidency.* The conflict reflects the growth of the presidency at the expense of the Congress and the courts, and the concomitant growth of the White House staff at the expense of the intelligence community and bureaucracies.

— *Economics.* The Committee to Re-Elect the President collected more money than legitimate politics warranted, leading to excesses. The undoing of Nixon stems from spiralling inflation and dwindling energy supplies, trends that explain why self-interested Republicans, with their constituents stuck in long lines at the gas pumps, might decide to make the most of an embarrassing but essentially trivial series of incidents.

Recalling the plethora of contexts available for Watergate interpretation raises the suspicion that vocational self-interest explains why the crime story came to dominate the pages and the airwaves. We come to the best case maximalists can offer: the press and the media foisted this particular view of Watergate upon America because it lifted investigative reporters to antiheroic heights. Don't journalists strike the muckraking pose whenever they can? Isn't this the one-in-a-million case where the pose proved unexaggerated?

Yet for all the flattery and profits journalists apparently reap by taking the crime story approach, their capacity to impose a genre, and swing stories into narrative lines advantageous to their image and then to one side of a big political fight, remains sharply limited. The multiplicity of interpretations abutting the main story line in Watergate journalism indicates that no one can exert authorial controls over news and opinion. The would-be authors in the press faced the same story-telling problems in purportedly igniting a crime-and-detection craze in American politics that the Nixon administration faced in attempting to extinguish it through the cover-up.

Bob Woodward and Carl Bernstein's book *The Final Days* and the movie version of *All the President's Men* were both released in April of 1976. This may well have marked the acme of press/media power for our time. But look at why. It was not because they were great men, so to speak. It was because customary audiences for news from Washington, Hollywood, and New York, already swelled by the political story of the century, now converged around two narrative figures—two lowly reporters turned national stars—and received simultaneously a reenactment of the story's beginning and a thorough revelation of its end. Moreover, the impact of this journalistic communion upon the policymaking capacity of the Ford administration, the 1976 elections, and the republic's sense of itself, while indubitably immense, was also simultaneous with the start of the conservative reaction against the media and the press.

The Final Days offended parts of the Watergate audience on grounds of taste and method. The book set a sales record for its publishing house (Simon & Schuster), entering the *New York Times Book Review* nonfiction list at number one; nonfiction paperback rights were soon auctioned to Avon for an unprecedented $1.55 million; but the authors were grilled on *Meet the Press* for liberties they had allegedly taken in narrating the last few weeks of the Nixon administration. In their book, Woodward and Bernstein reproduced what Nixon and the people around him had said and felt outside the public record (and off the White House tapes). Sometimes the authors used quotes, sometimes not, but there was no recognizable system of attribution in order to protect their sources from clever readers. In an explanatory preface, Woodward and Bernstein claimed every detail they included in the text had at least two reliable sources behind it ("reliable" meaning non-self-serving, in the reporters' judgment, and often documented in logs or notes). Where a meeting was not possible to reconstruct through the recollections of participants, the reporters turned to descriptions from people who saw the participants just after the meeting in question. One such meeting, many commentators presumed, depicted the president asking Henry Kissinger to get down on his knees and join him in prayer. It was hard to believe that Kissinger would relate such an embarrassing anecdote to the reporters, whereas Nixon had not granted them an interview. Woodward and Bernstein also revealed that the president had kept yet another set of tapes, a Dictabelt diary of intimate confessions and stray expressions of feeling.

Nixon's sons-in-law, David Eisenhower and Edward Cox, formally denied telling the *Post* reporters, among other things, that they had feared the president would commit suicide. Apart from their pointed disclaimers, however, immediate objections to *The Final Days* dealt with its lack of tact, not its credibility.

These scenes of the presidency jarred the role that institutional custom and decades of inspirational prose had created for the nation's leader. Yet once the Woodward and Bernstein accounts passed muster, they compelled acknowledgment in the discourse of the day. The story was true beyond disputation, and everyone in the republic knew it. No greater power travels through the news media. As Hannah Arendt (1977, p. 241) wrote in her essay about "Truth in Politics":

> Unwelcome opinion can be argued with, rejected, or compromised upon, but unwelcome facts possess an infuriating stubbornness that nothing can move except plain lies.

Thus, even as the story passed muster with the audience, the gauntlet the reporters had to run exposed the limits, and the largely symbolic nature, of press and media power. Speakers and writers in journalism are denied story-telling freedoms exercised in diaries, gossip, novels, and dramas. These constraints look fuzzy on paper, because they operate essentially as social conventions, but they are no less effective for being nebulous in description. The major barrier to a clean and unified narrative in journalism resides in the community's commitment to accuracy. Not every item we encounter will prove accurate, but that quality is uppermost on our minds when we talk and listen along news channels. A good story may incline us, like the sultan listening to Scheherazade, to suspend plans for action. We may even suspend some of our values as we go along with those advanced by the narrator. But we will cling to disbelief. What we come across in journalism must appease our sense of verifiability, or credibility. We would rather have reporters admit they have heard conflicting accounts, or were unable to confirm a source, or cannot be sure about what some event means, than have our sense of microcosmic truth violated by palpable claims of artistic license.[8]

Beyond the preeminent assumption of factuality, which limits journalistic story-telling through self-censorship, stylistic conventions moderate the use of narrative devices. For example, we don't like roles drawn and character imputed through interior monologues and unrecorded dialogues. The inner life of an individual has been construed off-limits to writers of hard news and opinion stories; and while language about emotions may be included in soft news profiles and features, excerpts from memoirs, and impressionistic or first-person essays, such works ought to be separated by time period and journal location from stories about political action. As a result, love enters journalism only when lovers have quarreled in court, or, as with King Edward VII, when love has been declared the reason for an action. This respect for privacy has been policed by (the threat of) libel suits, the objectivity movement in the profession, and by press criticism that becomes news.

We find ourselves in the middle of a great news story whenever politically momentous events gain additional momentum from the emotions stirred by their narration in journalism. Who moves, and who is so moved? The eddies of story power may be studied outward from the news narrative texts, in concentric circles of influence: nearest the center, the newsmakers depicted as characters in the story; then others with relevant financial, legal, military, and literary authority as potential sources, narrators, and new characters in the next installment; then good storytellers in the press and adept purveyors of the story in the media industry, as clearinghouses and symbolic targets for critics; then greatly interested publics, as expressers of opinion; then the inactive but interested masses in receipt of the story, who await the next installment; and finally the inactive and uninterested masses, who wish the entire story would disappear, yet must concede, as members of the community, that the story merits coverage until closure is achieved. Each of these circles is a part of the story audience. Like the distribution of wealth, the territorial boundaries of states, and the laws of the land, politicians involved in conflicts ignore the shapes and trends of audience awareness at their peril. The story is a political fact of life, with potentially great consequences.

NOTES

1. The author thanks Everette E. Dennis, Stephen F. Graubard, Richard E. Neustadt, Michael Schudson, Julie Talen, and Ronald Weber for comments on earlier drafts—of which there have been many—of this chapter. The Gannett Center for Media Studies provided invaluable resources toward the chapter's completion.

2. I court trouble in branding Irangate as a less interesting story than Watergate before it is over. Still, a Times-Mirror survey in early 1987 found that only 20% of Americans were paying close attention to the arms-for-hostages affair (Barnes, 1987).

3. This vivid metaphor, countering the crime story context with the image of lethal destruction, was coined by Nixon aide Alexander Haig.

4. K. and G. E. Lang (1983, p. 49) define this term as front-page or one-minute coverage for at least four of five successive days, and/or for three days in a row.

5. See *Editor and Publisher*, May 11, 1974; *Publisher's Weekly,* May 13 and May 20, 1974. National Public Radio and NBC staged readings, but in this era before video recorders, the diffusion by television could not have been as great as by print.

6. Defenders of the prowess of political marketing could rejoin that the president miscalculated, that better alternatives were open to him, such as burning the tapes or a ritual contrition. The poor strategy explanation for Watergate, however, requires more evidence than we currently have about the president's assumptions and intentions, and fails to specify what it was about Watergate in particular that stymied an otherwise shrewd media manipulator.

7. In his conclusion, Halberstam made it clear that he believed media executives, not the news figures, inherited the real power.

8. Yes, we may be fooled by a news account—but not willingly so, as when we attend magic shows and movies. Tell consumers of docudrama—*Washington: Behind Closed Doors* or *Blind Ambition*—that this scene never really happened, or that that character is a composite of four people, and there will be interest, but no outrage. We associate the form of the docudrama with entertainment, and when we are entertained we tolerate the exploitation of history. But when we learn that an elision appeared in a regular news slot, with neither a qualificatory preface nor an obvious sign of spoof or satire, we will blame the producers.

REFERENCES

Adler, R. (1976, December). Searching for the real Nixon scandal. *Atlantic.*
Anderson, P. (1968). *The president's men.* Garden City, NY: Doubleday.
Arendt, H. (1977). *Between past and future.* New York: Penguin.
Barnes, F. (1987, March). Over-reported, under-read. *Washington Journalism Review.*
Bernstein, C., & Woodward, B. (1974). *All the president's men.* New York: Simon & Schuster.
Carter, J. (1982). *Keeping faith.* Toronto: Bantam Books.
Cronin, T. E. (1980). *The state of the presidency.* Boston: Little, Brown.
Cutler, L. (1984, Fall). Foreign policy on deadline. *Foreign Affairs.*
Diamond, E. (1975). *The tin kazoo.* Cambridge: M.I.T. Press.
Drew, E. (1975). *Washington journal: The events of 1973-1974.* New York: Random House.
Epstein, E. J. (1975). *Between fact and fiction: The problem of journalism.* New York: Vintage.
Epstein, E. J., & Berendt, J. (1973, November). Did there come a point in time when there were 43 different theories of how Watergate happened? *Esquire.*
Forster, E. M. (1927). *Aspects of the novel.* New York: Harcourt, Brace and World.
Gallup, G. H. (1978). *The Gallup Poll: Public opinion 1972-1977.* Wilmington, DE: Scholarly Resources.
Grossman, M. B., & Kumar, M. J. (1981). *Portraying the president: The White House and the news media.* Baltimore: Johns Hopkins University Press.
Halberstam, D. (1979). *The powers that be.* New York: Knopf.
Hersey, J. (Ed.). (1974). *The writer's craft.* New York: Knopf.
Kennedy School of Government [Harvard University]. (1977). *The Saturday Night Massacre* (case 14-77-150).

Kissinger, H. (1982). *Years of upheaval.* Boston: Little, Brown.

Knappman, E. W. (Ed.). (1973, 1974). *Watergate and the White House* (Vols. 1-3). New York: Facts on File.

Kraft, J. (1981, May). The imperial media. *Commentary.*

Lang, G. E., & Lang, K. (1983). *The battle for public opinion: The president, the press, and the polls during Watergate.* New York: Columbia University Press.

Lichter, S. R., Rothman, S., & Lichter, L. S. (1986). *The media elite.* New York: Adler & Adler.

Lukas, J. A. (1976). *Nightmare: The underside of the Nixon years.* New York: Viking.

Magruder, J. S. (1974). *An American life.* New York: Athaneum.

Marcus, S. (1974). "Introduction." In *The Continental Op* (stories by Dashiell Hammett). New York: Vintage.

Martin, W. (1986). *Recent theories of narrative.* Ithaca, NY: Cornell University Press.

McCartney, J. (1973, July-August). The Washington *Post* and Watergate: How two Davids slew Goliath. *Columbia Journalism Review.*

McGeever, P. J. (1974). Guilty, yes; impeachment, no. *Political Science Quarterly*, pp. 289-299.

McLeod, J. M. et al. (1977, January). Decline and fall at the White House: A longitudinal analysis of communication effects. *Communication Research.*

Nixon, President, R. M. (1974). Submission of Recorded Presidential Conversations to the Committee on the Judiciary of the House of Representatives by President Richard Nixon, April 30, 1974 (The White House Transcripts). Washington, DC: Government Printing Office.

Nixon, R. M. (1978). *RN: The memoirs of Richard Nixon.* New York: Grosset & Dunlap.

O'Neill, M. J. (1982, May 6). A newspaper editor looks at the press. *Wall Street Journal.*

Ranney, A. (1983). *Channels of power.* New York: Basic Books.

Rather, D., & Gates, G. P. (1974). *The palace guard.* New York: Harper & Row.

Robinson, M. J. (1974, Spring). Impact of the televised Watergate hearings. *Journal of Communication.*

Robinson, M. J. (1977, Summer). Television and American politics, 1956-1976. *The Public Interest.*

Safire, W. (1980). *Safire's political dictionary.* New York: Ballantine.

Schattschneider, E. E. (1975). *The semisovereign people: A realist's view of democracy.* Hinsdale, IL: Dryden.

Schell, J. (1975, June 2). The time of illusion: I. *New Yorker.*

Schorr, D. (1977). *Clearing the air.* Boston: Houghton Mifflin.

Seymour-Ure, C. (1982). *The American president: Power and communication.* New York: St. Martin.

United States House of Representatives. (1974). 93rd Congress, 2nd Session. Committee on the Judiciary. *Impeachment of Richard M. Nixon, President of the United States* (Report No. 93-13055). Washington, DC: Government Printing Office.

Weaver, D. H., McCombs, M. E., & Spellman, C. (1975). Watergate and the media: A case study of agenda-setting. *American Politics Quarterly*, pp. 452-472.

White, T. H. (1975). *Breach of faith.* New York: Athaneum.

White, T. H. (1982). *America in search of itself: The making of the president, 1956-1980.* New York: Harper & Row.

Wildwood Productions. (1976). *All the president's men* [Film].

Wills, G. (1971). *Nixon Agonistes: The crisis of the self-made man.* New York: Mentor.

Woodward, B., & Bernstein, C. (1976). *The final days.* New York: Simon & Schuster.

Chapter 10

ON JOURNALISTIC AUTHORITY
The Janet Cooke Scandal

David L. Eason

FIVE YEARS AGO, A PULITZER PRIZE for journalism was returned for the only time in the 69-year history of the awards. Janet Cooke, a young, black reporter for the *Washington Post*, forfeited the prize for feature writing after it was revealed that the subject of her story, an eight-year-old heroin user named Jimmy, was a fabrication. It was neither the first nor the last fake story in the history of journalism but it was one of the most, if not the most, publicized inventions. There were some obvious reasons for this. The fabrication occurred in an age when the machinery of publicity is very extensive. It was revealed after the awarding of journalism's most coveted award. It occurred at one of the nation's leading newspapers, a newspaper that played a vital role in the events leading to the only resignation of an American president and a newspaper that through Watergate has come to symbolize aggressive, hard-boiled reporting. The spotlight on the newspaper was intense, and the *Post* made it more so by publishing its own account of how the fabrication passed from a reporter with little experience through the hands of its editors into the pages of the *Post* and, despite doubts and criticism from its readers and staff members, into the Pulitzer Prize contest. Janet Cooke and her creation, "Jimmy's World," quickly became a part of the folklore of journalism and ideological tokens in discussions of the news media.

The scandal surrounding "Jimmy's World" challenged the Watergate image of reporting that dominated popular culture in the 1970s. The

AUTHOR'S NOTE: From David L. Eason, "On Journalistic Authority: The Janet Cooke Scandal," in *Critical Studies in Mass Communication*, Vol. 3, pp. 429-447. © 1986 Speech Communication Association. Reprinted by permission.

Post account described a bureaucratic kingdom where editors and reporters vied for territory and status, often the same thing. Because the conventions of news routinely ban the discussion of the reporter's relationship to sources, institutional structure, and narrative conventions, the description of the process of story creation, selection, editing, and display opened up areas of the news process for public scrutiny.[1] The report, written by Ombudsman Bill Green, deemphasized the structural dimensions of news production and reflected "an unremitting home team psychology" (Boylan, 1981, p. 29), but it also humanized what for most of us are the alien processes of news-making by describing petty squabbles among the employees and personalizing the chain of command. More important, the Cooke scandal provided an occasion for journalists to reflect publicly on the social and cultural process whereby their accounts gain authority in society. This discussion took the form of a consideration of the changes that occurred within journalism in the 1960s and early 1970s. Like much of the rest of the country in the 1980s, journalists were still trying to make their peace with changes wrought by the period that for convenience sake we call the 1960s.

Janet Cooke and Jimmy functioned largely to organize what they were not, the boundaries of the permissible in journalism.[2] One a fictional being, the other an actual person, they shared a condition of otherness that for a short time made a profession real to itself. In one sense, the symbolic drama that surrounded them tells little about the authority to separate fact and fiction in news. No one stepped forward to defend Cooke, and no one defended the use of composite characters and fictionalized dialogue in reporting. Cooke crossed the boundary between fact and fiction, not only by creating a fake story but also by changing her own biography to create a false identity. The violation was taken to be so extreme that it did not inspire much reflection on the boundary where what we call facts and fictions grows hazy. Boundaries after all are ambiguous places, liminal zones made from the two sectors they divide. While boundaries take from both sectors, they belong to neither. To live continually on a boundary, whether experiential or material, is to live in a realm where, at worst, war and madness are common enemies, and where, at best, certainty is precarious. We try to avoid long periods in such realms. We build our houses in the middle of lots, throw water on our faces to emerge from the realm of half sleep and secure our own views of the facts by connecting with others who share them. In reflecting publicly on the Janet Cooke scandal, only an occasional journalist went near the boundary of fact and fiction to reflect for long on the role of language, narrative, values, ideology, or the interrelationship of institutions in the creation of news.

The commentary built a high wall well inside the boundary, enclosed within it a community of believers, and celebrated its oneness in disapproving of Cooke's violation. There were signs, however, that the veteran editors and writers who wrote the commentary doubted the reality of the united profession they portrayed. The commentary celebrated oneness in the abstract, but, in detail, divided the profession between the older members who held the journalistic tradition as sacred and the newer members whose allegiance to the traditional was suspect. Janet Cooke, young, female, and black, personified the ideas of the newer members, ideas that in the eyes of the veterans had to be controlled if the boundary between fact and fiction was to remain meaningful and the status of those who maintained the boundary was to remain secure.

In this essay, I will reflect on the boundary between fact and fiction with respect to the authority that maintains it. I do not take "facts" and "fictions" to be givens that we all recognize but rather the product of interpretive communities whose work is the making of the two categories and explaining how they interrelate. "Facts" and "fictions," like other cultural categories, are the result of social and symbolic processes that publicize, authorize, and legitimize the reality of a group.[3] The history of journalism is, in part, that of establishing, repairing, and transforming the authoritative base for accounts of "the way it is." As the work of Davis (1983), Schudson (1978), Schiller (1981), and others has shown, this history has often involved dramatic conflicts over the nature of facts and the authority that sustains them.

Journalists always enjoy a precarious authority with their readers. In the most stable of times, their accounts are frequently challenged. The last two decades, however, have produced sustained attacks on the very process whereby the facts of news are produced, attacks that question the legitimacy of the news media as a democratic forum. At stake has been not just the truth of a report on a particular event or issue but the role of the press in creating our political culture, a culture, most critics agree, that falls far short of our democratic ideals. Conservative critics argue that the media play a major role in the undermining of the authority of the state and business through a contrary stance and by giving legitimacy to oppositional groups. Leftist critics counter that the interests of the media are synonymous with those of other powerful institutions in society and that news media work maintains the control of these institutions. This debate has generated a body of critical studies that shows news to be a way of understanding the social world that reflects the values, routines, and conventions of journalists.[4] "Objectivity," once an important term in assessments of the news, has become a controversial standard. The term appeared rarely in the aftermath of the Janet Cooke scandal and usually to point out the gap between the ideal and the reality of news. Although the word *objectivity* had gone underground, ideas associated with the word lingered on in other guises. The scarcity of the term suggests that the Janet Cooke scandal provided a forum for journalists to consider their own authority at a time when objectivity was increasingly questioned as a cultural ideal but remained entrenched as a set of institutional practices. Making sense of Janet Cooke involved coming to terms with a history that had eroded a way of speaking about news but had made only slight impact on the way news was produced.

"JIMMY'S WORLD": THE BACKGROUND

On September 28, 1980, a Sunday, the *Washington Post* published a front-page story (Cooke, 1980) that told of the life of Jimmy, an eight-year-old user of heroin in one of Washington's black ghettos. The story, designed to draw attention to the heroin problem in the city, was formally an unexceptional human interest story. It laced the specifics of Jimmy's life with more general comments by experts about young people and drugs in the Washington area. Some of the content, however, was startling and the ending particularly so. The story's climax described Jimmy being injected with a syringe of heroin by his mother's lover, and accompanying artwork visualized the scene.

The week-long media event that followed the article focused on the conflicting authority of the newspaper and city government. Against an alarmed public that saw Jimmy not as a symbol of the drug problem but as an actual person and a city government that interpreted the article as an attack on its policies, the *Post* defended its own authority to print the news and not reveal its sources under the First Amendment. The *Post*, its attorneys, columnists, and editorial writers argued, had not only the authority but the duty to print the news and had performed its obligations as a demonstration of its concern for the community. Jimmy was not the *Post*'s creation but the creation of an incompetent city government and an apathetic public.[5] The city threatened to subpoena *Post* staff members but took no action, and the morality play ended as abruptly as it began.

The story resurfaced on April 14, 1981, when the *Post* announced in a front-page story that Janet Cooke had won the Pulitzer Prize for feature writing for "Jimmy's World." Two days later, the *Post* (Maraniss, 1981, p. A1) reported the discovery of the fabrication, the forfeiting of the prize, and the resignation of Janet Cooke. Benjamin Bradlee, the editor of the newspaper, apologized to the mayor of the city, and a *Post* editorial, "The End of Jimmy's World" (p. A18), apologized to its readers and promised a full investigation. On Sunday, April 19, the *Post* published its account of the fabrication, a two-and-a-half page story by Bill Green (April 19, 1981, pp. A12-A14), the ombudsman of the newspaper. Green's account told of the hiring of Cooke, her status as a reporter within the newspaper, the origins of the story idea, the writing of the story, the editorial process through which it passed, the controversy that occurred after its publication, the review process that led to its nomination for the Pulitzer Prize, and the actions that led to Cooke's confession.

Two days before the *Post* story appeared, the *Wall Street Journal* had published its own report ("Capital Offense," April 17, 1981, p. 1) on the scandal. The *Journal* story raised the questions that were to be debated repeatedly in the discussion of "Jimmy's World." "To what extent," the *Journal* asked,

> do the pressures facing big-city papers to recruit and promote promising minorities cloud the initial hiring procedures as well as the decisions as to which of their stories should be published? Are the competitive pressures of big-city newsrooms such that style and form are overtaking substance? Are editors tough enough? And to what extent will the media in general— not to mention the *Post* itself—be tarnished in their efforts to maintain public trust?

The *Journal* questions pulled up some of the seams that divided journalists: racial and gender identified minorities versus a white male majority, editors versus reporters, and individual goals versus institutional responsibility.

The scandal revealed the foundation of the news process to be a trust that sustains the authority to determine the facts. In the wake of the scandal, journalists did not retreat to the claim that the facts speak for themselves. Clearly, something other than facts had spoken here, and professional journalists, including the distinguished Pulitzer Prize panel, had believed them. Against the habits of news reading that transform conventions into facts, "Jimmy's World" asserted that facts are produced by consensus and that the consensus may be grounded in little more than the fit between style and expectation. The ties that bind together reporters and editors into a professional group and bind that group to its public are not facts, as Walter Lippmann recognized a half century ago, but conventions that signify certain rules were followed in the production of a report. "Jimmy's World" revealed a breach of trust among those authorized to report the news, a rupture, journalists feared, that would be exaggerated by an already skeptical public.

The questions raised by the scandal focused on the trust that sustains authority. Do newspapers trust minorities too much? Does competition among reporters pressure them to betray the trust put in them? Do editors trust reporters too much? Will newspapers be able to maintain the public trust? Exploring these questions sent journalists sifting through their recent past. When, they asked, had things begun to go wrong? They found the answer in the late 1960s and early 1970s.

JOURNALISTS: A COMMUNITY OF BELIEVERS

Journalists felt "assaulted," "humiliated," "befouled," "shattered, betrayed, angry and sad," in the wake of the scandal. Grieving, they "fought back tears" in a newsroom the "demonic" Janet Cooke and her creation Jimmy "haunted."[6] The dark mood lingered. Two months after the revelation, the president of the Investigative Reporters and Editors (Stein, July 11, 1981, p. 16) bemoaned, "The evil will not die down."

In a column in the *Post*, Judy Mann (April 17, 1981, p. B1) gave voice to the nature of the community that had been ruptured:

> The business and what it stands for is, to many of us, about as close as we come to having a religion. . . . Whether it is our particular job to cover local government, a foreign war, a cocktail party or a sports event, we are bound together by a common love of truth and the unspoken belief that truth will keep us free.

Held together by intentions and beliefs, the community requires trust in order to survive. As stated by Mann:

> Ours is a business based on trust and it is a tribute to our own faith in the way newspapers work that we trusted an extraordinary story by a colleague. The betrayal of our profession, the violation of truth, hurts professionally and it hurts personally. But for many of us, we are coming out of this with something of enduring value. We never knew just how deeply we care. (p. B1)

Much of the commentary focused on the violation of trust. Ellen Goodman (April 22, 1981, p. A23) reflected on the meaning of the violation for a profession with "only one credential: our credibility." "This is a society running short on trust," she wrote. "Most journalists deal with this fact every day. We're assigned the role of public trustee. . . .

So, we are all affected by any single reporter who fuels the public wonder: Is this true? Do I believe them? . . . It makes our jobs harder, it makes our lives harder. We feel it." Richard Cohen (April 19, 1981, p. D1) saw unjustified trust emerging from the need to believe in a society of strangers. "These lies work because people want to believe them. If you believe the stranger is a rainmaker, it's your fault. You fall in love and find out your wife had 17 husbands, it's your fault. You want too much to believe." The *Post*, however, was no stranger to its readers and could only deceive them because it had deceived itself. "After all," Cohen concluded, "we might have fooled the reader—but not until we fooled ourselves" (p. D1).

The picture that emerges from much of the writing on Janet Cooke is of a unified community of journalists betrayed by a person *Post* editor Benjamin Bradlee referred to as a "pathological liar," but there is another picture as well.[7] This one shows a community segmented by race, age, gender, and assumptions about the process of reporting.

TRADITION AND CHANGE:
A DIVIDED COMMUNITY

While journalists failed to articulate the unified community's history, they were less causal with that of the segmented community. They found its origins in the social changes of the 1960s and 1970s. In the picture of the divided community, Janet Cooke became a representative figure who personified changes in journalism during that period. She symbolized, on the one hand, issues related to the increased presence of minorities in the profession, and, on the other, changes in reporting routines and conventions.

JANET COOKE'S BLACKNESS

No attribute of Janet Cooke's received as much attention as her race in discussions of the scandal. Although it was generally pointed out that she was a young, attractive, charming woman, it was her race that captured the imagination of the commentators. There were, for instance, no gender-based interpretations of the scandal, but there were a number of racial interpretations. These analyses focused on the merits of affirmative action programs, the pressures on minorities in organizations dominated by whites, and the effect of black-white relations within the newspaper on the reporting of black affairs. On occasion, the place of women in newspapers was treated, but it was usually subsumed to more extended interpretations of race.

The *Wall Street Journal* ("Capital Offense," April 17, 1981, p. 19) raised the issue of minority recruitment and questioned *Post* editor Benjamin Bradlee about it. The *Journal* reported that Bradlee "concedes that there is pressure to hire women and blacks but says that 'we're past the stage in the struggle where we've changed standards.'" In the *Post* ombudsman's report (April 19, 1981, p. A14), Green acknowledged that minority recruitment had played some part in the episode. "Did race have anything to do with Cooke's ascendancy?" he asked. "Did she get choice assignments and move up because she was handsome and black? Was she employed for the same reason?" In answering his own questions, Green acknowledged, "There's some yes and some I-don't-know in any honest answer." Although Green maintained that race was minor when compared with other factors, some reporters felt accused and responded.

On April 18, 1981, Dorothy Gilliam (p. B1), in a column entitled "Janet Cooke: Journalist Who Happens To Be Black," took issue with the belief that Cooke's race had played a major role in the scandal. Gilliam argued that the "coded messages" of the scandal were that "blacks are brought into journalism unchecked" because of the pressure to hire them and that "Cooke's stunning looks have helped to pave her path in journalism." Gilliam countered the claims by arguing that competitiveness for positions was so intense that only "SuperBlacks" were hired and that Janet Cooke was a marvelous reporter. Acknowledging that blacks felt "hurt and used by the whole Cooke affair," Gilliam argued that the "taint (of the affair) is inclusive for all journalists, not just black journalists."

Eight days later, the *Post* published another column on the racial issue, this one (April 26, 1981, p. C1) by Herbert H. Denton, a black member of the national staff. Denton took exception to comments by white reporters on a television show that her editors believed Cooke because black Washington was "an unknown world" to the white editors. The idea that only blacks could cover black issues adequately, Denton argued, was "a mythology that many black journalists created in the 60s" and the idea "long ago went the way of the dashiki for all but a lingering fringe of blacks in this business." Newspapers hired black journalists in the 1980s, Denton argued, "simply because they are first-rate journalists."[8]

If it seemed in April that some journalists were too defensive on the race issue, by the end of the summer it was obvious they were not. Writing in *U.S. News and World Report*, James Michener (May 4, 1981,

p. 79) concluded that Cooke's status as a "twofer"—a black and a woman whom "management could cite twice in claiming it does not practice discrimination"—had led to her background not being checked thoroughly and suggested that it was possible "her stories were handled with more tenderness than would have otherwise been the case." The case could not be interpreted properly without acknowledging its implications for blacks and women, and he concluded that "the damage Miss Cooke has done to black and women reporters is incalculable." In *Commentary*, Naomi Munson (1981, p. 49) mixed an analysis of Cooke's career with affirmative action war stories from her 10 years in news—stories of blacks who couldn't be fired until another black was found and of incompetent journalists who were praised because they were "about the best to be hoped for" by a white majority. Munson supplied another set of answers to Green's questions about the importance of Cooke's color. Cooke, she argued, was "hired easily and quickly because she was black . . . was fostered and promoted, despite her problem with truth-stretching because she was black . . . and won her Pulitzer because she was black" (p. 49).

More sophisticated reflections on race relations within the news media focused on the predicament of middle-class black reporters as mediators between a predominantly white management and audience, and a black ghetto underclass. These arguments placed the racial issue within concern about social structure. Writing in the *Columbia Journalism Review*, C. Gerald Fraser (July/August, 1981, pp. 35-36), a black reporter for the *New York Times*, argued that journalist rules did not matter much when reporting about "people who have no status." "Fantasies about black people can be passed off as journalism because in the nations' newsroom very few facts are known about black people and because black people don't matter much." The *New Republic* ("Deep Throat's Children," May 2, 1981, p. 10) agreed that the Janet Cooke episode had occurred because the ghetto was for the *Post*'s ruling hierarchy "as exotic and remote a place as the furthest corner of the third world." The issue, however, was not race but exoticism, and the checks of the story "would have been the same if Jimmy has been a white kid from Appalachia." The magazine argued that "we are prepared to believe both the worst and the best about unknown regions anywhere, virtually on faith."

In the *National Review*, Richard Brookhiser (August 21, 1981, pp. 964-969) used a similar argument but emphasized why the story was produced. White liberals, Brookhiser argued, want tales of black misery and despair. Black middle-class reporters, in white mythology familiar with "life in the streets," are placed in the position of delivering the tales.

White liberals believe the stories because they are the stories they expect to be there. "Jimmy's World" is the inevitable result.

Those who saw the Janet Cooke scandal as a racial story questioned the legitimacy of black reporting. Sometimes this was done simply and crudely, as when the case was used for a springboard to attack affirmative action programs. Other commentators raised the more complex issue of the various community and professional authorities "internalized" by the black reporter. In this view, the black reporter was a site where the voice of her or his own past and community vied with the voices of the newspaper institution. To be successful as journalists, black reporters had to report—and imagine—the negative aspects of black life in order to fulfill white political and social fantasies. This was not a perspective found only among white conservatives. C. Gerald Fraser (1981, p. 35), reflecting on recent history, saw the emergence of blacks in the profession as a product of white fears following the urban riots of the 1960s. "Now that the disorders have subsided," he wrote, "the black reporter is less useful. To get somewhere today, he must not only be considered 'objective' but must prove his objectivity by reporting on the negative aspects of black life."

The racial dimension of the scandal raised questions about the relationship of the institutional world of the newspaper to the other worlds that make up a complex urban society and about the identities of those who move among these different worlds. The social conflicts of the 1960s and 1970s had increased awareness of the lines of difference and promoted new ones. They also stimulated curiosity about life in those other segments. Journalists fed this curiosity, becoming, as the *Columbia Journalism Review* ("Exploring Jimmy's World," July/August, 1981, p. 28) pointed out, amateur anthropologists.

The heightened awareness of the relativity of cultural worlds created a wealth of stories for journalists, but it also made their activity problematic in new ways. Subcultural groups demanded the right to define their own experience, and journalists, confronting these demands, had to face new questions. Could the white reporter understand the cultural reality of the blacks? Could the male reporter understand the experience of a woman? Could the middle-class person understand what it was to be poor? Could the old understand the young? Some of the new amateur anthropologists probed the problem of authority in self-conscious reports.[9] More typically, the problem was resolved by assigning black or women reporters to cover black or women's affairs. "Jimmy's World" was such a case. Herbert Denton's protests to the contrary, there is enough evidence to suggest that the white upper-level editors at the *Post* did defer to Cooke and her black editor Milton Coleman because they were black, that in their estimation color was more important than class as a determinant of their knowledge of "life in the streets." While such deferments are common in a pluralistic world, what they often ignore, as they did here, is that identities and knowledge emerge in socioeconomic worlds, not merely racial worlds.

When objectivity was more binding as a cultural ideal in journalism, reporters could tell themselves that the goal of reporting was to transcend racial and socioeconomic background to see the event as any reporter would see it. Although a casual examination of the history of the press in this country will reveal the inadequacies of this conception for understanding what the press did in a given case, it did furnish the reporter with a language for rationalizing personal feelings and defending the report. The unraveling of the social fabric has called attention to the relativity of perspectives for determining what was going on in a given situation. This awareness, along with an undermining of trust in authority, produced not a radical change in journalism but a contradictory mode of operating that clung to remnants of the idea of objectivity mingled with a new cultural relativism. Minority reporters were expected to see the world as other reporters would see it in some instances and to see it as minority representatives in others. They simultaneously were expected to reflect the middle-class values their professional status provided while understanding a black culture of poverty of which they may or may not ever have been a part, but from which they were now distanced by income, education, and status.

The 1960s and 1970s had undermined the authority of the newspapers dominated by white middle-class men with certain segments of society. Despite criticism from these sectors, the structure of the news report reflected only an occasional deference to subcultural realities, and the position of the newspaper within the social structure and the role of the journalist remained largely unchanged. Those within the newspaper, as well as those without (Marx, 1980), experienced the contradictions between a culture celebrating subcultural difference and individual liberation and a social structure where institutional practices and role relationships remained inflexible.[10] While news thrived on the culture of difference, the institutional and organizational frameworks through which the news was presented changed little. In a nation where most cities are dominated by one newspaper or one-company newspapers, a relativistic journalism seemed impossible to imagine for both journalists and readers. Newspapers continued to present "the facts" and, when unchallenged, were able to believe that their accounts were binding.

Although reader disenchantment increased, objectivity—named or unnamed—remained the main norm for rejecting reports. Positioned in society to provide authoritative consensual accounts of events, newspaper accounts became as suspect as those authorities they legitimized and delegitimized. In the aftermath of the Janet Cooke scandal, some journalists struggled to name the contradictions involved in providing consensual images of a conflicted society. The majority, however, focused on changes in journalistic techniques that had gone too far and sought refuge in a nostalgic interpretation of the journalistic past. Although the attraction for a simpler context for journalism did not focus on racial and gender issues, it did recall a time as preferable when such questions could be ignored.

ROUTINES AND CONVENTIONS: TURNING BACK THE CLOCK

After the scandal, much attention was focused on changes in the use of sources and the writing of reports, changes commentators saw emerging in the 1960s. Although sometimes only implicitly and at other times in underdeveloped ways, all of the commentaries related these changes to the problem of authority in journalism. *Newsweek* ("A Searching of Conscience," May 4, 1981, p. 51) made the problem explicit:

> In Vietnam, journalists found themselves challenging their own government's statements—and Watergate became an all-out adversary story. The *Washington Post's* tenacity in the Watergate chase embarrassed, then inspired the rest of the news media. When the dust finally settled, journalists began to see themselves as heroes—guardians of truth and morality in a corrupt society.

Out of this context, two submerged traditions in reporting, literary and investigative journalism, became more prominent (Schudson, 1978, pp. 187-190). The first tradition, associated in the scandal with the New Journalism of Tom Wolfe, Truman Capote, Gay Talese, Norman Mailer, and Gail Sheehy, claimed the authority of a higher truth for journalism and grounded that claim in the aesthetic transformation of depth experience. The second, associated with the reporting of Bob Woodward and Carl Bernstein, challenged the authoritative claims of government and other powerful institutions through the collection of facts from public records and dissatisfied institutional workers who usually remained, like "Deep Throat," anonymous sources. In each case, the claims to truth were often less dependent on verification than upon the reputation of the reporter.

The Janet Cooke scandal actually had very little to do with the New Journalism. "Jimmy's World" was a traditional human interest story based on anonymous sources. Although, in her confession, she did suggest that Jimmy was a composite character created from a variety of details she had collected, it seemed obvious to most critics that an eight-year-old heroin user was so exceptional that he could hardly be justified as representative of a life-style in the way that Gail Sheehy (1973) had justified her character "Red Pants" as reflecting the life of a prostitute. Nonetheless, the literary techniques of the New Journalism were criticized almost as often as the unnamed sources of investigative reporting. The predominant thrust of this commentary—so predominant that few alternative conceptualizations were published— was that journalism had lost its way in the 1960s and 1970s and that it needed to turn away from these new practices and reconnect with the better traditions of its history.

The version of journalism history that emerged from these reflections was a highly romanticized one, the story of a profession that until recently had gotten better and better. Peopled by legendary figures such as Boss Clarke of the *New York Sun* around the turn of the century and Homar Bigart and Eddie Folliard from the postwar period, journalism after 150 years of progress had recently lost its way. Occasionally, a different interpretation was offered. *Newsweek* ("A Searching of Conscience," May 4, 1981, p. 51), for instance, pointed out that "U.S. journalism as a whole didn't really start to get respectable until the 1940s and 1950s" and quoted David Halberstam's remembrance that "the journalism I went into in the mid-1950s was a sort of dark corridor where only screw-ups went." Such interpretations, however, were rare. Far more characteristic was the column by Haynes Johnson (April 19, 1981, p. A3) that the *Washington Post* printed on the day of the ombudsman's report. Arguing that the Janet Cooke affair had "left a grievous open wound that would be long in healing and never, I believe, forgotten." Johnson reflected on how a tradition for skeptical reporting that had progressed from the circulation-building hoaxes of newspapers in the 1930s to the hard-edged skeptical figures such as Boss Clarke, an editor around the turn of the century, to the highly educated young journalists of the present had fallen on such hard times. The central figure in Johnson's tale was Clarke, "the grizzled night editor" of the *New York Sun* at the time of the San Francisco earthquake. As news from the quake came across the wires, Johnson wrote, Clarke "quietly made the rounds of his editors."

He wanted to make sure they kept all unchecked rumors reported from the scene out of the paper. "You can be sure we'll get the one that says looters are cutting off the fingers of the dead women to get their rings," he told them. "I've been spiking the canard ever since the Johnstown flood."

Scarcely an hour later, he sidled up to his editors with a flimsy of telegraph copy from one of his reporters in San Francisco.

"Thar she be," he said, waving the report about looters cutting off women's fingers to get rings. Then with a flourish, he spiked it. (p. A3)

Boss Clarke's lessons had been lost in recent years. Entertainment and gossip had intruded, investigative reporting "and its cloak of anonymous sources" had become "a license for distortion," certain techniques of the New Journalism such as the use of composites had eroded public trust, and television docudramas further had blurred the line between fact and fiction. Although he did not refer to objectivity, Johnson urged journalists to return to the profession's "most valued tradition . . . that of looking at news with the hardest of skeptical eyes." That tradition suggests, Johnson argued, that if there are doubts about a story, then Boss Clarke's example should be followed: "Just say *Thar she be* and spike it."

Three days later, Meg Greenfield (April 21, 1981, p. A19) affirmed Johnson's warnings in the *Washington Post*. Greenfield used the occasion of the scandal to "unload some gloomy thoughts about the degraded conditions of political reporting in one respect: the increasingly slithery nature of the 'reality' much of that reporting seeks to convey." Her targets were the fictionalizers in reporting, the newspaper, magazine, and television reporters, the authors of books of political commentary, and the creators of "that dog's breakfast" docudrama. From the time of the Pentagon papers onward, "print journalism and commentary and history-writing as a whole have fallen more and more into the same profligate, blurry ways." Acknowledging that those seeking "a deeper and more sophisticated reality than the one we used to purvey in the old days have added a positive dimension to political commentary," she nonetheless urged that journalists needed "to be more humble . . . in our estimation of what we are about . . . and far more rigorous in the standards we set for achieving it." Many of these themes were echoed throughout the summer in the newspaper trade publication, *Editor and Publisher*, which ran stories on the need to use fewer anonymous sources, reported on efforts at newspapers to revamp their source policy, and affirmed editorially that newspapers should engage in soul-searching but should stop self-flagellation.[11] In July, *Editor and Publisher* reran on its editorial page (July 11, 1981, p. 8) "A

Newspaperman's Credo," written by Max Lerner and published originally in 1961. Although the column rehearsed the traditional ethical virtues of the journalist, it contained few points relating to the role of literary technique, unnamed sources, or the relations between reporters and subcultures in the production of this report. The code argued points few would challenge, but offered little counsel on the difficulties of the time. It was a remembrance of a quieter time when authority and certainty were clearer.

In May, following the announcement of the resignation of *New York Daily News* columnist Michael Daly for a fabrication, the *Wall Street Journal* ran a front-page story (Blustein, May 14, 1981) focusing on the use of the techniques of New Journalism. The story was somewhat more measured in assessing the New Journalism than the columns in the *Washington Post*, acknowledging that techniques such as narration, dialogue, and scene-setting could be used with integrity in journalism. Still, the "sacred rule of journalism," as John Hersey (1980, p. 2) had explained it the previous autumn in the *Yale Review*, was that "none of this was made up." Although Hersey's essay was written prior to the Janet Cooke scandal, it addressed the problems the conventionalists saw in the scandal. The blurred lines between the fact and fiction in contemporary culture, Hersey wrote (p. 23), involved high stakes, "our grasp on *reality*, our relationship with the real world."

Hersey argued that the New Journalism was a response to a failure of belief in objectivity, but it reversed the error, believing only in subjectivity. The result was that "what is, or may be, going on in 'reality' recedes into a backdrop for the actor-writer; it dissolves out of focus and becomes, in the end, fuzzy, vague, unrecognizable, and false" (p. 23). Acknowledging that there was a relationship between the delegitimizing of authority that the public lying of government officials had produced and the blurring of the boundary between facts and fictions in journalism, Hersey argued, the two enjoyed a symbiotic relationship. "Each in its ways has contributed to the befogging of public vision, to subtle failures of discrimination, and to the collapse of important sorts of trust" (p. 24).[12]

There is a poignancy to the reflections of the conventionalists. Reality, in Greenfield's words, does seem slithery, and a culture of greater consensus has some appeal, at least when considered in the abstract. There also can be little doubt, as Hersey argued, that journalism is not a neutral agent in transforming our notions of facts. Reporting, after all, does not merely register some reality outside itself but is a symbolic process for naming and evaluating the world, for creating our collective reality. Journalism, however, is only one of the ways we do so; it is part of a larger social fabric where it influences and is influenced by our other ways of making sense. In the conventionalists' account, the problem of journalistic authority is, in large part, isolated from its social context. Positioned against a backdrop of a more stable time when journalists knew what was real and described it conventionally, the problem of journalistic authority becomes simpler and more manageable. In the process, however, the concrete social world where dissensus exists for very real reasons evaporates or recedes and a nostalgic glow covers a history truncated into professional history.

Nostalgia has been one of the ways journalists have dealt with their past since the nineteenth century (Schudson, 1978, pp. 84-85). Perhaps the desire for the better days of the past is one of the ways editors and reporters, like the rest of us, cope with the increasing bureaucratization of their lives. Perhaps it is merely an essential sentimentality that must accompany a profession that takes its identity from being tough, aggressive, and uninvolved. Whatever its causes, this yearning for a simpler, more stable time was in step with large segments of American society in the 1980s. Fred Davis (1981, p. 106) argues that the wave of nostalgia that rolled over the country in the late 1970s and in this decade was a response to the "wide-ranging, sustained and profound assault concerning the 'natural' and 'proper' " that occurred in the 1960s and 1970s. Nostalgia, Davis argues, is a response to a crisis of identity, "the means for holding onto and reaffirming" (p. 107) badly bruised conceptions of who we are.[13]

The "assault on the 'natural' and 'proper' " was the journalistic story of the 1960s and 1970s. Reporters found the story among youth, gays, women, blacks, Indians, and a variety of ethnic groups. It was at political conventions, demonstrations, prisons, in the family, schools, in Vietnam, and in government. The story vitalized journalism, creating a continual series of exciting "nows." In a society where so much was happening, journalism, a means to know, seemed more important than usual to both the journalists and the public. Even as it revitalized journalism, the assault on conventionality undermined it. In a world that seemed to be unraveling, the conventions of journalism themselves became suspect. Objectivity, a strategy whereby the journalists would provide "both sides" of the story and allow the public to decide on the correctness of the positions, increasingly seemed to a highly differentiated public to be a way of elevating one side over the other, an alliance, when seen from the left, between press and government, and, when seen from the right, between the press and oppositional groups.[14] Alternative forms of journalism, particularly those with liberal orientations, as well as media criticism, were successful in building audiences critical of the mass media's reliance on governmental authority. As the evidence mounted of governmental deceit in Vietnam, the news media too seemed to learn this liberal lesson and slowly became more critical of government. When it finally turned on its central source, it did so with the emotion of a lover wronged. Watergate precipitated a wave of exposure that predominated the middle 1970s (Huntington, 1981, pp. 188-196). The period of exposure produced its excesses and it seems safe to say that "Jimmy's World" was one of them.

After the Janet Cooke scandal, conventionalists directed their hostility toward the young who had entered journalism during the years of exposure, toward phenomena marginal to daily journalism such as the New Journalism, and toward an investigatory posture that had been central to undermining government authority. Journalism, they argued, was in disorder and the solution to its problems lay in its past. The disorder was real, even if these arguments for its causes and solutions seem inadequate. The 1960s and 1970s ruptured the news media's relationship with both government and its audience, but the news media did not substantially alter its news processes or redefine its relationship to either. In response to the cultural fragmentation of its audience, it put more emphasis on life-style sections. In response to its loss of trust in government, it proceeded contradictorily in an accentuated form of its traditional relationship, a form that, extending a usage by Richard Sennett (1981), can be called disobedient dependence. In covering the day-to-day affairs of government, the news media proceeded largely as by custom, relying heavily on governmental authority for its own legitimacy. At the same time, however, many newspapers devoted increased resources to exposing the errors of government. Dependent upon governmental authority for its conventional coverage and disobedient to the same authority in its exposés, the press advertised its own freedom and independence from government while remaining conventionally bound to that authority for the bulk of its news. Unwilling to assert its own independence, the news media dramatized the contradictions of its own social and political placement to an increasingly alienated audience.

AFTER OBJECTIVITY?

The contradictions of accentuated disobedient dependence did receive voice after the scandal. Writing in the *Los Angeles Times*, Sandy Close (April 26, 1981, sec. IV, p. 5) argued that "the real danger to journalism's credibility does not stem from any lack of sincerity or honesty of individual journalists" but from "a growing gap between what the public wants and needs" journalism to do. Journalism, however, "having been badly burned by dependence on 'government sources' for explanations of crises such as Vietnam," had "been obsessed with uncovering duplicity by officialdom, as if that will produce a quick fix to set the system right. But the quick fix—whether it is the resignation of a reporter or a President—only deprives the public of a deeper explanation of the context in which the lie occurred, or the pressures that produced it." The dilemma of journalism, Close argued, was that it was linked to the very sources it sought to expose:

> Thus the reporter depends on the source for describing and confirming the reality he seeks to report; the editor depends on the reporter for discovering the source; the reporter depends on the editor for making the assignment leading to the source; and the editor depends on the good faith of both the reporter and the source. What results is a network of passivity of everyone involved. What results from this passivity is that no one participant in the process is expected to do anything like thinking. Indeed, thinking is itself almost a dirty word, equated with ideology or bias, a blot on the blank tablet of "objective journalism." (p. 5)

Close suggested that the news media needed "to demote the 'magic source' as the final authority," work toward presenting a "multiplicity of voices," engage in a more teamlike spirit in the pursuit of knowledge, and enter the risk-taking realm "of every other institution whose members have to think about what they are doing." The solution to journalism's problems, Close argued in the spirit of John Dewey, was not to return to the safety net of past practices embedded in authoritative institutions but to confront radically new situations and issues with "serious thought, action and even risk" (p. 5). Beyond objectivity, in this view, lies a world where reporters must stake a claim to knowledge, take responsibility for their actions, and engage in argument.

Close, however, was not in tune with the spirit of the time. Nostalgia proved a more appealing response to the contradictions of journalistic life. The habits of journalism were grounded in an ideology of consensus that located journalism as a mediator between an authority that could be trusted and a public divided along simple political lines. However this ideology might conflict with the history of the press and with contemporary culture, the centralized power of the news media and its marketing strategies were dependent upon such a view. The conflicts of the 1960s and 1970s had challenged the cultural ethos that justified and explained what journalists did even as it had further entrenched journalists as centralized voices within the social structure. The result was the experience of contradictions.

In a society where reality definitions were increasingly recognized to be the product of institutional, racial, and gender subcultures, journalists were to present consensual facts. In a culture that valorized subjectivity, journalists were to be objective. In a culture increasingly oriented toward communication effects, journalists were to present the facts. In a culture where traditional authorities were being undermined, journalists were to rely on them and then expose them. In a culture where there was no outside, journalists were somehow to take up residence there. While journalists attempted to create a world consistent with the centralized position of the news media in society, the larger culture asserted the inadequacy of those rules. On the margins of journalism, people sought to resolve the contradictions by asserting that journalism itself was a political act or through literary journalism that built the authority of the individual reporter and made reporting an art. Some of these strategies filtered into the mainstream where, increasingly, celebrity columnists were used to give authority and where life-style sections sought to capture the varieties of life in segmented society. It was, however, in the realm of the social and the political where there seemed to be no refuge. Investigative reporting supplanted official reality with a conception of an underlying one, but in the 1970s more and more work produced fewer and fewer results. "Jimmy's World" was the apotheosis of this truth. Many weeks of work produced not one real child drug addict, and, in the wake of the controversy when the story was published, the *Post* sent six reporters into the field to find another Jimmy. Again, none was found. Unwilling to accept a journalism where reporters must make claims, engage in argument, and take responsibility for their positions, journalists needed to believe there was a truth that was neither aestheticized nor politicized. They needed to believe it, because their job was to produce such truth. Visionaries such as Close could seek release from the contradictions of the field by an imaginative leap, but, for most journalists, nothing in their histories, including their educations, had prepared them to believe such visions. Sometimes they sought release from the contradictions in a return to an idealized past, and occasionally an idealized future, but most often in the magic everyday life performs, through un-self-conscious habitualization.

Janet Cooke focused attention on one of the outcomes of the contradictions, a world where individuals were no longer sure of the boundary between fact and fiction, or, in another reading, a world where individuals no longer felt compelled by authority to obey those boundaries. The exposure of "one of their own" allowed journalists to resolve their own internal contradictions symbolically, at least momentarily, by expulsion of the guilty and a reconstitution of the community's history. Janet Cooke's meaning was not explicit in the act of expulsion; it only became fixed in the symbolic drama that followed, a drama where the dominant voices called into question the changes that journalism had thought it could merely chronicle but that had ultimately eroded its own center. Janet Cooke was physically sent outside the community, but her symbolic significance was to reconstitute for a moment the myth of the outside observer. In the symbolic space of "outside," the changes of two decades could appear to be a minor eruption in a 150-year history of the mass commercial press, the tiny segments that made up that phantom—the public—could fade to reveal a coherent unit, and the individual reporter, up close a highly differentiated being traversed by race, class, region, and transition could look much like an earlier human with a more limited range of experience and a more coherent character. In the symbolic space of "outside," however, there were only journalists dancing a ritual war dance of consensus, telling each other stories about who they were. In the eyes of others, these facts of the profession were themselves fictions. In the eyes of others, as public opinion polls show, journalists continue to lose credibility. Still having the power to direct attention, they lack the authority to make their own makings of themselves—"fictions" in its originary sense—the facts of others.

NOTES

1. On scandals and news, see Molotch and Lester (1974).

2. Sociological interest in the role of the deviant in creating social solidarity dates from Durkheim (1960). An important study in this tradition is Erikson (1966).

3. See Berger and Luckmann (1967) and Carey (1975).

4. See, for instance, Schudson (1978, pp. 160-194), Gans (1980), Tuchman (1978), Gitlin (1980), Hall, Critcher, Jefferson, Clarke, and Roberts (1978), and Hackett (1984).

5. See the following *Washington Post* news stories: Simons (September 30, 1980, p. A1; October 1, 1980, p. A1), Simons and Knight (October 2, 1980, p. C1), Cooke and Simons (October 5, 1980, p. A1), Morgan and Schaffer (October 5, 1980, p. A22), and Richburg (October 16, 1980, p. C1). *Post* editorials on the issue are "An Addict at Eight" (September 30, 1980, p. A18) and "Telling the Story of a Child Addict" (October 1, 1980, p. A16). Columns include Cohen (September 30, 1980, p. C1), Gilliam (October 4, 1980, p. B1), Green (October 3, 1980, p. A12), Raspberry (October 3, 1980, p. A13), Gold (October 6, 1980, p. C11), and Cohen (October 12, 1980, p. B1).

6. The *Post* printed press reaction from around the country on April 17 and 18. See

Tyler and Simons (April 17, 1981, p. A3) and Tyler (April 18, p. A3). Also see, in addition to the columns analyzed below, Green (April 24, 1981, p. A26).

7. For an extended description of the scandal that treats the unified community as taken for granted, see the National News Council's report (1981).

8. Also see Jones-Miller (1981).

9. See the discussion of New Journalism as cultural phenomenology in Eason (1984).

10. Bell (1976) deals with these themes, though the point of view is more reactionary. For another approach to contradiction in contemporary journalism, see Schudson (1983).

11. See the following stories and editorials: "Fact or Fiction" (April 25, 1981, p. 6), "Truth and Accuracy" (May 2, 1981, p. 6), "Pulitzer Hoax" (May 2, 1981, p. 33), "Newspapers Revamping News Source Policies" (June 6, 1981, p. 76), "Reporter vs. Editor Responsibility" (July 4, 1981, p. 6), "Next Pulitzer Deadline Set" (June 6, 1981, p. 80), and Stein (July 11, 1981, p. 16). Also see Shaw (April 19, 1981) and Safire (April 20, 1981).

12. Also see Fishkin (1985).

13. For another interpretation of the place of nostalgia in contemporary life, see Jameson (1984).

14. The social and cultural conflicts of 1960s live on in historical interpretation. For contrasting ideological viewpoints on the period, see Sayres, Stephanson, Arnowitz, and Jameson (1984) and Matusow (1984).

REFERENCES

An addict at eight. (1980, September 30). *Washington Post*, p. A18.

Bell, D. (1976). *The cultural contradictions of capitalism*. New York: Basic Books.

Berger, P., & Luckmann, T. (1967). *The social construction of reality*. Garden City, NY: Anchor.

Blustein, P. (1981, May 14). Some journalists fear flashy reporters color, overwhelm fact. *Wall Street Journal*, p. 1.

Boylan, J. (1981, July/August). The ombudsman's tale. *Columbia Journalism Review*, pp. 28-34.

Brookhiser, R. (1981, August 21). Yellow journalism, black faces. *National Review*, pp. 964-969.

Capital offense: How Washington Post and the Pulitzer board were duped by writer. (1981, April 17). *Wall Street Journal*, pp. 1, 19.

Carey, J. W. (1975). A cultural approach to communication. *Communication, 2*(1), 1-22.

Close, S. (1981, April 26). News "sources"—the crutch that cripples. *Los Angeles Times*, sec. IV, p. 5.

Cohen, R. (1980, September 30). Eight-year-old shoots up: A question of caring. *Washington Post*, p. C1.

Cohen, R. (1980, October 12). Jimmy the addict: Not gone, just forgotten. *Washington Post*, B1.

Cohen, R. (1981, April 19). Putting the creator of "Jimmy's World" in context. *Washington Post*, p. D1.

Cooke, J. (1980, September 28). Jimmy's world. *Washington Post*, p. A1.

Cooke, J., & Simons, L. M. (1980, October 5). Children and drugs. *Washington Post*, p. A1.

Davis, F. (1981). *Yearning for yesterday*. New York: Free Press.

Davis, L. (1983). *Factual fictions*. New York: Columbia University Press.

Deep Throat's children. (1981, May 2). *New Republic*, pp. 8-12.

Denton, H. (1981, April 26). Janet's race. *Washington Post*, p. C1.

Durkheim, É. (1960). *The division of labor in society* (G. Simpson, Trans.). New York: Free Press.

Eason, D. L. (1984). The new journalism and the image-world: Two modes of organizing experience. *Critical Studies in Mass Communication, 1*, 51-65.

The end of Jimmy's world. (1981, April 16). *Washington Post*, p. A18.

Erickson, K. T. (1966). *Wayward Puritans: A study in the sociology of deviance*. New York: John Wiley.

Exploring Jimmy's world. (1981, July/August). *Columbia Journalism Review*, p. 28.

Fact or fiction. (1981, April 25). *Editor and Publisher*, p.6.

Fishkin, S. F. (1985). *From fact to fiction: Journalism and imaginative writing in America*. Baltimore: Johns Hopkins University Press.

Fraser, C. G. (1981, July/August). Black thoughts. *Columbia Journalism Review*, pp. 35-36.

Gans, H. (1980). *Deciding what's news*. New York: Random House.

Gilliam, D. (1980, October 4). Hopelessness fashions its own environment. *Washington Post*, p. B1.

Gilliam, D. (1981, April 18). Janet Cooke: Journalist who happens to be black. *Washington Post*, p. B1.

Gitlin, T. (1980). *The whole world is watching*. Berkeley: University of California Press.

Gold, B. (1980, October 6). Whose rights anyway? *Washington Post*, p. C11.

Goodman, E. (1981, April 22). Credibility: Our only credential. *Washington Post*, p. A23.

Green, B. (1980, October 3). The only promise that was kept. *Washington Post*, p. A12.

Green, B. (1981, April 19). The ombudsman's report on "Jimmy's world." *Washington Post*, pp. A12-A14.

Green, B. (1981, April 24). Picking up the pieces. *Washington Post*, p. A26.

Greenfield, M. (1981, April 21). Reality is good enough. *Washington Post*, p. A19.

Hackett, R. A. (1984). Decline of a paradigm: Bias and objectivity in news media studies. *Critical Studies in Mass Communication, 1*, 229-260.

Hall, S., Critcher, C., Jefferson, T., Clarke, J., & Roberts, R. (1978). *Policing the crisis: Mugging, the state, and law and order*. London: Macmillan.

Hersey, J. (1980). The legend on license. *Yale Review, 70*(1), 1-25.

Huntington, S. P. (1981). *American politics: The promise of disharmony*. Cambridge: Harvard University Press.

Jameson, F. (1984). Postmodernism, or the cultural logic of late capitalism. *New Left Review, 146*, 53-92.

Johnson, H. (1981, April 19). A wound that will be long in healing and never forgotten. *Washington Post*, p. A3.

Jones-Miller, A. (1981, June). Too many Cookes? *Quill*, p. 10.

Lerner, M. (1981, July 11). A newspaperman's credo. *Editor and Publisher*, p. 8.

Mann, J. (1981, April 17). The respect for truth deeper than we thought. *Washington Post*, p. B1.

Maraniss, D. A. (1981, April 16). Post reporter's Pulitzer Prize is withdrawn. *Washington Post*, p. A1.

Marx, J. H. (1980). The ideological construction of post-modern identity models in contemporary cultural movements. In R. Robertson & B. Holzner (Eds.), *Identity and authority* (pp. 145-198). Oxford, England: Basil Blackwell.

Matusow, A. (1984). *The unravelling of America: A history of liberalism in the 1960s.* New York: Harper & Row.

Michener, J. (1981, May 4). On integrity in journalism. *U.S. News and World Report*, pp. 79-80.

Molotch, H., & Lester, M. (1974). News as purposive behavior: On the strategic uses of events, accidents, and scandals. *American Sociological Review, 39*, 101-112.

Morgan, T., & Shaffer, R. (1980, October 5). Cries for help go unheard. *Washington Post*, p. A22.

Munson, N. (1981). The case of Janet Cooke. *Commentary, 72*(1), 46-50.

National News Council. (1981). *After "Jimmy's world": Tightening up in editing.* New York: Author.

Newspapers revamping news source policies. (1981, June 6). *Editor and Publisher*, p. 76.

Next Pulitzer deadline set: 1981 feature debate rolls on. (1981, June 6). *Editor and Publisher*, p. 80.

Pulitzer hoax: The bastard progeny of "reliable sources." (1981, May 2). *Editor and Publisher*, p. 33.

Raspberry, W. (1980, October 3). Did we need to know about Jimmy? *Washington Post*, p. A13.

Reporter vs. editor responsibility. (1981, July 4). *Editor and Publisher*, p. 6.

Richburg, K. R. (1980, October 16). Mayor says city ending search for "Jimmy." *Washington Post*, p. C1.

Safire, W. (1981, April 20). Bradlee's world. *New York Times*, p. 2.

Sayres, S., Stephanson, A., Arnowitz, S., & Jameson, F. (Eds.). (1984). *The 60s without apology.* Minneapolis: University of Minnesota Press.

Schiller, D. (1981). *Objectivity and the news.* Philadelphia: University of Pennsylvania Press.

Schudson, M. (1978). *Discovering the news.* New York: Basic Books.

Schudson, M. (1983). *The news media and the democratic process.* New York: Aspen Institute.

A searching of conscience. (1981, May 4). *Newsweek*, pp. 50-55.

Sennett, R. (1981). *Authority.* New York: Vintage.

Shaw, D. (1981, April 19). A matter of confidence. *Los Angeles Times*, sec. IV, p. 5.

Sheehy, G. (1973). *Hustling.* New York: Dell.

Simons, L. M. (1980, September, 30). D.C. authorities seek identity of heroin addict, eight. *Washington Post*, p. A1.

Simons, L. M. (1980, October 1). Addict, eight, is in hiding mayor says. *Washington Post*, p. A1.

Simons, L. M., & Knight, A. (1980, October 2). Search for boy addict grows. *Washington Post*, p. C1.

Stein, M. L. (1981, July 11). Other reporters admit knowledge of fake stories. *Editor and Publisher*, p. 16.

Telling the story of a child addict. (1980, October 1). *Washington Post*, P. A16.

Truth and accuracy. (1981, May 2). *Editor and Publisher*, p.6.

Tuchman, G. (1978). *Making news.* New York: Free Press.

Tyler, P. E. (1981, April 18). Nation's editors plumb "Jimmy's world." *Washington Post*, p. A3.

Tyler, P. E., & Simons, L. M. (1981, April 17). Jimmy episode outrage, sadness. *Washington Post*, p. A3.

Chapter 11

WHAT IS A REPORTER?
The Private Face of
Public Journalism[1]

Michael Schudson

WHAT FIRST STRIKES A READER of Harrison Salisbury's autobiography, *A Journey for Our Times*, is that it begins with two pages of "Acknowledgments." An autobiography is always an acknowledgment. One written at the end of a long, public career cannot help but be a series of acknowledgments, some certainly heartfelt, some painful, some politic. It is nonetheless a surprise to find Salisbury (1983, p. lx) thanking his parents and aunt "for creating the family archive and writing the letters that enabled me to reconstruct so much of my early life" and thanking his sister for preserving this archive. He then makes explicit what the reader already senses: "I have approached my memoirs like a reporter and have drawn on many sources to refresh, correct and extend my recollections." He is a reporter first and last and he knows it.

But what is a reporter? That is not so obvious a question as it appears. Is a reporter a kind of historian? A political activist or reformer? A skilled stenographer? A writer? Reporting as an occupation is an invention of the nineteenth century, a result of and a contributor to a democratic market society and an urban commercial consciousness. But it has evolved a life of its own and a unique self-consciousness. It is through that self-consciousness, reflected in the autobiographies of Lincoln Steffens (1866-1936) and Harrison Salisbury (1908-), that I seek some insight into the meaning of news reporting as a vocation with a distinctive outlook and a distinctive meaning.

AUTHOR'S NOTE: The quotes from Harrison E. Salisbury are excerpts from *A Journey for Our Times* by Harrison E. Salisbury, a Cornelia and Michael Bessie book, copyright © 1983 by Harrison E. Salisbury. Reprinted by permission of Harper & Row Publishers, Inc. and Curtis Brown Ltd.

Autobiographies, of course, provide direct evidence not of the life 'of the writer but of how the writer conceives his or her life. An autobiography is necessarily an apology and the autobiographical project shows us primarily "the effort of a creator to give the meaning of his own mythic tale," as George Gusdorf (1980, p. 48) puts it. What is revealing, in examining the autobiographies of Steffens and Salisbury, is that journalists of different eras repair to different myths. This is a difference between the two individuals, to be sure, but it is also a difference that reflects the changing career of journalism itself.

In 1908, the year Salisbury was born, reporting in anything like the modern sense was just three generations old. While newspapers date back to the early 1700s in this country, reporting as a specialized journalistic activity did not begin until the 1830s. Even after the Civil War, the activity that is today the archetypal act of the journalist—the interview—was a novelty. And as late as World War I, American journalists were teaching their European colleagues that it was not uncivil but professionally responsible to interview powerful government officials (Schudson, 1978, pp. 66, 143, 202). The reporter, and reporting, were inventions of the nineteenth-century middle-class public and its institutions. Reporting is not an ancient art. It is a historically specific, historically created activity. It does not necessarily transfer well or easily to other cultures. It does not maintain itself untouched as the world around it changes. What reporters report on, how they report, what they aim for, and how they go about their work varies from one era to another. But some features of reporting, bequeathed to contemporary journalists by the nineteenth century, mark the authority and character of news-gathering in ways that still shape the world of reporters and the world of the rest of us who read and listen to the news. We may get some insight into this by inquiring after what a reporter is, asking about, if you will, the ontology of this novel occupational type.

For a general reader of Salisbury's memoirs who sails right by the acknowledgments, there is still no doubt, from the first sentence of the first paragraph of the first chapter, that Salisbury is a reporter and sees, or at least portrays, even his own life through the reporter's eyes:

> To a workingman, head tucked into collar against the wind, hurrying home in the dark Minnesota November, the figure of a small boy slowly stomping across the snowy lawn beyond the yellow arc of gaslight was almost invisible, a blur against the crepuscular shadows of the gabled house. (1983, p. 1)

We are not surprised to learn in the next paragraph that this small boy, marching back and forth as if he were standing guard in the snow, is

Salisbury, age nine. We are shown him at first as someone else might see him. Who that someone else is is a matter of some surprise: a workingman hurrying home after work. This workingman could be just a figure to give the whole scene a Victorian nineteenth-century flavor (the gaslight certainly does that), but there is more to it than this. Salisbury's father was a doctor's son who found himself trapped in an office job in an industrial plant that meant little to him besides his paycheck. He was a workingman. Salisbury's father-in-law had been a miner in the coalfields of Illinois. Salisbury finds a natural identification with the worker, not a Marxist romance but a plainspoken, simple respect. And so he first pictures himself to his readers watched, nonjudgingly, and watched over, by a worker. What a reporter is depends in large part on who a reporter reports to. Who is the audience? Who is the public for the reporter's words?

Salisbury, called "Bunny" by his parents, age nine, seen or not seen by a workingman passing by, is outside in the snow near his home on Royalston Avenue in Minneapolis. It is November 1917, shortly after the Russian Revolution. What he is doing there is problematic. Salisbury the memoirist reconstructs a conversation after Bunny goes inside. His father asked him what he was doing in the yard. "Just playing," he replies. But what he was playing at was imagining himself a member of the Children's Regiment, standing guard at the Winter Palace, wearing a helmet with a red star. Was this "just playing"? The memoirist writes, "I've looked back a hundred times at that nine-year-old youngster, particularly during my long years in Russia, wondering whether, in fact, I was 'just playing' " (1983, p. 2).

I will worry the same question here. The question is about imagination, about play, about how children or the reporters they grow into construct a career for themselves and a world for their readers. It is a question, again, of what a reporter is, because no reporter just "gets the facts." Reporters make stories. Making is not faking, not lying, but neither is it a passive mechanical recording. It cannot be done without play and imagination.[2]

Lincoln Steffens was also concerned with "play" in his autobiography. Born 42 years before Salisbury and half a continent away in San Francisco, his effort in the first pages of the autobiography is not to pose a question but to assert an answer, to propose a theory— that his is the story of a happy life and one that has come full circle from his own golden infancy to his pleasure at being, for the first time, in his sixties, the father of an infant son who laughs when he tumbles out of bed.

Certainly this is how Steffens deals with the serious topic of child's play. For Steffens, the magic and beauty of childhood is in play, fantasy, and imagination. For the young Steffens, books were a great source of fancy. Riding around Sacramento on his pony, he would be Napoleon or Richard the Lion-hearted or Byron and lose himself in his daydreams. One day, as he tells it, his father brought home an artist, W. M. Marple. Marple wanted to be taken to the dry basin of the American River, which, as it happens, was Lincoln's favorite stomping ground, a playground filled in his imagination with Indians, Saracens, and elephants. Marple set up his easel and painted while young Joseph Lincoln watched. Not impressed with the realism of the painter's work, he criticized it. Marple replied that he was not interested in the details of the brush-baked mud. "I see the colors and the light, the beautiful chord of the colors and the light." Steffens then admitted to his Indians and Saracens and felt embarrassed. "Your golden light is really there and my Indians aren't." The painter replied,

> Your Indians are where my gold is, where all beauty is, in our heads. We all paint what we see, as we should. The artist's gift to see the beauty in everything, and his job is to make others see it. I show you the gold, you show me the romance in the brush. We are both artists, each in his line. (Steffens, 1931, p. 44)

For Steffens, play creates reality, imagination finds and makes worlds. At the same time, imagination is the consolation afforded disappointed hopes. The young boy keeps discovering that each adult he gets to know is "playing he is really something else besides what his job is" (1931, pp. 66). They are all, in their minds, enacting life scripts they would like to be different or reenacting life stories that might have taken a more favorable turn.

Salisbury and Steffens—two different reporters, two different people, two different eras of journalism, even two different kinds of journalism—Steffens a magazine writer in his heyday as a muckraker; Salisbury, a foreign correspondent for United Press and later the *New York Times*. It would make no sense to try to extract from these different lives some qualities we could describe as "essence of journalist." But by examining how they present themselves in their autobiographies, how and what they remember of their lives as reporters, we can learn something about the contours of twentieth-century journalism. What does a reporter report—and how? To whom does a reporter report? What is the reporter's objective? What does this imply for the inner life of the person who is a journalist? What does the prominence of reporting in contemporary life imply for all of us?

WHAT A REPORTER FEELS

Let me go back some distance to a prehistoric journalist for contrast. Benjamin Franklin was a printer, not a reporter, and his journalism was of a very different order from that to which we are accustomed. Indeed, "reporting" was not a part of his task as conductor (the term *editor* was not in use) of a journal (the term *newspaper* was not widely in use either), nor was the journal necessarily the place for the promotion of political opinions. Not that Franklin entirely refrained from political jousting in the *Pennsylvania Gazette*. But he was as likely to launch his plans for civic improvement by pamphlet publication as by placing the article in his journal.

For Franklin, journalism—printing—was a trade. It was a trade that suited him, but not in any central respect an expression of or a mold for his soul. He is, in his autobiography, as Robert Sayre (1964, pp. 23-25) has shrewdly observed, a kind of trickster figure who takes on different masks, different trades, different persona, and passes on—in some measure untouched by them.

There is nothing of the sort in Lincoln Steffens, an artist in his own line. For Steffens, becoming a reporter meant becoming a distinct human subspecies. Writing to a friend in 1897 as a young, ambitious, and rather successful reporter for the *New York Evening Post*, he took a characteristic stance:

> I have no longer any inclination to answer you the moment I receive your letters. It seems so hopeless. You are living your own life out, while I am living that of others, hundreds of others. My thoughts and my feelings, my purposes and desires and doings are of no moment; they hardly engage my own attention, never any protracted reflection. My observations are worth while. Others are the objects of them, so they interest me,—I can work them over and there is a market for what I say. So I am the spectator. I am not grumbling, mind. But my concern is with anybody but myself, and my life is the life of the millions, the Greater New York. (Nevins, 1938, p. 129)

This last is a bit strong. Despite some reporting on crime and on the Jewish ghetto on the Lower East Side, Steffens had devoted most of his career to reporting on Wall Street. So his life was scarcely the "life of the millions." The whole letter seems a concealed put-down: "I am not concerned with myself, you are preoccupied with navel gazing while there is a whole world out there to know." And yet the letter expresses a genuine, one could even say breathless, sense of enthusiasm for the work of the journalist, the spectator, the watcher. And for Steffens, this *is* ontology. Journalism is not one trade among many. It is a distinct way of experiencing the world. It is a separate consciousness.

But what is it to be an onlooker? For Steffens, it is an activity that reaches far beyond itself. The events he witnesses are to be understood not as important in themselves but as revelatory of deeper significances, underlying laws of human behavior. He is not merely an observer—observing is an active, constructive, reforming activity. He wrote Ray Stannard Baker what he hoped for his magazine work: "I have great ideas of what can be done by telling the facts and telling the stories of life about us. I would have the *American* report and report and report, till men had to see in what a state of serviture they are in, and fight for very shame" (Nevins, 1938, p. 177). For Steffens, the people he witnesses are instances and he is in search of the general law, and the truth of the general will will set people free.

For Salisbury, in contrast, general laws do not exist except in the instances. He takes pride in his Minnesota, commonsense, down-to-earth turn of mind. He is skeptical of grand theories of human behavior. "I am wary of precise rules. Precision puts human conduct into a straitjacket. We are a disorderly species. Clean-cut cases are rare, and unless we recognize that there must be exceptions, we bind ourselves to rigidity and nonsense." Salisbury wrote to me, responding to an earlier draft of this chapter, "Stef was a crusader and quite a public figure. I am, as you note, basically a reporter, not an exhorter. I try to dig out what is what and present it and let the facts (as I see them) move people's minds" (Salisbury, 1986).

For Steffens, his life is a life of his own exploits. He is his own hero. Rarely does any outside event impinge on his recollections. He tells, in the book's opening paragraph, how the San Francisco earthquake of 1868 pitched him, two years old, out of bed—unhurt and, as usual, smiling, and tells how his mother repeated this story over and over as evidence that Joseph Lincoln, Jr., was a remarkable boy. Nowhere else in the book does an event of general magnitude affect him—and even here, of course, he suggests that the effect was on his mother more than on himself. The world's events are, for him, a textbook. They instruct him. They influence his theories. But they do not touch him.

Salisbury, in contrast, regularly marks his own passage through life in terms of the world's passage through history. He recalls the cries of the newsboys, the "bushwhackers," the night the news came of the Titanic, the family awakened after everyone had gone to bed—at least he thinks he recalls it, acknowledging some doubt on the subject. The sinking of the Lusitania he remembers clearly. Much more important, he remembers the news that "Minnesota's Slim Lindbergh" had touched down in Paris. "It was an extraordinary moment, the biggest moment for me since the armistice of November 7, 1918, the 'false' armistice which I and everyone in Minneapolis thought had ended World War I" (Salisbury, 1983, p. 14).

Minnesota's "Slim" Lindbergh was a kind of alter ego for young Salisbury. "I could never have flown across Lake Minnetonka, let alone the Atlantic, but my emotion was there never quite to vanish" (p. 15). It is, of course, the one thing the reporter of Salisbury's temperament can never do—fly, be the center of the world's attention, soar beyond what others have done rather than following close behind them. Reporters may be close to the history-makers but they are not the history-makers. Salisbury knew this from the beginning of his career, writing to a friend in 1933 that he found working for United Press "a grand seat for viewing things over the world from the grandstand" and that "I think that after all the grandstand is the place I would rather view them from" (p. 62). This sharp distinction between reporter and participant, so vital to the contemporary journalist, is not something Steffens was clear about—in Los Angeles, in Washington, in Paris. Steffens lived, as he saw it, on the frontier of knowledge. Salisbury lives in the folds and furrows of history. Steffens seeks a future; Salisbury, a location. What makes them exemplary journalists is that they both seek—both expand out over their jobs—though Salisbury did not manage this, truly, until Russia. He had, retrospectively, a destiny; Steffens had, prospectively, a mission.

It would not be fair to say that Steffens represents an active and Salisbury a passive view of reporting. Salisbury was and is a man of great energy, his 75-word-per-minute leads his trademark, stubbornness a key virtue he admired in himself and others, enterprise—and not a little imagination—something he exhibited in his reporting. But he certainly found the job of reporting created a unity for his life, provided him a whole world, in ways it did not and could not for Steffens. In part, this reflects a general development in which professional lives have become more and more absorbing and defining. In part, it indicates a modesty of ambition in a world where specialized roles are more carefully constructed than in Steffens's heyday. In part, I suppose, it indicates a growing tradition in journalism itself. Steffens could imagine himself a pioneer. Salisbury's exploits were ones he could always see as part of a continuity in journalism. While editor at his college newspaper, Salisbury's heroes were the likes of Upton Sinclair, Ida Tarbell, Frank Norris, and—of course—Lincoln Steffens. He thought of himself as a muckraker, at first; later he thought of himself simply and proudly as a reporter. It may be generally true that muckraking more often recruits people to journalism than keeps them there.

WHAT A REPORTER KNOWS

Both autobiographers describe, in cinematic detail, a street scene of the reporter as a young man. This follows something of a tradition in American autobiography. Benjamin Franklin, of course, in one of the most famous scenes in American literature, describes himself as the newly arrived Boston printer walking through the streets of Philadelphia, poor but prosperous in outlook, two loaves of bread under his arms. Philadelphia is for this young man not a city to describe nor a city to understand but a city in which to work. Franklin includes the scene of the young man as a comic interlude and as a moral lesson—behold how far I have come since then! Steffens offers a scene of Pittsburgh we can compare. He goes to Pittsburgh in the heyday of his muckraking articles for *McClure's* Magazine. Pittsburgh, he recalls,

> looked like hell, literally. Arriving of an evening, I walked out aimlessly into the smoky gloom of its deep-dug streets and somehow got across a bridge up on a hill that overlooked the city, with its fiery furnaces and the two rivers which pinched it in. The blast ovens opened periodically and threw their volcanic light upon the cloud of mist and smoke above the town and gilded the silver rivers, rolling out steel and millionaires. (Steffens, 1931, p. 401)

He was afraid because it was the first city he "muckraked" without knowing ahead of time a reformer or friend who could guide him through it.

> As I wandered, a stranger, through that vast mystery of a city, looking for a place or a person to begin my inquiries, I wanted to run away. I could not. I had to stay. "We" had announced that I was to investigate and expose the corruption of that invisible government which looked so big and strong, so menacing and—so invisible. (p. 402).

This is a very different entry into a city—not to be a part of it but to take it apart. Steffens assumes, from the outset, that the only truth worth getting to would take digging and the wits to deceive the dissemblers. And all this in a place that looked like hell.

Salisbury has a street scene of his own. He leaves the Twin Cities for the first time to take up a job with United Press in Chicago. He comes to

Chicago with a whole set of associations ahead of him. "I kept thinking in capital letters. The Big Test. Sandburg's Chicago, Frank Norris's Chicago, Colonel McCormick's Chicago, Al Capone's Chicago. The Big Time." The train pulls in at 7:00 in the morning, a chill January day in 1931.

> I put on my camel's hair coat, my throat sore from the hot air, the feverish naps, the cigarettes. I picked up my bags and walked through the great waiting room and out over the bridge, dirty ice floating on the green puke of the Chicago River, men and women, mostly men, hurrying head down against the wind, I hurrying too, under the "L" and up Monroe Street to the Great Northern Hotel. I got a room, paid in advance, three dollars. I gave the bellhop a dime tip, my first tip. I remember coming down to the street and out into the cold, the wind blowing off Lake Michigan. Not eight o'clock yet and on my way to the office, my throat ached, my eyes ached, my head ached. I breathed in the cold air, big breaths, threw back my shoulders, put my head up, held it high and walked east toward the lake. I leaned into the wind and walked through the crowds pouring down from the "L," starting their day's work. They did not know me. They did not know who I was. They did not know what I way going to do. (Salisbury, 1983, p. 96)

Salisbury walks through the Loop, down Michigan Avenue,

> tall and skinny, six feet tall, 142 pounds, a long cantering gait, my ankle-length coat swirling around me, a comic figure, likely to be splintered by the wind, but not splintering, not aware of the comedy, deathly serious, stalking Chicago like a camel-coated panther. I was going to take this city. I was going to take Chicago. Words out of some book I had read. Well, that was my fantasy. (p. 96)

There is what we might call a reflexivity in Salisbury's self-portrait that is missing in Steffens, an ironic edge, an irony created not only by the bemused view of an old man looking at himself as a young man (after all, Steffens shows no such bemusement) but by the sense that the young Salisbury was reenacting rather than acting, that he was living out a dream he had evidently already read about. The dream is serious but the fact that the young Salisbury was a dreamer keeps it at one remove. (Salisbury would have the feeling of the Chicago street again in 1944 on first arriving in Moscow:

> What I knew that night, huddled under my mountain of blankets, sweat turning me into a soggy mass, was that I had started on a new path. I did not know where it would lead or what it would bring, but I had finally cut

loose. I was on my own. I felt very much as I had that frosty January morning thirteen years before when I had stalked up Michigan Boulevard. Russia was the big one and I was going to make it my own. [p. 211])

In classical tragedy, there is a vital "scene of recognition" where all comes clear and Oedipus or Lear stands face-to-face with the truth about himself. He knows, in a moment of tragic insight, who he is. It is a culmination and a turning point. Reporters, as they tell their stories to us, have no such turning points. Their scene of recognition is a scene of challenge, of a new assignment, another task, another world to conquer, yet one more Philadelphia or Pittsburgh or Chicago before him.[3]

Steffens's and Salisbury's street scenes share the reporters' conviction that life is a confrontation with the world outside. It is not that the reporter has no inner life but that he is relatively uninterested in it. Indeed, both reporters suggest that such interest would be self-indulgent. Reporting, for Steffens and for Salisbury, is a challenge to manhood. The job is to penetrate, to get beyond appearances, to find the facts that make the meanings. But Steffens is confronting politics; Salisbury is confronting a career in journalism and a name for himself. Steffens still has an aim outside reporting; Salisbury is the more consummate professional—his only aim is defined within reporting itself, a passion to master the trade.

Salisbury, in this regard, is the more modern reporter. He has no great use for ideas and a "fierce antagonism to ideologues" (p. 249). As a young man, he liked to think of himself as "a hard-hitting, two-fisted, call-them-as-they-come reporter." For him, the detail, the fact is all. His "Minnesota turn of mind" (p. 348), his "commonsense approach" dominate. He learned, he reports, to understand Russia by relying less on codes and doctrines and textbooks "and more and more on reality" (p. 348). He is not anti-intellectual. He makes apparent his respect for scholars who taught him about Russia and his respect, indeed, his love, for the Russian poets he came to know. But "ideas" are sentimentalized for him; they are romantic, they are poetic, they do not seem critical to his understanding of what goes on in the world. They are, in a sense, similar to his experience with great works of literature as a preteen, reading volume after volume: "I read them all, serially in continuous wonder shelf by shelf, between the ages of nine and thirteen I grew up knowing what culture was—it was the books on the walls of my grandfathers's study" (p. 7). Ideas, for him, though beloved, remain on the walls of the study.

Steffens seems different. He had a sense that a "science of ethics" lay just beyond him, and his muckraking days were spent in search of a "theory of corruption." In short, Steffens saw himself as an intellectual; intellectuals were not for him, as for most journalists today, a different species. But his was a simple, simpleminded in retrospect, theory; not so much a theory as a simple thesis that processes of corruption are the same in different cities and different countries and have to do not with the moral qualities of individuals but with the social organization of business and politics. (In retrospect, it all would have been easier for Steffens had he studied sociology and not psychology, but sociology was not yet born when he was in school and he did not become better acquainted with it later.)

Despite Steffens's passion for facts and for science, he was well aware that he had some information as a reporter and some news that he did not put into the public domain. It is worth looking at these aspects of his work. If a reporter's job is to get the news out to the public, we may be able to define reporting better by seeing what news the journalist fails to carry through to print.

For Steffens, first of all, he would not print information given to him "confidentially" by a source for fear of losing the source (Steffens, 1931, p. 184). The reporter, in pursuit of an ongoing or long-term commitment to provide information to the public, made short-term compromises that kept information from the public.

Second, Steffens as a young reporter withheld information about criminal activity on Wall Street because he simply could not believe it. "I was too imbued with the Wall Street spirit . . . I was a Wall Street man myself, unconsciously, but literally." Information does not fall upon a blank slate. No reporter is a blank slate but an uneven terrain in which some information will settle and some will not be absorbed at all. For Steffens, the information on Wall Street criminality was such that "I would not, could not, take it in" (p. 194). Steffens also reports how Jacob Riis responded to news at police quarters of a raid on a homosexual resort. When the situation was explained to him, he could not believe it, he denied the existence of homosexuality. "Not so. There are no such creatures in this world." He would not report the raid (p. 223).

Third, Steffens learned that some information would never be printed by any paper. News of police brutality against strikers never made the papers. From his own account, Steffens never tried to buck this system. He accepted the reality, if not the necessity, of it (p. 207). When writing on political reform in New York, Steffens realized that no one he talked to had any good idea how to get to the bottom of corruption, how to make a real difference. It was his job to find such people—"it was my job as a reporter to seek them out and report them," but, he wrote, "within the limit of my search I found not one." And then he adds a curiously acquiescent clause: "I could not interview radicals, of course, there were not many of them anyhow, they were only faddists: cooperators, socialists (a few), anarchists, whom nobody would listen to" (p. 249). Here he reports his failure as a reporter, followed by a set of excuses—there weren't very many radicals (and presumably they didn't represent many others), those who existed were not very serious anyway, and even if they were serious, "nobody" would listen to them. Well, not "nobody" of course. Steffens suggests here that he, for one, recognized that they might have something important to say. But of course "nobody" is a metaphor standing for a smaller body of people: Steffens's editors, first of all; and then his readers, the wealthy and established readers of the *Evening Post*; and perhaps also the wider elite circles of power in the city. That is the "nobody" who would not listen.

Finally, Steffens refers more philosophically to a large category of information: "What reporters know and don't report is news—not from the newspapers' point of view, but from the sociologists' and the novelists'." (p. 223). It is a sober recognition all too often denied or ignored by reporters—that "news" is a peculiar form of information, a peculiar genre, by no means the totality of what might be interesting but only what might be interesting from a certain point of view.

We might define a reporter in these terms: a reporter is someone faithful to sources, attuned to the conventional wisdom, serving the political culture of media institutions, and committed to a narrow range of public, literary expression. This is scarcely a flattering definition, but there may be more honesty in it than more celebratory definitions of journalism would care to admit. It also leads naturally to a set of questions that would be good starting points for a systematic study of journalism. Who are the reporter's sources? Where does the reporter pick up conventional wisdom? What is the economic, political, and social structure of media institutions? What is "news" as a genre of literature and public expression?

Salisbury would add a fifth limitation to the four Steffens acknowledges: the reporter is constrained by the competition and camaraderie of other reporters. (And this would lead to a fifth question in our sociology of journalism: Who are journalists and what are their background and training?) Steffens identified with science and with reform, not with "journalism." Salisbury, in contrast, is part of a profession of journalism he identifies with and in which he wants to succeed. He is part of a circle of journalists. Conversations with other reporters recur throughout his book—in Steffens's, most reported conversations are with politicians. For Salisbury, the search for truth is a collective search as it never was for Steffens. It is a story of friends and comrades in arms. And it is a story of competition. Salisbury is passionately competitive—and this is what led to one of his compromises with truth, withholding information that there was a plot to assassinate the mayor of Chicago—in hopes of getting a jump on the competition in reporting the assassination when it happened. It is also the occasion of a comical, but perhaps not so comical, admission: that when he heard the news, via Associated Press, that the war in Europe was over, he found that "to a competitive UP man like myself, the disaster of an AP exclusive on the war's end overshadowed the event itself. All day I called one diplomat after another, looking for confirmation—or better yet, denial" (Salisbury, 1983, p. 291).

This suggests a sixth question for a sociology of journalists and journalism, but the hardest one of all to answer: What does it all mean? What does this fact-gathering, competitive, implicated, news bureaucracy mean for how people, journalists or their readers, come to experience the world?

WHAT THE REPORTER WANTS

It's time to return to Salisbury's workingman. Because my concern with these autobiographies is not only with looking at how two notable journalists constructed or imagined their selves as professionals but, equally, how that relates to their construction of a public. Few phrases have been bandied about in recent years in social scientific circles as frequently as "the public sphere"—but with little recognition that the public sphere is a historically constructed entity. To take Jürgen Habermas's definition, it is "a realm of our social life in which something approaching public opinion can be formed." Habermas accords great importance in the evolution of a public sphere to the rise of the newspaper in the eighteenth century. For Habermas, a decisive change came when newspapers changed from haphazardly publishing news to leading public opinion as instruments of political parties. The press was then "an institution of the public itself, effective in the manner of a mediator and intensifier of public discussion, no longer a mere organ for the spreading of news but not yet the medium of a consumer culture." Habermas (1974) sees the life of the public sphere as represented by the newspaper to be rather limited—from the late eighteenth century to the transformation of the political and public press into a commercial press, beginning in the 1830s.

But it is not a question of the life and death of some ideal-typical "public sphere." It is a question, rather, of the changing character of publicness once the conviction that there is and should be a "public" was established in the Age of Revolution in the eighteenth century. And the role of the reporter, the journalist, is absolutely essential in contributing to—or failing to contribute to—the public sphere.

What is the task of the reporter?

For Steffens, the task is to find the truth and thereby change the world. For Salisbury, it is to keep the faith. To find the truth, for Steffens, is a scientific task and a political task. For Salisbury, to keep the faith is an act of homage to the past and an act of defiance toward those who will not honor it.

Salisbury feels a deep connection to his parents and their heritage, to Minnesota, to a Progressive political tradition (although he has been a life-long Republican), to a patriotism in which no holiday in the calendar, sacred or secular, could match the fourth of July. His great-great-uncle Hiram, a farmer in the early 1800s, celebrated no holiday except the fourth of July (Salisbury, 1983, pp. 20-21). It was the same for Salisbury as a boy, the Glorious Fourth. And he misses the special qualities the day once had.

But even as a boy Salisbury sensed a world he cared about slipping away. He mourned the demise of the passenger pigeon in 1914, and "for years I kept hoping I might discover a survivor" (p. 20). Salisbury's effort for much of his life has been devoted to discovering survivors. In Russia, he hoped to discover survivors of revolutionary hope and humanist commitment that he learned of from a neighbor across the street in St. Paul, a Russian émigré committed to the revolution. (He did not really find what he sought but "came to realize that nowhere in that gray wasteland would I ever taste the wine of the Revolution as pungent and pure as that of my childhood in the Oak Lake Addition" [p. 6].) In his travels in the 1960s and 1970s across America he kept looking for survivors or survivals of dreams and hopes and desires. It is no accident that he is a Civil War hobbyist, enthralled with that terrible era and remembering, perhaps, that his father, as he grew older, "looked like Lincoln, not so tall, but with Lincoln's deep-set eyes and melancholy" (p. 42).

With Steffens, whose journalistic career was focused on American cities and American national politics rather than international affairs, connections to the wider world are less personally crucial. Salisbury is something of the traveler and anthropologist, intent on understanding the peculiarities of different peoples. Steffens, who studied in German universities including some time at Wilhelm Wundt's lab, the first psychological laboratory in the world, was more the social scientist seeking laws of invariance to explain the variations of human behavior. Steffens, indeed, ultimately became bored with muckraking and at the end of his muckraking days, in Boston, in the year Salisbury was born, he turned over much of the legwork to a young assistant, Walter Lippmann, because he was bored: "I had reported the like so often that my mind or my stomach revolted at the repetition" (Steffens, 1931, p. 606). Oddly enough, it is Salisbury, with the more scholarly sense of his subject—the Soviet Union—who never got bored. Disappointed, pessimistic, and angry, but not bored. Steffens, with more scientific ambition and a more formal, organized mind, was more lost as a journalist, groping for a stance between the scientist, the reformer, and the scold.

Steffens is intent on explanation. Salisbury is content with "getting the facts." Steffens sometimes delights in the role of observer and outsider but at other times chafes at it; Salisbury slides into it comfortably. Steffens is restless, Salisbury—for all his evident energy—comes across as "old shoe" in his memoirs. Steffens is a public figure and he tells us in chapter after chapter how the political and business bosses of the great American cities confided in him and used him as a father confessor. Salisbury's friends are journalists or poets or his own family, outsiders to the political struggles Salisbury chronicles. The image Steffens gives us is his heart-to-heart talks with Teddy Roosevelt; the image Salisbury leaves us is his waiting, alone or with other reporters, outside the Kremlin for news of Stalin.

The 1890s was the age of the reporter. Not now, not even in Salisbury's account of traveling to Hanoi as the first American reporter there during the Vietnam war. Here he soft-pedals his own efforts; where Steffens is his own hero, Salisbury, in Salisbury's writing, is, if not an antihero, then at least someone more on the sidelines than in the center of history, Rosenkrantz or Guildenstern, not the prince. And yet, his trip to Hanoi was an act of imagination of a sort very rare in journalism (or in any field). It was the sort of nonpartisanship that makes journalistic objectivity inevitably an impertinence and a challenge to authority. He showed forcefully the unending capacity of the objective stance to be seditious. In doing so, he raised a question in action about what audience a journalist should imagine and what loyalties he should hold dear. (This is a question, by the way, that Ronnie Dugger has raised again recently, criticizing the American press coverage of the Reagan-

Gorbachev summit in Geneva, arguing that the press behaved like sportswriters, writing everything from the point of view of the home team. "As professional journalists, what are our international responsibilities? . . . perhaps, if we ask the question, and answer that reporters do have responsibilities to the human race no less than national leaders do, we will make our way to the second summit as more than sportswriters for the home team" [Dugger, 1986, p. 4].)

In going to Hanoi, to what was Salisbury loyal? To journalism? To his family and regional tradition? To the working man? To his own career? To his alter ego, Lindbergh the flier and the pioneer?

To all of them, I think. What may be important for thinking about the ethics of journalism is that loyalty to journalism and to "career" would not have been enough. Salisbury's objectivity in this instance was anathema to many journalists, including even the *Washington Post* that editorialized in criticism of Salisbury's decision to go to Hanoi (Halberstam, 1979, p. 534; Hallin, 1986, p. 147). Description is always an act of imagination. Salisbury was willing to play in this case as well as to work, to locate a personal destiny consistent with one reading of journalistic ethics but unrecognized by the conventionality in which all professions and all ethical codes come slothfully to lounge until challenged. The journalist with a destiny is willing to go beyond the ethics of the profession, an ethics always limited and limiting, even in the best of circumstances. Salisbury, I suspect, has been a leading journalist not just because he committed himself to his profession—though he did—but because he never let that commitment obscure the fact that his father looked like Lincoln, his great-great-uncle celebrated the fourth of July, and his fellow Minnesotan flew solo across the Atlantic.

Salisbury has a refined sense of the past and of continuity. Steffens, one of Salisbury's heroes, had no such thing. This is a difference between scientific optimism and realistic pessimism; between a man who thought journalism could serve up truth and another who sees journalism as a modest chipping away at falsehood; between someone whose sense of the line between advocacy and observation was incidental and someone for whom it is cardinal. But even Salisbury's stance is not of scientific detachment but of personal integrity. The reporter faces more constraints on fact-gathering and more limits on publication than any scientist would tolerate. The reporter, in the face of this, seeks an ethical ideal, and Salisbury finds his in a dedication to observing.

The difference is not just between two individuals but between two eras in journalism. The shift from Steffens to Salisbury is a shift from an individual with a mission to an individual with a role (the detached reporter), a role within a profession that has a collective mission or, at least, a collective responsibility.

Salisbury (1983, p. 534) ends his memoirs describing himself as a "pilgrim" in

> an unending quest for knowledge—knowledge of Russia, whose shadow falls across the planet which in my lifetime has grown so small, so dangerous, so enigmatic; knowledge of America, so filled with promise, so shackled by frustration, yet still pregnant with hope for her people and for the world.

The world, however small it seems to Salisbury, is larger than it was for Steffens. Steffens believed in a unity of humankind, he believed in simple solutions, he believed in the capacity of truth to settle matters. Salisbury is much more aware of human differences, the peculiarities of both Russians and Americans. He is more intent on describing differences and hoping this will help than on finding underlying truths and knowing this will be decisive. Steffens's optimism is naive; Salisbury's hopefulness plaintive. But between them, I think, they define the range of possibilities to which a journalism of dedication and vision can aspire.

The old debates of the 1960s—objective journalism versus advocacy journalism—have abated enough for us to see that the terms were never quite right. No one has ever observed these abstractions in practice. No journalism worthy of the name fails to seek trustworthy facts collected according to the best standards of objective reporting. But neither is there a journalism worth more than a radio headline service that is not also an act of play and imagination.

Nor are these old debates adequate to the question Salisbury's memoirs raise—without nearing an answer—about the audience. The question of the audience never came clear in the 1960. Who is the reader? What is the public sphere in which the journalist works, serves, and that he helps to establish? Neither Steffens nor Salisbury give us guidance about this. They are exemplary reporters who held to the presuppositions of their craft in their age. When they escape those presuppositions, as both of them had the will and instinct to do, they are, with so many of the rest of us, adrift without a language adequate to describe or celebrate their best actions.

NOTES

1. I want to thank Dan Martin for research assistance on this essay and Helene Keyssar for a careful and critical reading of an earlier draft. Harrison Salisbury also provided very helpful comments on an earlier draft. I am grateful to William May of

Southern Methodist University for providing the occasion and the encouragement, through a forum on the public role of the news media, for this essay.

2. Somewhere the anthropologist Victor Turner has written that "making is not faking," but I cannot locate the source. The general point, for newspapers, is developed in a number of recent studies of the media, most recently in Manoff and Schudson, 1986.

3. I am grateful to Helene Keyssar for drawing my attention to "scenes of recognition" in tragedy.

REFERENCES

Dugger, R. (1986, September/October). The administration's long knives and the hazards of nationalism. *Deadline.*

Gusdorf, G. (1980). Conditions and limits of autobiography. In J. Olney (Ed.), *Autobiography: Essays theoretical and critical.* Princeton, NJ: Princeton University Press.

Habermas, J. (1974, Fall). The public sphere: An encyclopedia article. *New German Critique, 1.*

Halberstam, D. (1979). *The powers that be.* New York: Knopf.

Hallin, D. (1986). *The uncensored war: The media and Vietnam.* New York: Oxford University Press.

Manoff, R., & Schudson, M. (1986). *Reading the news.* New York: Pantheon.

Nevins, A. (Ed.). (1938). *The letters of Lincoln Steffens* (vol. 1). New York: Harcourt Brace.

Salisbury, H. (1983). *A journey for our times: A memoir.* New York: Harper & Row.

Salisbury, H. (1986, September 26). Personal correspondence.

Sayre, R. (1964). *The examined self: Benjamin Franklin, Henry Adams, Henry James.* Princeton, NJ: Princeton University Press.

Schudson, M. (1978). *Discovering the news: A social history of American newspapers.* New York: Basic Books.

Steffens, L. (1931). *The autobiography of Lincoln Steffens.* New York: Harcourt Brace.

Chapter 12

RUPERT MURDOCH AND THE DEMONOLOGY OF PROFESSIONAL JOURNALISM

John J. Pauly

ASIDE FROM THE STORIES they are paid to tell, professional journalists also invent myths about themselves. One such myth stresses the socially edifying features of their occupation. According to that story, journalists gather and disseminate the vital information democracy needs to function. Reporters share a devotion to their craft, which they conduct in the light of widely accepted ethical codes. Apprentice journalists are imbued with these same ideals during their education at American universities (Birkhead, 1982, 1984). Through this story runs an ethos—a conception of journalism as news work conducted by public-spirited, independent professionals—and an aesthetic—a taste for particular narrative forms and styles of occupational identity (Pauly, 1985a).

Such is the stuff of awards banquets, publishers' speeches, and round table forums on freedom of the press. But this morality pageant is often played out against the backdrop of darker forces and figures. The antagonists against whom journalists joust may vary—the Political Demagogue manipulating the masses, the Conniving Bureaucrat withholding documents, the Lumpen Reader watching television. But few figures so dominate journalists' occupational dramas as the Press Baron. Witness the case of Rupert Murdoch. He has evoked more vituperation than any press owner of the last 40 years. Murdoch's critics chant an endless litany of his failures—his intrusive newsroom habits, his ruthless tactics with unions, his cowardly betrayals of his editors, his bankrupt conception of his profession, his contempt for his readers. Yet such stories may tell as much about the mythic sources of professional journalists' identity as about Murdoch himself. To paraphrase Erving Goffman (1963, p. 6), Murdoch provides professional journalists with someone to be normal against. His incessant presence marks the dark border at which enlightened journalism imagines itself standing watch.

A key element of Murdoch's mystique has been his outsider status. Even in Australia, his homeland, Murdoch for some time played the role of upstart. Though his father, Keith Murdoch, was the most famous Australian journalist of his generation and the younger Murdoch grew up amid relative wealth, the father was more a manager than an owner. When Keith Murdoch died, he left his family a modest estate, including small papers in Adelaide and Brisbane. Compared to Australia's older press families, like the Fairfaxes and Packers, Murdoch was a small operator indeed. His recent bid to buy the Herald and Weekly Times (HWT) group that once employed his father marks for Murdoch a triumphal return. (Paradoxically, now that Murdoch has taken American citizenship to acquire Metromedia, some Australian critics object to his offer for the HWT group because it would place control of a powerful network of newspapers in the hands of a foreign citizen ["Murdoch to Purchase," 1986]).

When Murdoch entered the English market in the late 1960s and the American market in the early 1970s, he was very much an outsider. To the well-established press lords of England, Murdoch was just another "colonial" seeking prestige and a peerage in the mother country (Grundy, 1969; " 'New Boy' on Fleet Street," 1971). Murdoch's entry into the American market at first attracted little notice. His founding of a supermarket weekly, then the *National Star*, and the sensationalist style of his San Antonio papers branded him as a curious but unthreatening figure ("The Talk of the Town," 1974; "The Three S's," 1973). When Murdoch later purchased the *New York Post, New York* magazine, and the *Village Voice,* critics would predictably treat him as *nouveau riche,* a tabloid hustler who had overstepped his social bounds.

Murdoch's methods of financing his empire have enhanced his image as an overambitious upstart. Unlike most current media owners, Murdoch maintains personal control of his holdings. Such control protects News Corporation against hostile takeovers, but it also limits Murdoch's ability to issue stock to raise capital. Thus Murdoch has borrowed heavily from a variety of English, Australian, and American banks. His operations are, in the Australian term, highly "geared" or leveraged. For example, Murdoch's purchase of Twentieth Century Fox and Metromedia expanded the worth of his worldwide empire to well over $4 billion. But his debt on those holdings was over $2.5 billion, even before the billion or more he offered for the HWT group in Australia (Barnes et al., 1986). When Murdoch's cash flow tightens, he sells nonessential holdings like the *Village Voice*. This manner of operations sometimes puzzles financial analysts; what does he intend?, they ask (Kirkland & Kinkead, 1984; O'Hanlon, 1984; Sloan, 1986). Critics, seeing his enormous debt and apparently careless style of acquisition, predict his imminent failure, the collapse of his holdings (especially in the United States), and his reduction to a lower, more appropriate status.

Sometimes Murdoch creates alarm by acquiring then transforming publications that have loyal but unprofitable audiences. In England, for example, Murdoch's ownership of the tabloid daily *Sun* still irks the Left. When Murdoch bought it, the *Sun* was a dying vestige of the once-stalwart working-class *Herald*. For the Left, Murdoch's *Sun* daily recalls their soured hopes for a mass-circulation Labour newspaper. Even today, as the Left tries to mount the weekly *News on Sunday,* the debate continues as to what a working-class paper should look like. Should the *News* adapt parts of the Murdoch formula or reject it outright (Johnson, 1987; Pilger, 1987)? The debate over Murdoch's takeover of the *Times* was even more ferocious. That paper had a special meaning for both the Left and the Right. For the Left, the *Times*, despite its cautious politics, encouraged serious journalism and professional autonomy. For the Right, Murdoch's attempt to make that shambling and eccentric dinosaur a moneymaker smacked of crass commercialism and foretold an abandonment of the *Times'* historic role as a dignified forum for serious commentary (Grigg, 1985; Pearce, 1982; Rothmyer, 1983).

In the United States, Murdoch has never purchased a property with the cachet of the *Times,* but he has still aroused anger. The *Post,* for example, had barely weathered the storms that sank other New York dailies in the 1960s. Yet the *Post* still retained many Jewish middle-class readers who remembered it as an outspoken liberal critic of McCarthyism. Some critics thought Murdoch's takeover demeaned that paper's heritage as the country's longest continuously published daily, the paper of Alexander Hamilton and William Cullen Bryant, for so long the voice of genteel reason.[1] Likewise Murdoch's purchase of *New York* magazine seemed to some the dethronement of a hip, upscale editor at the hands of a grubbing, untutored foreigner (Sheehy, 1977).

The vision of Murdoch as Outsider has been clearest in the work of cartoonists and headline writers. He has been portrayed as a barbarian, a killer bee, a Godzilla-like "creature from down under," King Kong, a Tasmanian devil, Dracula, Dr. Frankenstein, and the Grand

Acquisitor. Chicago journalist Mike Royko once tagged him "The Alien"(Crain, 1984). Headlines ask "Who's afraid of Rupert Murdoch," casting him as the Big Bad Wolf who seduces the innocent child of legitimate journalism (Lewis, 1983; Parry-Jones, 1981). Abe Rosenthal of the *New York Times* once denounced him as "a bad element, practicing mean, ugly, violent journalism" (Welles, 1979, p. 51). A near-hysterical editorial in the *Columbia Journalism Review* ("Doing the Devil's Work," 1980, p. 23) accused him of "doing the devil's work," and indicted him as "a social problem—a force for evil." Time and again critics have portrayed Murdoch as the dark Other, a vulgar Prince of Darkness, the Antichrist of Professional Journalism.

Those who condemn Murdoch claim good reasons for their opinions. Some argue that Murdoch's newspapers pose an economic threat to more legitimate and trustworthy publications. Such fears have solid grounds in England and Australia. Before becoming an American citizen, Murdoch was one of Australia's richest men. Aside from his dailies in Sydney, Melbourne, Adelaide, and Canberra, his weeklies and numerous country and suburban papers, he owned two television stations, large record and book publishing companies, enormously successful magazines, and a variety of hotel, resort, and transportation interests (Kiernan, 1986, pp. 323-325). Similarly, in England, one-third of the national papers read each week are Murdoch-produced. He owns both the largest circulation weekly and daily (the *News of the World* and the *Sun*) and the most prestigious weekly and daily (the *Sunday Times* and the *Times*), plus a variety of other provincial newspapers and printing, transport, and paper interests.

In the United States, where the anti-Murdoch rhetoric until recently burned the hottest, Murdoch is far less an economic threat. He owns no opulent and powerful dailies such as the *New York* or the *Los Angeles Times*, the *Chicago Tribune*, or the *Washington Post*. He has lost an estimated $10 million or more on the *New York Post* every year that he has owned it. His supermarket weekly, the *Star,* has been consistently profitable, but his other newspapers have returned modest profits or lost money. Murdoch's newspapers typically face powerful chain competitors (Hearst in San Antonio, the New York Times, Tribune, and Times Mirror companies in New York, and formerly the Tribune Company in Chicago). Murdoch also delights in reminding critics that in no market has he owned a monopoly paper, unlike Gannett, Knight-Ridder, Newhouse, Scripps-Howard, and other American newspaper chains. Of his recently acquired television stations, half are UHF and all rank fourth or lower in their markets, not nearly as profitable as the powerful owned-and-operated stations of the Big Three networks or as established as their affiliates.

The argument that Murdoch economically threatens the American press seems even more dubious when one examines Murdoch's actual strategies. In markets like New York, Chicago, and Boston, Murdoch has pursued a market strategy more commonly found in England or Australia but largely eschewed by monopolistic American newspapers. Murdoch pushes circulation and street sales, hoping to gather readers who feel no allegiance to the dominant dailies. Advertisers, however, have remained skeptical of this strategy. The *Post,* though its circulation approached one million for a time, has never been able under Murdoch to capture more than 7% or so of the newspaper advertising revenues of the New York market (Jones, 1984). (When Murdoch bought the *Chicago Sun-Times,* its rival, the *Tribune,* controlled 75% of that market's newspaper advertising revenues [Friendly, 1983, p. 10]). Most American papers, of course, now cater to upscale audiences, even at the cost of some circulation. Even the *New York Daily News,* for so long the nation's largest daily, has considered cutting back on its circulation to save printing and delivery costs and better identify an audience for which advertisers would pay (Henry, 1982, pp. 19-20). Until now, the vast majority of Murdoch's profits have come from his English and Australian operations. In the United States, Murdoch's profits have mostly come from the *Star* and San Antonio papers, from greenmail, as in the foiled buyouts of Warner Communications and St. Regis, or from resale of his properties at a profit, as with the *Village Voice* and the *Chicago Sun-Times.*[2]

Murdoch's drive for numbers may succeed in television. He claims to have gathered affiliates for a fourth network that would cover 80% of the U.S. population, but it remains to be seen whether he will be able to produce enough attractive, cheap programming to keep those allegiances ("Tally ho, Rupert," 1987). Murdoch's strategy may be to gather a global audience for "satellite brand" consumer advertising. The combination of stations in major American markets, Fox's production facilities and film library, Australian stations, and Sky Channel's satellite-cable system in Europe might gather in a single buy an international audience for consumer advertisers like Coke, Gillette, and McDonald's. Business writers and analysts, while they sometimes question Murdoch's strategies, do acknowledge the possibility of such an international market, and they respect his record of success (Bass, 1986; Livingston, 1986; Maddox, 1986).

Just as some American critics fear Murdoch's economic threat, others condemn his political influence. Murdoch is not at all shy about using his papers to support candidates he likes, sometimes even by slanting news coverage. In Australia, he first promoted then tormented

Prime Minister Gough Whitlam (Leapman, 1983, pp. 64-72). He has staunchly supported Margaret Thatcher in England and Ronald Reagan in the United States (though that hardly distinguishes him from the vast majority of press owners in either country). The *New York Post* has supported Ed Koch and Al D'Amato, condemned liberal candidates like Elizabeth Holtzman, and led the attack on Geraldine Ferraro's husband. Many have denounced Murdoch as a flak for conservative views, and Murdoch himself sometimes plays the part in his public statements, echoing popular conservative slogans (Murdoch, Bradlee, Thimmesch, & Lichter, 1984).

Yet it seems misleading to say that Murdoch's central passion is politics, as a number of commentators have insisted (Brogan, 1985; Diamond, 1980; Stephens, 1982). To the extent that Murdoch holds a political position, one might label it a commercialized populism that, at the moment, has a right-wing tinge throughout much of Europe and the United States. His support for particular candidates seems entirely opportunistic. When politicians like Thatcher, Reagan, and Koch somehow garner widespread popularity, Murdoch's papers jump on the bandwagon to boost circulation. While being a publisher affords him the same access to elites that all major publishers enjoy, it is hard to find evidence of Murdoch's direct influence on the American public. Much of the evidence that does exist rests on the single example of the *New York Post,* but such arguments are peculiarly contorted. On one hand, critics enjoy noting that the audience does not read papers like the *Post* carefully enough to attract advertisers. On the other hand, critics assume that the *Post*'s readers take seriously the political commentary they read there.[3] In any case, it is difficult to prove that Murdoch's American properties have dramatically influenced politics, especially outside of New York City, or that such influence has been in a direction substantially different from that of the vast majority of American newspapers.

Murdoch's current infatuation with conservatism may not even be a permanent commitment. He was infatuated with socialist ideas in college, and through much of the 1960s was a supporter of liberal causes. In recent years, the Right has taken up Murdoch as a hero with the same gusto that the Left decries him as a villain (Irvine, 1984, p. 9). Murdoch has been invited to play the role of "entrepreneur" at conferences (Murdoch, Newhouse, & Forbes, 1984). A teaser headline from the conservative weekly *Human Events* ("Will Murdoch Launch Fourth Network?," 1985, p. 1), discussing Murdoch's acquisition of Metromedia, asks whether Murdoch's will be a fourth network for conservatives. Those expectations are likely to be disappointed. Any

Murdoch network will probably feature game shows, syndicated features along the lines of "Entertainment Tonight," and inexpensively produced sitcoms and movies. Such is hardly the stuff of a right-wing revolution.

If Murdoch's political and economic effect on the United States thus far has been minor, then what threat does he pose? What he threatens is the social legitimation and psychological repose of professional journalism. Murdoch neither shares the canons of *professionalism*, as that word is used by most American journalists, critics, and journalism educators, nor does he feel obliged to pay lip service to those ideals. He freely admits that his downscale newspapers are different, but vigorously asserts that they are every bit as journalistic. Miffed at Murdoch's refusal to honor their public ideals, professionals indict Murdoch on two counts. They charge that he blurs the distinction between information and entertainment, and that he is indifferent or hostile to the autonomy of his editors (Riggenbach, 1984).

American journalists consider serious professional work as that which informs rather than just entertains its audience. Journalists articulate this distinction across a variety of practices and discourses. The preference for hard news to feature stories (which for so many years was in part a preference for the male news work of politics and business as opposed to the soft feminine news work of "social" reporting) rests on the information-entertainment distinction. So do the invidious distinctions of intermedia occupational rivalries; newspaper journalists consider themselves more professional than television reporters, who are more concerned with appearance, demographics, and visual sensation. This respect for "information" also serves well in the practice of news work. It creates the impression of a high-minded, scientific and progressive occupation. It protects news workers from the discomfort of their role as meaning brokers by declaring their detachment from any of the groups among whom they move (Carey, 1969). And it confirms journalists in their contempt for an unresponsive audience that would rather read box scores and fashion advice than intricate interpretations of sewer commission proposals, school board elections, or party caucuses. In short, the information-entertainment distinction, though intellectually feeble, helps defend a particular style of professional practice. That faith in information is part of the psychological contract by which journalists make palatable their roles within large, advertising-driven news organizations.

Murdoch seemingly ignores the information-entertainment distinction, offering readers whatever stories they will pay for. When a particular formula works, he stays with it. Though often portrayed as the typical Murdoch property, the *New York Post* actually remains the exception to this rule, for it is still unclear just what alternative marketing strategy any competitor of the *Times* might use (Benjaminson, 1984, pp. 1-53). In other American markets, Murdoch adapts his methods to circumstances. A 1984 Northwestern University study found no significant changes in the *Chicago Sun-Times* after Murdoch's takeover ("Chicago Sun-Times Has Changed Little," 1984). Most astonishingly of all, Murdoch allowed complete freedom to the *Village Voice* while he owned it. The *Voice* regularly strafed its owner in print for several years. Murdoch neither liked nor quite understood the *Voice*'s audience, but because he made money off it, he left the *Voice* alone. It is hard to imagine a Ben Bradlee, an Otis Chandler, an Abe Rosenthal, or Murdoch's other critics allowing such vigorous dissent in a paper they owned or edited.[4]

Moreover, Murdoch hardly introduced entertainment to the American newspaper. Publishers and editors, however, distinguish their brand of marketing from Murdoch's. A 1977 panel of editors ("Rupert Murdoch," 1977) willingly admitted that Murdoch's style of "promotional journalism" would push them to make their papers more personal, spritely, and readable, but they smugly proclaimed that the Murdoch style would never displace their own brand of "professional" journalism.[5] Even the *New York Times*, before Murdoch's arrival, had remade itself into a more supple, stylish paper, to much the same reaction that later would accompany Murdoch's revision of the *Times* of London.[6] There's even some evidence that Murdoch learned from America, borrowing his promotional techniques from aggressive American network executives like ABC head Leonard Goldenson, whom he met with in the late 1950s and early 1960s (Kiernan, 1986, pp. 76-78).

American journalists' defense of the distinction between information and entertainment obscures the fact that "informative" news is a narrative protocol. The term *information* carries social weight. It does not merely denote a set of indisputable facts, but argues that some sciencelike styles of imagination, such as news, be privileged in public discourse. Yet dozens of newsroom studies continue to affirm that news is the product of specific social and organizational practices, ranging from bureaucratic procedures for gathering news, to economic decisions about deploying resources, to reporters' habits of writing for one another.[7] When critics attack Murdoch for offering entertainment not information, they are in part chastising him for not honoring the stylistic conventions that journalists use to defend the social importance of their occupation.

These attacks on Murdoch also ignore, more obviously, the extent to which all advertising-driven publications disguise entertainment coverage as consumer information. Theater, movies, television, travel, dining out, sports, hobbies—all of these and more are newspaper staples. Yet such stories are not thought to compromise the informational integrity of a publication, except when they appear in a Murdoch paper. Much of the criticism of the *Star* aptly illustrates the point. When that supermarket tabloid started in 1973, it tried to compete with the UFO/Cancer-Cure/Return-of-Elvis formula of competitors like the *National Enquirer*. By the early 1980s, however, the *Star* had increasingly become a tabloid of celebrity news. Today its stories read like the features found in the entertainment and life-style pages of any daily newspaper, except that the *Star* is generally more interesting and better written than most American newspapers. As a recent tongue-in-cheek review of the supermarket tabloids for *Utne Reader* (Reid, 1987, pp. 58-59) noted, "*Star* suffers from coherent graphic design, crisp writing, good use of color, and a sensible advice column. Who wants slick trash?"

In attacking publications like the *Star* or the *Post,* Murdoch's critics condemn him by synecdoche. At one level, using this rhetorical strategy—letting the part represent the whole—allows journalists to defend their own preferred conception of their occupation. In this mode, critics can portray those tabloids as "typical" Murdoch publications, and depict his journalists as mere servants of the trivial and demented, while *they* remain serious-minded defenders of the public's right to know. Forgotten in such an analysis, of course, are the many assignments that require "serious" journalists to interview the Chamber of Commerce's Miss Teen Personality, document the annual Christmas rush at the airport, or promote the newspaper-sponsored boat show or charity marathon.

At another more important level, using synecdoche allows critics to represent Murdoch's papers using those parts they dislike. The essence of Murdoch's papers, critics argue, is entertainment; the essence of professional papers is information.[8] The very complexity of the newspaper encourages such rhetorical contention and moral posturing over its "character." Because mass-circulation dailies comprise vast and varied symbolic materials, different groups can argue that the "essential" part is the one that they most enjoy or that sustains their sense of identification. Thus the professional journalist emphasizes the investigative role of the newspaper out of all proportion to the actual number of such stories undertaken. Editors value the bold, outspoken editorial that, though unread, always threatens to influence public opinion. Readers meander contentedly through the baseball standings, comics, television and movie listings, advice columns, and department store ads. The daily newspaper flourishes precisely because it allows producers and consumers alike to carve out their own symbolic social spaces in a way that does not undermine the merchandising principles that make such newspapers profitable.

Murdoch's behavior also calls into question a second central ideal of professional ideology—editorial independence. When the term *independence* began to be widely applied to the daily newspaper in the midnineteenth century, it carried a variety of inflections (Pauly, 1985b). It echoed Americans' frequent declarations of their independence as a free people. As journalism historians have long noted, the term also declared the freedom of advertising-supported dailies from their party subsidies and commitments. But the praise of an independent press, which resounds after the Civil War, contained a larger social symbolism as well. The related terms *independence* and *impersonality* traced the trajectory of a press evolving toward more complex forms of collective organization and away from dominance by individuals. By the twentieth century, *independence* had become a keystone of journalists' professional identity, a psychological comfort against and social legitimation for the compromises the editorial side of the daily newspaper made with its business side. The myth of editorial autonomy not only protected the self-regard of the news worker, but also affirmed the higher social goals claimed on behalf of the daily newspaper as an agent of civilization, and on behalf of news as a form of imagination.

Murdoch's unapologetic behavior exposes once again the fragile economic underpinnings of news workers' claims of autonomy. As Harold Evans (1984) learned firsthand, no editorial independence exists if the publisher chooses to exercise the prerogatives of ownership. Murdoch's proprietary attitude means that his journalistic employees must find new grounds for their own identities. Though he occasionally speaks about the social role of the press, Murdoch's behavior suggests that he does not take newspapers all that seriously. He buys and sells them to make money. Murdoch is a gambler, and he acquires media properties for the sheer love of the game. His interest is in the economic performance of his properties, regardless of how his employees might hope to dramatize the larger social meanings of their occupations. Newspaper writers who work for absentee conglomerates can afford the luxury of considering themselves aspiring Walter Lippmanns. Murdoch's employees quite soon understand that he expects them to be Hildy Johnsons.

Even more, perhaps, Murdoch's behavior lays bare the larger economic assumptions that have historically undergirded the myth of editorial autonomy. Editors seemed independent only because most

American newspapers had little competition (and because, perhaps, editors quietly accommodated themselves to the narrow boundaries of their freedom). In monopoly conditions, dailies could allow journalists more generous leeway. Statements of professional values, such as the report of the Commission on Freedom of the Press (1947), often portray professionalism as a countervailing force, a response to the depredations of an increasingly monopolistic press. But it may be just as useful to think of professionalism as a simulation of social responsibility made possible by the political and economic power of monopoly dailies. Murdoch disturbs the generational expectations of his critics. He seems an anachronism, a throwback to an earlier era of press barons, a barrier to the long, slow progress toward higher ideals of professionalism.[9]

Murdoch's circulation practices also raise troubling issues about the relationship between daily newspapers and the communities they purport to serve. Murdoch's papers often suggest how deep the fault lines of class, race, and ethnicity may run in American cities. Anthony Smith (1978) has accused Murdoch of breaking down the illusion of classlessness that mass newspapers had once helped sustain. In any case, Murdoch has embarrassed some big city newspaper owners by making visible those demographically disenfranchised classes of readers that monopoly papers could once afford to ignore.[10] Murdoch's papers in New York, Boston, San Antonio, and, formerly, in Chicago may not suit advertisers well, but their large circulations suggest that many readers are simply not interested in the style of newspaper that professional journalists are content to publish.

In the United States, Murdoch has been accused of driving out "good" journalism. Murdoch is accused of "forcing" his reluctant competitors into the dirt with him to maintain their circulation base and, implicitly, the economic viability of their more noble brand of journalism. That argument, of course, repeats the tired and suspect accusations of Dwight MacDonald (1962) and other mass society critics that a kind of Gresham's Law operates in the realm of culture. Here again synecdoche operates: Murdoch appeals to mass tastes because he wants to; others do it because they have to. Yet Murdoch has never opened a door that other media owners have not rushed through (or previously knocked on themselves). For instance, most of the other Fleet Street papers have now won dramatic concessions from their unions and introduced state-of-the-art printing plants.[11] (Even the Left's plan for the weekly *News on Sunday* became feasible only because Murdoch broke the union stranglehold on staffing and technology use.) And if Murdoch had sought and received a permanent waiver of the FCC's cross-ownership rules in order to keep his New York or Chicago papers, would the New York Times, Times Mirror, Washington Post, and other newspaper conglomerates have restrained their acquisitive instincts, in the name of democracy?

For better or worse, Murdoch's papers tap a vein of resentment toward "quality" papers that casually ignore economically undesirable segments of the audience. One need not accept Murdoch's portrayal of his own sentiments as more "democratic" than those of his "elitist" critics. In the end, Murdoch's narrow conception of the needs of his working- and lower-middle-class audience serves those groups no better than the imperial indifference of the great dailies. Yet it should be noted that while professional journalism claims to defend democracy, it does so on its own terms. By narrowing the conception of journalism to news work, and the social role of the newspaper to providing "information," professionalism guards against alternative conceptions of democracy. It would be impossible, for example, to win professional approval for a press conceived of as "a full and representative expression of the views and interests of all classes in the community" (Hirsch & Gordon, 1975, p. 25). Such a definition would call into question matters of ownership and social class that professionalism would rather not debate. Journalists' resistance to even moderate forms of community response, such as press councils, suggests that they would not welcome a more fully participatory model of journalism. A publication devoted to dialogue rather than consumerism might empower its audience, but it would never be commercially profitable enough to sustain professional journalists' political privileges, social ambitions, or sense of moral grandeur.

This argument should not be capsulized and dismissed as an attempt to show that Rupert Murdoch has been made a scapegoat for the failures of the American press. Any talk of the "failures of the press" accepts the claim that the news organizations are institutions, not merely industrial organizations that impart a particular social character to reporting practices and printing technologies. The language of scapegoat also assumes a widely accepted, taken-for-granted set of fixed taboos that are violated, leading to a ritual absolution of guilt and affirmation of the original values. Certainly the debate over Murdoch ends by reaffirming professional values, but like debates over earlier press barons, this one will likely end in acceptance rather than sacrifice. Indeed, over the last year or so, Murdoch has gained more respect in the United States, or at least garnered less violent criticism than he once did. Though Murdoch's move of his English printing plant to Wapping has ignited extraordinary conflict, leading to armed confrontations at the plant gate, lawsuits, and the refusal of Labour leaders like Neil Kinnock even to talk to Murdoch papers' reporters, American observers have treated the move as a technological inevitability (Hitchens, 1986; Jenkins, 1986). Murdoch himself has seemingly lost some of his defensiveness and begun to grant more interviews. Perhaps the image of Murdoch as tabloid hustler is no longer sustainable now that, by *Forbes* magazine's count ("The Forbes Four Hundred," 1986), he is the 47th wealthiest citizen in the United States.[12] With his horns receding, Murdoch may soon take his place in the pantheon of journalism along with other great American press barons. After all, if the sustained mediocrity of Gannett or the illegal high jinks of the Annenbergs can create distinguished schools and institutes for the promotion of professional journalism, surely there must be hope for Rupert Murdoch as well.[13]

NOTES

1. Though newspapers try every means to drive out their competitors, publishers and journalists alike usually mourn each latest newspaper death. By professing the importance of failed newspapers, they symbolically affirm a plural marketplace that their business office is just as happy no longer exists. For a discussion of the Boston *Globe*'s contribution to the *Herald*'s pre-Murdoch woes, see O'Brien (1983, p. 150).

2. Murdoch made more than $40 million on the Warner deal and $37 million on St. Regis. For a convenient account of those battles, see Kiernan (1986, pp. 275-281).

3. Lower-class readers are often assumed to be duped by the "sensationalist" papers they read. What's more likely is that reading such papers is, for them, a rather different experience than reading the *New York Times* is for political and cultural elites. Tabloid reading is part of the action of city life, just another game one plays to pass the time, certainly not one of the foundation stones on which the republic rests. In their own dramas of occupational identity, journalists tend to stress the newspaper's role as vehicle for serious political information, but the newspaper, as an organization, depends on the casual curiosity, nervous rhythms, and impulsive buying habits of urban consumers.

4. One thinks, for example, of the discomfort that the relatively mild protests of a Sydney Schanberg or a Raymond Bonner caused at the *New York Times*.

5. One example of the editors' tendency to dismiss Murdoch as a geek: The article starts with a Roger Simon column that equates Murdoch with William Loeb, the bizarre and vindictive owner of the tiny Manchester (NH) *Union-Leader*.

6. In commenting on the changes Murdoch made to the London *Times*, *New York Times*' writer R. W. Apple Jr. ("Times of London," 1984, p. 2) disingenuously defended the border between information and entertainment by noting that American newspapers, some years before, had added "extra" feature sections, without cutting back on their political and foreign coverage.

7. The literature on newsmaking is now too voluminous to cite in a single note. The work of Herbert Gans, Gaye Tuchman, Todd Gitlin, Leon Sigal, Bernard Roshco, Mark Fishman, Robert Darnton, David Altheide, Edward J. Epstein, and others is by now familiar. A convenient introduction to the topic is Bennett (1983).

8. Few critics have studied in depth the actual content of Murdoch's papers, rather than just the headlines. Aside from the Northwestern University study, one of the only other studies has been Pasadeos's study (1984) on sensationalism in Murdoch's *San Antonio News*. He concludes that Murdoch did sensationalize the *News,* though it is hard to know what significance to attribute to the category *sensational* when it includes "news stories on crime, violence, armed conflict, death, accidents, disasters, scandals and other crises, as well as articles on contests and promotions" (p. 11). Even some critics admit that Murdoch has sometimes improved his papers' coverage in particular areas. Brogan (1985, p. 13) cites improvements in the *Post*'s city hall, sports, and spot news reporting, though he dislikes its Washington news and failure to cover Harlem and the Bronx.

9. Ben Bagdikian has said that Murdoch "has set back American journalism 100 years. [Murdoch's conception of journalism] cheapens the whole idea of what news is" (Kiefer, 1984, p. 4).

10. For a sympathetic accounting of Murdoch's early policies in San Antonio, see Smith (1976). Smith suggests that Murdoch's papers created an uproar because they called into question the clean, official image the town fathers hoped to project.

11. The *Mirror, Daily Mail, Telegraph, Guardian, Financial Times,* and *Observer* already have moved or plan to move off Fleet Street ("The Weekly Worker," 1987).

12. Even at number 47, Murdoch still lags far behind ex-Metromedia mogul John Kluge (2), two Cox sisters (15-16), two Newhouses (18-19), Walter Annenberg (23), the Tisches of Loew's theaters (28-29), and former magazine owner William Ziff (31). *Forbes* ("The Forbes Four Hundred," 1986, p. 154) notes that "58 members of The Forbes Four Hundred have fortunes derived principally from media enterprises."

13. I would like to thank Karen Fossum for helping with the bibliographic research for this article.

REFERENCES

Apple, R. W., Jr. (1984, October 6). Times of London lets its hair down. *New York Times*, p. 2.

Barnes, P. W., Cieply, M., & Landro, L. (1986, February 21). Big picture: Rupert Murdoch's bid to form TV network faces huge obstacles. *Wall Street Journal*, pp. 1, 12.

Bass, I. (1986, May). The sky's the limit. *Marketing and Media Decisions, 26.*

Benjaminson, P. (1984). *Death in the afternoon: America's newspapers struggle for survival.* Kansas City: Andrews, Michael & Parker.

Bennett, W. L. (1983). *News, the politics of illusion.* New York: Longman.

Birkhead, D. (1982). *Presenting the press: Journalism and the professional project.* Ph.D. dissertation, University of Iowa.

Birkhead, D. (1984, Winter). The power in the image: Professionalism and the communications revolution. *American Journalism, 1.*

Bradshaw, J., & Neville, R. (1977, February). Killer bee reaches New York. *More, 7.*

Brogan, P. (1982, October 11). Citizen Murdoch. *New Republic, 187.*

Brogan, P. (1985, June 24). Post-Murdoch Post. *New Republic, 192.*

Carey, J. W. (1969). The communication revolution and the professional communicator. In P. Halmos (Ed.), *The sociology of mass media communicators.* Sociological Review Monograph 13. Keele, England: University of Keele.

Chicago Sun-Times has changed little under Murdoch. (1984, June 23). *Editor and Publisher, 117*, p. 13.

Commission on Freedom of the Press. (1947). *A free and responsible press.* Chicago: University of Chicago Press.

Crain, R. (1984, October 11). Murdoch hasn't trashed "Sun-Times." *Advertising Age, 55,* p. 60.

Diamond, E. (1980, June). Rupert Murdoch. Power without prestige: The outside outbacker. *Washington Journalism Review, 2.*

Doing the devil's work. (1980, January/February). *Columbia Journalism Review, 18.*

Evans, H. (1984). *Good times, bad times.* New York: Athaneum.

The Forbes four hundred. (1986, October 27). *Forbes, 138.*

Friendly, J. (1983, December). Aussie hits Windy City. *Washington Journalism Review, 5.*

Goffmann, E. (1963) *Stigma.* Englewood Cliffs, NJ: Prentice-Hall.

Grigg, J. (1985, July-September). Profile of *The Times. Political Quarterly, 56.*

Grundy, B. (1969, November 22). Murdoch and Sun. *The Spectator, 223.*

Hall, S. (1978). Newspapers, parties and classes. In James Curran (Ed.), *The British press: A manifesto.* London: Macmillan.

Henry, W. A., III (1982, March). The decline and fall of the New York *Daily News. Washington Journalism Review, 4.*

Hirsch, F., & Gordon, D. (1975). *Newspaper money.* London: Hutchinson.

Hitchens, C. (1984, February 24). Minority report. *The Nation, 238.*

Hitchens, C. (1986, February 22). Minority report. *The Nation, 242.*

Irvine, R. (1984, February 11). Why liberal media fear Rupert Murdoch. *Human Events, 44.*

Jenkins, S. (1986, October). New money on Fleet Street. *Atlantic, 258.*

Johnson, P. (1987, January 10). What do the workers want? *The Spectator, 258.*

Jones, A. S. (1984, December 10). Headlines blaring, city's tabloids step up battle. *New York Times,* p. B6.

Kiefer, F. (1984, February 23). Publisher Murdoch's empire—all tastes considered. *Christian Science Monitor,* pp. 3-6.

Kiernan, T. (1986). *Citizen Murdoch.* New York: Dodd, Mead & Company.

Kirkland, R. I., Jr., & Kinkead, G. (1984, February 20). Rupert Murdoch's motley empire. *Fortune, 109.*

Leapmann, M. (1983). *Barefaced cheek: The apotheosis of Rupert Murdoch.* London: Hodder and Stoughton.

Lewis, A. (1983, December 29). Pretty teeth, dear. *New York Times,* p. A19.

Livingston, V. (1986, October 13). Murdoch's media reach invites global advertising schemes. *Television/Radio Age, 34.*

MacDonald, D. (1962). Masscult and midcult. In *Against the American grain.* New York: Random House.

Maddox, B. (1986, January/February). Sky king. *Channels, 5.*

McClintock, D. (1977, January 7). Publisher's paradox: Reserved, soft-spoken, Murdoch is antithesis of the papers he owns. *Wall Street Journal,* pp. 1, 16.

Munster, G. (1985). *A paper prince.* Victoria, Australia: Viking.

Murdoch to purchase Australian news group. (1986, December 4). *New York Times,* pp. D1, D8.

Murdoch, R., Bradlee, B., Thimmesch, N., & Lichter, R. (1984, June 28). Is there a liberal media elite in America? American Enterprise Institute symposium, Washington, DC.

Murdoch, R., Newhouse, S. I., Jr., & Forbes, M. (1984, October 21-29). The entrepreneurs. American Magazine Conference, Magazine Publishers' Association, Nassau, Bahamas.

"New boy" on Fleet Street. (1971, May 10). *Newsweek, 77.*

O'Brien, G. (1983, May). Rupert buys hub rag. *Boston Magazine, 75.*

O'Hanlon, T. (1984, January 30). What does this man want? *Forbes, 133.*

Page, B. (1981, January 30). Into the arms of Count Dracula. *New Statesman, 101.*

Parry-Jones, E. (1981, February 19). Who's afraid of Rupert Murdoch? *The Listener, 105.*

Pasadeos, Y. (1984, Summer). Application of measures of sensationalism to a Murdoch-owned daily in the San Antonio market. *Newspaper Research Journal, 5.*

Pauly, J. J. (1985a). Reflections on writing a history of news as a form of mass culture. *Working Paper No. 6.* Milwaukee: University of Wisconsin-Milwaukee, Center for Twentieth Century Studies.

Pauly, J. J. (1985b, October). *The ideological origins of an independent press.* Paper presented to the American Journalism Historians Association convention, Las Vegas, Nevada.

Pearce, E. (1982, May). Dial M for Murdoch. *Encounter, 58.*

Pilger, J. (1987, January 2). The birth of a new Sun? *New Statesman, 113.*

Regan, S. (1976) *Rupert Murdoch, a business biography.* London: Angus and Robertson.

Reid, J. (1987, March/April). Supermarket tabloids. *Utne Reader.*

Riggenbach, J. (1984, July). Rupert Murdoch: That's entertainment. *Inquiry, 7.*

Rothmyer, K. (1983, September/October). Letter from London. *Columbia Journalism Review, 22.*

Rupert Murdoch: What do American editors think of him? (1977, April). *The Bulletin of the American Society of Newspaper Editors.*

Schanberg, S. H. (1982, July 13). The Tasmanian devil. *New York Times,* p. A25.

Shaw, D. (1983, May 25). Murdoch: Press loves to hate him. *Los Angeles Times,* pp. 1, 13-16.

Sheehy, G. (1977, July 14). A fistful of dollars. *Rolling Stone.*

Sloan, A. (1986, March 10). Understanding Murdoch—the numbers aren't what really matters. *Forbes, 137.*

Smith, A. (1978, November 18). Murdoch trap: Press lord of mass ignorance. *The Nation, 227.*

Smith, G., Jr. (1976, November). Weirdo paper plagues S.A. *Texas Monthly, 4.*

Stephens, M. (1982, July/August). The New York City scene II—clout: Murdoch's political *Post. Columbia Journalism Review, 21.*

Stevenson, M. (1983, October). The state of America's newspapers. *American Spectator, 16.*

Tally ho, Rupert. (1987, January). *Channels, 6.*

The talk of the town: New boy. (1974, February 25). *New Yorker, 50.* -

The three S's. (1973, December 15). *Forbes, 112.*

Tyrrell, E., Jr. (1984, January 2). Who's afraid of Rupert Murdoch? *Washington Post,* p. A21.

The weekly worker. (1987, January 24). *Economist, 302.*

Welles, C. (1979, May 22). The Americanization of Rupert Murdoch. *Esquire, 91.*

Will Murdoch launch fourth network? (1985, May 18). *Human Events, 45.*

Zwar, D. (1980). *In search of Keith Murdoch.* Melbourne: Macmillan.

ABOUT THE CONTRIBUTORS

S. ELIZABETH BIRD teaches journalism, anthropology, and folklore courses at the University of Iowa. Her current research explores the relationship between media and oral traditions with special emphasis on a cultural study of supermarket tabloids.

JAMES W. CAREY is currently Dean of the College of Communications, University of Illinois, Urbana-Champaign. He formerly held the George H. Gallup Chair at the University of Iowa. He has published over 75 papers on popular culture, communications technology, and communications history and theory.

MICHAEL CORNFIELD teaches courses on media, culture, and politics at the University of Virginia. His Ph.D. dissertation, in political science at Harvard University, analyzes feature stories about President Harry Truman. This is his first academic publication.

ROBERT W. DARDENNE is Assistant Professor in the Department of Communication at the University of Tennessee-Chattanooga, and a doctoral candidate at the University of Iowa. He is researching the development of the news genre over about the last 200 years.

DAVID L. EASON is Associate Professor in the Department of Communication, University of Utah. He is also editor of *Critical Studies in Mass Communications*.

STEWART M. HOOVER is Assistant Professor of Communications at Temple University in Philadelphia. His research has focused on the impact of communication technology on cultures and subcultures in North America and in the developing world. He has also researched and taught in the area of communication law and policy.

ELIHU KATZ is Professor of Sociology and Communication at the Hebrew University and Distinguished Visiting Professor at the Annenberg School of Communications, University of Southern California. In addition to work on the "Dallas" project, he is engaged (jointly with Daniel Dayan) on a study of "media events."

TAMAR LIEBES is Instructor in Communications at the Hebrew University and Lecturer in the Department of Cinema at Tel-Aviv University. Her other papers on the "Dallas" project have appeared in *Studies in Visual Communication, European Journal of Communication, Intermedia,* and in the forthcoming volume of *Progress in Communication Science.*

HORACE M. NEWCOMB is Professor of Radio-Television-Film at the University of Texas at Austin. He is the author of *TV: The Most Popular Art* (Doubleday/Anchor: 1974), coauthor (with Robert S. Alley) of *The Producer's Medium* (Oxford: 1983), and editor of four editions of *Television: The Critical View* (Oxford: 1987). He has written about television for the *Baltimore Sun, Christian Century,* the *Wall Street Journal, Channels,* and the *Village Voice.*

JOHN J. PAULY is Associate Professor of Communication at the University of Tulsa. His research on the history and sociology of mass communication has appeared in *Critical Studies in Mass Communication, Communication Research, American Quarterly, American Journalism,* and the *Journal of Business Communication.*

JIMMIE L. REEVES is Assistant Professor of Speech Communication at Auburn University. Since obtaining his Ph.D. from the University of Texas at Austin, he has published articles in the *Village Voice* and has served as a guest editor for a special issue of the *Southern Speech Communication Journal.*

MICHAEL SCHUDSON is Professor of Communication and Sociology at the University of California, San Diego. He is the author of *Discovering the News: A Social History of American Newspapers* (Basic Books, 1978) and *Advertising, the Uneasy Persuasion: Its Dubious Impact on American Society* (Basic Books, 1984). He is the coeditor (with Robert Manoff) of *Reading the News* (Pantheon Books, 1986). He is presently concerned with issues in the history of political communication.

ROGER SILVERSTONE is Lecturer in Sociology and Director of Graduate Studies in the Department of Human Sciences, Brunel University, Uxbridge, Middlesex, UK. He is the author of several articles and two books, *The Message of Television: Myth and Narrative in Contemporary Culture* (Heinemann Educational Books, London, 1981) and *Framing Science: The Making of a BBC Documentary* (British Film Institute, London, 1985). Both books deal with matters relating to the place of television in culture.

DAVID THORBURN is Professor of Literature and Director of Film and Media Studies at MIT. He is the author of *Conrad's Romanticism* (1974), essays and reviews on literature and popular culture, and the forthcoming *Story Machine*, a cultural history of prime-time television to be published by Oxford University Press.

THOMAS H. ZYNDA is Assistant Professor in the Department of Theatre and Communication Arts at Memphis State University. He has written on television's role in representing historical experience, and is currently studying television dramas of violence.